Writing a Proposal for Your Dissertation

Guidelines and Examples

SECOND EDITION

STEVEN R. TERREL

KAY NEO

Throughout the years, my wife, Dalia, and I
have dedicated ourselves to adopting dogs from rescue shelters.
Some of them have gone on before us—Benny, Baxter, Bella,
and Bosley—but Barney and Harper are sleeping on the floor
here right next to my chair. Thanks, guys.

Acknowledgments

Every author should be as blessed as I am to be working with C. Deborah Laughton, Publisher for Methodology and Statistics at The Guilford Press. As I've said on many occasions, her untiring support, professionalism, charm, and her true caring for those she works with, makes my life as an author enjoyable and fulfilling.

To Paul Gordon—your cover for the first edition of this book was amazing, and the cover of this edition even more so. One of my colleagues said it best; "Oh, I like this! . . . the metaphor of how a potentially bad idea (crumpled paper) can actually turn into a great idea! It also alludes to the iterative nature of the dissertation. Love it!" I've also had the pleasure of working with Jeannie Tang, Senior Production Editor at Guilford. This was our first time working together, and your great skill in reviewing my work, providing guidance, and keeping me on schedule was much needed and greatly appreciated. Thank you both so very much.

An author has to rely on the insight, expertise, and feedback from the reviewers. I could not have asked anything more from the group working with me; their guidance was outstanding. My utmost thanks to Katherine K. Rose, Professor, College of Professional Education, Department of Human Development, Family Studies and Counseling, Texas Woman's University; Lené Levy-Storms, Associate Professor, Departments of Social Welfare and Medicine/Geriatrics, Luskin School of Public Affairs, University of California, Los Angeles; Tobin Hindle, Scientist and Graduate Program Director, Department of Geosciences, Florida Atlantic University; Pam Kocher Brown, Kinesiology Professor and Director of the EdD in KIN program, University of North Carolina at Greensboro; Steven B. Mertens, Professor, Middle Level Education, Illinois State University; John S. Carlson, College of Education, Child and Adolescent Psychological Services, Michigan State University;

and Kelley Brock-Simmons, Associate Professor, Chair of Graduate Programs, and Director of EdD Programs, Brenau University.

In the ethnography section of this text, I wanted a picture of Domino Park in Miami, where many Cuban immigrants gather to socialize, debate, discuss current events, and, as you might guess, play serious games of dominos. I found exactly what I was looking for in a work by Jake Rose. His only stipulation in giving me his permission to use it in this book was that I send him a copy. Jake, it's on the way.

Finally, I've moved to a new university since the first edition was published. I am looking forward to working with the faculty, administration, and staff at Middle Georgia State University for years to come.

Contents

Chapter Three   Writing the Review of Literature   56
                     for Your Dissertation Proposal

Chapter Four   The First Part of Your Dissertation Research Method   80

Chapter Five   Quantitative Research Methods   107

Chapter Six   Qualitative Research Methods   161

Chapter Seven   Mixed Methods Research Designs   212

Introduction

Your Dissertation Proposal

From the outset, did you notice something in the title of this book that may be different from those of other books you may have read about writing a doctoral **dissertation**? In case you didn't, unlike many other authors, I want to focus solely on writing the **dissertation proposal**, the first part of the dissertation that sets the stage for the research to be conducted, and ultimately the final **dissertation report**. In general, the proposal usually consists of stating a research problem and purpose, asking research questions, stating hypotheses if needed (i.e., ideas or explanations you will test), reviewing the literature about the problem area, and creating a detailed plan, called the research method, which will be the guideline for your study.

To be clear, this isn't a research **methodology** book per se. Obviously, talking about different research designs and methodologies is part of the process, but my primary focus is helping you to write a good proposal. While I do go into some detail about such things as statistical tests, instrument development, different research designs, and so on, it's all within the scope and context of getting a good start on your dissertation. In cases where you need more detail about a specific topic, I've supplied helpful references in each chapter. You'll find that outstanding authors, such as Earl Babbie, Kathy Charmaz, John Creswell, Lorraine Rumbel Gay, Sharlene Hesse-Biber, Clark Moustakas, Robert Stake, Robert Yin, and many others, will provide you with all of the information you will need.

My reasoning for focusing solely on the dissertation proposal is this: I don't want to discourage you but, surprisingly, only about 50% of students entering a doctoral program in the United States ultimately graduate. The reasons are many: they might run out of money, their personal life intervenes, they have academic problems, and so on. In my more than 30 years of experience, I've found that the biggest hurdle to graduation is writing the dissertation proposal, and more specifically, being able to identify or focus on a problem area to investigate. Most of my

1

students are academically capable of writing a dissertation or they wouldn't be in a doctoral program in the first place; they just need something to help them understand the process and get them started.

That's my goal in this book: to help you understand what it takes to get started and write your proposal. In doing so, I've included a lot of material that I think you'll find very useful. There are chapters dedicated to specific parts of the dissertation: the **problem statement**, and the **review of literature (ROL)**, for example, and separate chapters focusing on quantitative data (i.e., numeric), qualitative data (i.e., text based), and mixed methods (i.e., where both quantitative and qualitative data are collected) research. There are review questions throughout, definitions of many of the terms you'll encounter in your research, an extensive reference list, and examples of everything we discuss. Finally, at the end of the book you'll see examples of a quantitative, qualitative, and mixed methods proposal based on the true story of a toxic waste recycling plant in a small southern town.

In short, I've given you a good set of tools with which to work. Before we talk in more detail about a dissertation, however, let's talk about how we get to the point where we actually need to write one.

An Overview of the Dissertation Process

When I was taking my doctoral coursework, I did not have a good understanding of what a dissertation really is. The coursework prepared me with the knowledge and tools I needed, but I didn't really know and understand how to use these, or what was expected of me until I was at the point where it was time to get started. At that time, by working with my **dissertation chair** and other faculty members, I moved forward and was ultimately successful. Since then, I've worked with doctoral students throughout my career, and many seem to share those same feelings. When I'm talking with these students, I start by describing the format of a typical dissertation.

The Format of the Dissertation

As you're writing you'll be asked to follow your school's guidelines for writing your dissertation. Different universities may have different formats, or sections, to be included in a dissertation, but the most common approach includes five chapters:

- Chapter 1: Introduction
- Chapter 2: Review of Related Literature
- Chapter 3: Methodology
- Chapter 4: Results
- Chapter 5: Conclusions

The first three chapters taken together are the proposal that guides your research and must be approved before you begin your actual research study. Chapter

1, the introduction, focuses primarily on the research problem statement you will be investigating. Chapter 2 is a review of the related literature (i.e., ROL) focusing on what is already known about your problem area, as well as opportunities for future research. Chapter 3 describes, in detail, the methodology that you will follow while investigating your problem area. In short, the proposal is a detailed plan for the research you want to conduct. After you have finished your proposal, it can guide your study—following that, you will present your results and conclusions in Chapters 4 and 5, respectively. The five chapters, taken together, are your dissertation report.

Just So That You're Aware, There Are Other Dissertation Models

Up to this point, we've talked solely about the **five-chapter dissertation** model. It is, by far, the most widely used approach, but a limited number of universities and schools may require anything from four to nine chapters. How you write your dissertation depends upon the guidance of your advisor, the discipline you are studying, and the guidelines published by your institution. You'll find that the content of each of these formats generally remains the same; the primary difference is how the material is presented.

Since the five-chapter model is the most commonly used approach to writing a dissertation, we will focus on writing a proposal based on the traditional first three chapters. Of the other formats, the **four-chapter dissertation** model is becoming more widely used in a limited number of cases. Because of that, we discuss the four-chapter model in Appendix F.

What Else Is New in This Edition?

After using the first edition of this text for over 5 years and listening to feedback from students, faculty members, and other readers, I have included additional material I believe you will find useful in helping you develop your dissertation proposal.

First, throughout the book, I have included examples from a broader array of professions and organizations not widely discussed in the first edition. For example, readers in the corporate world, information systems professionals, and health care workers will also find the book more relevant and valuable.

There are several places in the text where material has been added to introduce new, or further develop existing, material from the first edition. For example, while discussing the development of a problem statement, I have included new sections on working with a dissertation advisor in your research area and replicating previously conducted research. The discussion of purpose statements has been expanded to better explain how they relate to the overarching focus, goal, aim, or intent of your study, as well as steps in writing purpose statements for quantitative, qualitative, and mixed methods research. Examples such as the effect of strength training on the range of kickers' field goal attempts and reducing recidivism due to training programs in prison are included.

The chapter focusing on writing the ROL has been greatly expanded to include a more detailed approach to preparing for and writing the ROL. This consists of a broader strategy for identifying appropriate literature, including a new section on peer-reviewed work, new coverage of web-based bibliographic databases, a more detailed discussion of journal articles and professional publications, and the use of popular press articles and books related to the topic of your paper. I have included additional material on establishing the validity of these sources, followed by a more focused approach to outlining, synthesizing, and writing the review. I've paid close attention to the different ways references can be formatted, as well as the use of web-based technology to help avoid grammatical and formatting issues.

Throughout the chapters focusing on quantitative, qualitative, and mixed methods research proposals, I have added to the discussion of ethical research, data collection, analysis, and research designs. All material in the book is supported by a broader and more detailed reference list and glossary. I think you will find these and other changes helpful but, for now, let's move forward.

Putting It All Together

For many students, the most challenging part of writing a dissertation is developing a sound, valid proposal that will ultimately guide their research. To keep things simple, think about the idea of a road map. You could use it if you wanted to drive to a location but did not know how to get there (i.e., the problem), reading literature such as travel guides and maps about possible routes (i.e., the ROL), and using what you've learned to plan your route (i.e., the methodology). This would result in a specific set of instructions to reach your destination. A well-developed map will successfully lead you to where you want to go; an inaccurate map might lead you astray. This same logic underlies the proposal for your dissertation; you want to develop a sound plan for conducting your research.

Before we move forward, let's look at how I followed this process in my own dissertation. In my case, I was working with math teachers in an elementary school trying to raise historically low math scores. Here is the sequence I used:

1. Problem (Chapter 1). I defined my problem as low levels of math achievement by fifth-grade students.

2. The Review of Literature (Chapter 2). By reading literature in the field, I found that different types of achievement feedback may affect a student's intrinsic motivation to learn a given subject, resulting in higher achievement. I also learned that providing feedback to students about their progress and performance in a timely, informational, and noncontrolling manner may positively affect intrinsic motivation.

3. Methodology (Chapter 3). I proposed creating a computer program to allow teachers to input grades and show students their weekly achievement, compared to prior weeks, using a standard bar graph. My idea, based on the literature, was that

students would be able to see their math achievement in a much timelier manner than traditional report cards; it would provide feedback in a manner more understandable than traditional letter grades; and, unlike the strong emphasis placed on traditional report cards, it might be perceived as less controlling. These three things, taken together, should increase levels of intrinsic motivation in math and lead to higher achievement scores. I proposed measuring student motivation at the start of the school year, having teachers distribute the graphical report cards to their math students weekly, and measuring motivation at the end of the school year. Correlating this with existing math scores would give me the data I needed to analyze in Chapter 4 and discuss in Chapter 5.

In short, I developed a plan for my dissertation, a step-by-step guide, focusing on the problem and based on the literature, that would guide me as I conducted my research.

Getting the Faculty Involved

With that understanding, let's dig deeper into the process that underlies writing a dissertation. First, as I started conceptualizing and writing my dissertation proposal, I established a **dissertation committee**. I started by identifying a faculty member, known as the dissertation chair, who helped focus and guide my work. He also helped me identify two other faculty members who were subject-matter experts and who would agree to serve as members of my committee. We worked together to help ensure I made it successfully through the dissertation process.

I worked closely with my dissertation chair and committee to ensure the validity of what I was doing from the outset. Their feedback was instrumental in helping me create a plan that showed I was ready to move forward with my research. Once I finished my proposal, as is the case at many universities, I had to "defend" my work. This involved presenting my proposal to an audience consisting of the committee, other faculty members, and anyone else throughout the university interested in my work. Once finished, audience members were encouraged to ask questions, many of which led to an interesting conversation about my work. The key was that I wanted to demonstrate my knowledge in the field, the problem I had identified, and the methodology I had developed to investigate it. On a side note, I have never witnessed a **dissertation defense** where the student failed. This isn't to say it couldn't happen but, as my chair told me, he wouldn't allow me to defend my work until he and the committee felt I was ready! His exact words were something to the effect of "If you look bad, guess who else looks bad?" Keep in mind that it's ultimately up to you to write a valid proposal for your work.

Once the proposal is approved, you will conduct your study and then, in Chapter 4, detail the results of the analysis of data collected during the research. Chapter 5 presents a discussion of the results or conclusions, in the context of the research questions or hypotheses, based on the data analysis from Chapter 4. Again, all five chapters, taken together, is your dissertation report.

Recap: What We Are Going to Do in This Book

As I've said, even though we just looked at the dissertation from an overarching perspective, in this book I want to focus solely on writing the dissertation proposal. This means we'll look at, in detail, the first three chapters of the dissertation. This isn't a research methodology book per se. While we will talk about different research designs and methodologies, my primary focus is to help you write a good proposal that will successfully guide you. While I do go into some detail about such things as statistical tests, how to conduct interviews, instrument development, different research designs, and so on, it's all within the scope and context of getting you off to a good start. In cases where you need more detail about a specific topic, I supply helpful references in each chapter.

Writing Words of Wisdom

Just a couple more words of wisdom before we move forward. First, keep in mind that first impressions are lasting impressions. Carefully proofread your work to ensure that it is free of grammar, spelling, or formatting errors before you submit it to your chair or committee. Always ensure that you're following writing reference guidelines, such as the American Psychological Association (APA), Modern Language Association (MLA), or the Chicago Manual of Style (CMS), that are called for by your school. If you have problems or concerns, it's very likely that your university has reference librarians and writing coaches to help you. In other instances, online writing labs, such as Purdue OWL (*https://owl.purdue.edu/owl/purdue_owl.html*) or Grammarly (*www.grammarly.com*), can be very useful.

Always ensure that you have not included material that is not correctly referenced. While this might be inadvertent, it can happen. To avoid this problem, since they are subject-matter experts, ask your committee members to point out any issues they may see. You might also ask your committee members to identify others outside of the committee who might proofread your work. Many students have taken advantage of technology growth in this field and use one of the great online resources, such as *https://turnitin.com,* to identify potential problems.

As you're writing, remember that your readers may not just be other academicians, they could be anyone interested in the subject matter you're investigating. For example, depending on your topic, you might have teachers looking for a new approach to student engagement, mental health counselors interested in the latest approaches to therapy, or business managers focusing on increasing employee morale. Also, just as you're going to rely on the completed dissertation work of others in your field to guide you, other students will look at your work for guidance. This is especially true when they are looking to support the background and significance of a problem they want to investigate.

Your goal should be to ensure that your dissertation proposal is an understandable presentation of your research problem, your literature review, your proposed methodology, your plans for data analysis, and how you will present your results.

Make sure that what you write comes across as authentic, understandable, and enlightening. To paraphrase a quote attributed to Albert Einstein, "If you cannot explain it simply, you don't understand it well enough."

Having said all of this, now it's time to get started!

Do You Understand These Key Words and Phrases?	
Dissertation	Five-chapter dissertation
Dissertation chair	Four-chapter dissertation
Dissertation committee	Methodology
Dissertation defense	Problem statement
Dissertation proposal	Review of literature (ROL)
Dissertation report	

CHAPTER ONE

Developing the Problem Statement for Your Dissertation Proposal

The Problem Is the Problem

As I said in the introduction, many students wrestle with "the problem is the problem"; they just can't seem to get started. My experiences with doctoral students are not unique; many experts believe that defining a clear, researchable problem is the most difficult part of any research study. Given that, in this chapter, we focus on learning how to identify a specific problem, or research opportunity, and then develop and write a good problem statement. In subsequent chapters, we will see exactly how the problem statement sets the stage for the rest of the dissertation proposal wherein we will include a statement of the purpose of the study, research questions and hypotheses, the review of related literature, and the research method for investigating the problem. By understanding this process, you will be well on your way to writing a quality dissertation proposal.

Finding a Good Research Problem

Problems or opportunities for research are all around us. For many students, the real issue isn't finding a problem to investigate, it's narrowing down the many possibilities—things you've studied in your coursework, personal experiences, issues at your workplace or institution, or by reading about a topic in which you are interested. Other potential areas for investigation can be found by attending professional conferences, speaking with experts in your field, or by replicating the work of others to better understand or apply the results of research they have conducted. We will look at several examples but, before we do, let's talk briefly about the reading required as part of identifying your problem.

Reading the Literature in Your Field Underlies Everything You Do

As I've pointed out several times up to this point, a formal *review of literature (ROL)* is an essential component of a good dissertation proposal. As I mentioned in the introduction, that leads some students to believe that all of the literature they read will be included in the formal ROL, but nothing could be further from the truth. Every part of a good dissertation is influenced and supported by what you read.

For example, in many cases, students identify a potential dissertation problem based on readings in a specific area of interest. As we'll see later in this chapter, however, a good problem statement also discusses the **background of the problem**, as well as why investigating the problem is important: the literature helps in writing both of these sections. In short, the literature you read at this point helps you write a strong problem statement.

The formal ROL, usually in Chapter 2 of a dissertation, expands upon that knowledge and provides the reader with a deeper understanding of the problem area, discusses prior research that has been conducted, and provides a basis for a sound research methodology upon which to investigate the problem. While this may sound somewhat confusing, the key lies in reading other high-quality proposals, dissertations, and journal articles. It will become readily apparent how writers use the literature to support their problem area and then how it is used to better define, understand, and guide the research itself. In this book, we go into greater detail when we get to those sections, but for now let's get back to finding a good research problem.

A Problem Based on Experience

Experience-based problems can be identified in almost any field: education, medicine, business, agriculture, psychology, and so on. In short, an experience-based problem can be identified in any case where we want to investigate a problem to find a solution, develop new technology, improve health care, and so forth.

Let's begin with a straightforward, easy-to-understand problem. In this case, imagine we are working at a university where the attrition rate from the doctoral program is higher than the historical average of doctoral programs throughout the United States; this is clearly a problem I could investigate:

> Our school has an attrition rate greater than 50%.

This type of problem is a *practical* or *applied* research problem because it focuses on a specific issue—attrition—within a group or organization, in this case, our school. In short, it tackles a real-world problem and attempts to solve it.

In another case, I might focus on a practical problem in the gym where I work out:

> Regardless of the amount of exercise they do, participants in aerobics classes do not lose a significant amount of weight.

Since I live in a state with a large population of older citizens, I might focus on the following problem:

Drivers over the age of 65 are involved in more automobile accidents
than drivers in other age groups.

In this example, you might be thinking, "Of course that's true. Older drivers have a slower reaction time, their eyesight tends to be poorer and, because they tend to drive less daily, their driving skills may not be as sharp as younger drivers." If we know the answer already, then why is this a valid research problem for a dissertation? Unfortunately, older drivers are involved in more accidents than most other age groups and this has led to preventative measures, including more frequent license renewals being implemented. Wait a minute though, did I just say, "most other age groups"? Yes, and as you might guess, according to the National Highway Traffic Safety Administration, there are about an equal number of accidents caused by drivers age 24 and younger. Reasons such as lack of experience, being distracted by their phones, speeding, and being with friends seem to relate directly to this problem. Information of this type, gleaned from the literature or other sources, such as publications from the Department of Motor Vehicles, might cause you to have to modify your problem statement:

Drivers over the age of 65 are involved in more automobile accidents
than drivers ages 25–65.

Theoretical or Basic Research Problems

We may also investigate *theoretical* or *basic* research problems: those that come from conflicts or contradictions in previous findings or a desire to extend the knowledge about a specific problem area. This is a perfect example of using the literature to help demonstrate the background and **significance of the problem** statement. For example, let's say we have found conflicting research regarding how to support dissertation students in an online environment; we could easily write a problem statement such as:

There is conflicting research on how to support dissertation students
in an online environment.

This problem statement implies that multiple studies (i.e., literature focused directly on the problem area) have been conducted about supporting online dissertation students; apparently there is no consensus on the best approach. For example, these studies may have been based on traditional learning theories, such as behaviorism and constructivism—our job would be to conduct further studies using the same constructs to help better explain or support prior results. We might attempt to replicate one or more of the studies to determine whether the results could be different using another population of students or different pedagogical tools based on the same learning theories. We could also attempt to extend the prior work by investigating a different approach.

In another case, one of my students was interested in using laboratory simulators to teach basic concepts in his undergraduate anatomy and physiology classes for students majoring in nursing. He searched the literature and found that many studies had been conducted using laboratory simulators in other disciplines—unfortunately, none of them dealt with anatomy and physiology in classes taken by nursing majors. Because the results of using laboratory simulators might vary from field to field, it led him to state:

> *There have been no studies investigating the effect of laboratory simulators on achievement by undergraduate nursing students in anatomy and physiology classes.*

In another case, we might find, because of health concerns with insects, molds, and bacteria, that many farmers are irradiating crops before they are packaged. This simply means that these crops are exposed to low levels of radiation to eliminate these perceived threats. While most farmers see no harm in this process, critics of this practice are concerned with the safety of eating irradiated crops and call for long-term studies in animals and humans. This is clearly a problem that could be investigated:

> *There is a lack of research on the long-term effects of irradiated crops and their effect on the health of humans.*

Using Suggestions for Future Research

Whether a student is still taking coursework or starting the dissertation, I always reinforce how important it is to be an expert in their field. They simply won't be able to move forward with a research study until they are intimately familiar with the history of the problem area, current issues, and any future research being called for. In order to do so, I tell them, they must "read, read, read, and then read some more." While reading, an area of research interest may present itself; in other cases, I tell the student to look at the final section of the articles they have found interesting. In more cases than not, they'll find a section titled "Suggestions for Future Research," "Articles of Interest," "Future Trends," "Conclusions," or other similar headings. In many instances, in that section, the article's author points a doctoral researcher in a direction they may want to go.

To demonstrate this, in one of my classes, I chose a random journal and opened it to the first article. In it, the author had written about exploring the career aspirations of undergraduate students majoring in math. His findings showed that most math students felt they were adequately prepared for a job in their field, but he went on to point out that the results were tentative, exploratory, and came from a small sample. He suggested future research that would focus on environmental or developmental factors that might influence a student to major in math. For a student interested in math education, this article might be a gold mine of inspiration.

Speaking with Experts in the Field

I've found, through the years, that once you have identified a broad topic to work with, many people who are the acknowledged experts in that field are more than willing to help you. For example, when I was writing my dissertation, I was interested in working with elementary school children to help raise their motivation in math and science classes. One of the things holding me back was a survey instrument that was no longer in print, so I contacted the original author directly. She was very gracious and sent me a copy with permission to use it; she even went so far as to follow up by asking how my work was progressing and offering her insight (A. Gottfried, personal communication, July 15, 1991).

Based on successes such as that, I have encouraged my students to reach out to experts for help; very few of these students' inquiries have been ignored, and the success stories are wonderful. One student was led through a civil rights museum by an actual freedom rider from the 1960s, one had a world-famous cardiac surgeon agree to serve on his dissertation committee, and another worked with a person famous in the equestrian world. While he wasn't my student and he wasn't working on a dissertation, one of the best success stories I have ever seen involved our son Andy during a high school science class.

From an early age, Andy dreamed of a career as an astronaut. He had a general idea for a science fair project related to astronautics, but he could not narrow his focus to one specific aspect of the problem. I told him he should identify one of the astronauts involved in the work he was interested in, and send an email asking for help. Andy, never shy, went directly to the top and emailed one of the shuttle commanders from a Hubble space telescope mission. To make a long story short, though he never became an astronaut, our son received a tremendous amount of guidance and information simply because he wasn't too shy to ask a leading professional for his help (L. Shriver, personal communication, May 5, 1997).

Working with Your Dissertation Advisor in Their Research Area

Many college professors have a research agenda in which they are actively involved; many times, this is a requirement for tenure at their school. In my case, for many years I have been very active in science, technology, engineering, and math (STEM) research. We've primarily focused on how we can raise the STEM interest and awareness of young, minority middle school females. Luckily, I've had a number of students who, after reading or hearing about the work we're doing, ask me about getting involved. I meet with these students to get their background, ask why they want to be involved in the study, what do they expect to learn from the study, and how they can contribute. One of the key questions I ask is whether they are really interested in the topic, or are they just looking for something to work on. So far, I've been lucky enough to find students who really want to work with me, for all the right reasons. In short, if you identify a professor who you are interested in working with, you should reach out to him or her. Before you do, however, be prepared:

1. Ask yourself—are you really interested in this field and are you willing to devote the amount of time and energy necessary to conduct research in the field?

2. Be up-to-date with the literature in the field—this is especially true of the work your potential chair has been involved in, and his or her publications and presentations.

3. Get to know your potential chair professionally prior to discussing your dissertation. It's a good idea to know their professional interests—organizations they belong to, positions they have held in academia, awards they may have received, and so on.

4. Finally, ask yourself—I will be asking this professor to dedicate a lot of time and effort to work with me. Am I willing to show them my appreciation by working diligently to finish my dissertation?

Attending Conferences or Professional Meetings

This idea is basically the same as speaking to experts in your field but, in this case, it is limited to a specific venue. For example, each year there are literally thousands of conferences dedicated to almost any discipline you can imagine. Personally, I have attended quite a few information systems, business, counseling, psychology, and education conferences. While I am there, I see many people whose names I recognize from the literature I have read. This offers a student several ways to learn more about a potential problem area.

First, look at the conference program and identify sessions you are interested in attending—at the end of the sessions there is usually an open period where anyone can ask questions. That's your big chance: ask the presenter specific questions about the topic you are interested in. You will be surprised how often the speaker appreciates an insightful question and provides informational feedback.

I have also found that approaching an author outside of a formal session, introducing yourself, and asking questions focusing on the author's area of expertise is very productive. In my case, I've had students approach me to ask about articles I have written. I am always so flattered that they've read my work that I am more than glad to spend a few minutes talking with them. Most authors I know feel the same way when students approach them.

Finally, many of the larger organizations have special interest groups, often called SIGs, devoted to a specific topic or field of study. I always enjoy going to presentations and social events hosted by SIGs whose focus interests me. Meeting and talking to people who, up to that point have only been names in the literature, is always refreshing and informative. In fact, I have developed quite a few relationships that have evolved into friendships outside of the professional meetings and conferences. For example, one of my well-published friends is more than willing to talk to anyone if you respond positively to his suggestion "to continue our conversation over dinner"!

Replicate Previously Conducted Research

When we talk about replicating a previously published study, many people seem to think we're planning to simply copy the work of another author. While this is true to a certain degree, and replication is a valid way to develop a problem statement, it is also the trickiest. I have had many students who read something interesting and wanted to conduct essentially the same study. While this is a potentially good place to start, I always ask them, "Why should you conduct the same research a second time?" In far too many cases, students are not able to clearly answer that question—let me explain what I mean.

I recently had a student from our college of business come to my office to tell me about a study conducted by a friend, a recent doctoral graduate from another university, that focused on increasing corporate telemarketing sales. In his friend's case, he had looked at differences in productivity between telemarketing employees working in traditional offices and colleagues working in home offices. Upon seeing the productivity in his friend's company grow significantly with in-home offices, my student wanted to conduct the same study in his company.

This sounds like a good problem to investigate, right? Yes, it could be, but I asked my student several questions: "Why do you want to do that? What makes your company different from the one where the research has already been conducted? Does your company offer a different product or service? Are their differences in the employees or customers, such as income, that would call for you to conduct the study again? If everything is equal, can't you just assume that your results would be the same as his?" In short, I was asking him to give me his reasoning for replicating his friend's investigation. He admitted that he had not thought about those things, and we agreed that he should do a bit more background work before committing to that direction. That's not to say that my student wouldn't be able to find work to support his idea, it's just that he needed to show why his proposed study was significant.

In another case, I had a student tell me about a study investigating technology acceptance that she would like to replicate. I asked her the same questions as those above, and she was able to support her desire to move forward. She pointed out that the original study investigated technology acceptance in a corporate environment, and she wanted to work with primary school teachers. She felt that gender gaps within the two types of organizations might have an effect on the results. She supported this by showing that females made up about 76% of primary school teachers, but only 22% of corporate executive-level positions. Because a limited number of studies had been conducted focused in this area, and none that she could find directly addressed her proposed area of study, she was able to support her desire to replicate the original work.

Characteristics of a Good Problem

Regardless of how we identify a problem, before we move forward with our investigation, we need to ensure it meets six criteria. As you're reading these, keep in mind that we're not going to look at them in any specific order; all of these characteristics must be met before we can move forward (Terrell, 2021).

1. The problem must be interesting to the researcher.
2. The scope of the problem must be manageable by the researcher.
3. The researcher must have the knowledge, time, and resources needed to investigate the problem.
4. The problem can be researched through the collection and analysis of data.
5. Investigating the problem has **theoretical** or **practical significance**.
6. It is ethical to investigate the problem.

Let's look at examples of each of these characteristics to ensure that we know what we need to do.

The Problem Must Be Interesting to the Researcher

Many times, I run into students who simply want to finish their dissertation and really don't care what they work on, as long as they're working on something. Unfortunately, this approach often fails simply because they are not interested enough to see the problem under investigation through to the end. For example, I once had a student who was near her wits' end trying to find a topic for her dissertation. She was a very bright student, so I asked her to work with me on a project investigating the abysmal failure rate of students taking algebra at a community college. She jumped at the chance to work on the project, not necessarily because she was interested but because she saw it as a way to graduate. Unfortunately, she did not finish the project with me; she simply did not have the interest, energy, and enthusiasm she needed to work on something for which she really didn't have a commitment. Two good things did come from her experience with me: she did graduate after she found a suitable project and I ultimately finished what I was working on. Both of us met our goals because we were working on a project we were interested in.

The Scope of the Problem Must Be Manageable by the Researcher

As I said earlier, when my students tell me they cannot find an interesting problem to work on for their dissertation, in many instances I tell them, "It's not that you can't find a problem, it's just that you can't find one with a scope you can manage." For example, look at the following "problem statement" presented to me by one of my students:

Many inner-city children throughout the United States come from single-parent homes and live at or below the poverty level. Research shows that these students are more likely to drop out of high school than their peers from different socioeconomic backgrounds.

The problem here is certainly clear: students from lower socioeconomic, single-parent homes are more likely to drop out of high school than students coming from more affluent, traditional families. This certainly seems to be a serious problem, one that bears investigating. While important, however, is this something that my student could investigate as written? Of course not! The scope is much too broad; in this case, it seemed my student was suggesting an investigation of students throughout the country. In cases like this, I tell my students not to attempt to "boil the ocean"; if the issue is so large that it cannot be easily investigated, focus on narrowing it down into something more specific and manageable.

My student might be able to reword this proposal as a more manageable practical problem statement by simply stating:

Many children in our school come from single-parent homes and live at or below the poverty level. Research shows that these students are more likely to drop out of high school than their peers from different socioeconomic backgrounds.

By narrowing down the first statement, the student was able to create a problem statement that could more easily be investigated. Let's look at another example:

Initiations for admission into fraternities and sororities are problematic throughout the United States. Published reports have shown that problems such as alcohol abuse, physical harm, and other criminal activities are often related to these rites of passage.

Instead of asking what's wrong with this problem statement, it might be easier to ask if there is anything right with it! First, the idea of investigating problems at institutions throughout the United States is monumental. Following that, trying to define exactly what we mean by "alcohol abuse" would be debatable: some schools are well-known for partying, others have very strict student conduct codes that limit or prohibit drinking alcoholic beverages. Finally, what does "physical harm" mean? While I knew that a symbolic "paddling" from my fraternal big brother was part of the process, other institutions may forbid such behavior at any level. In short, in this case, the physical scope of the problem (i.e., the United States), as well as the broad scope of some of the areas to be investigated, would preclude this from being a viable problem statement.

Believe it or not, issues with the scope of a problem occur more often than you might imagine; I suppose that some students believe that the bigger the problem, the more impressed I'll be. When that happens, I tell them three things:

1. Don't try to investigate all of the world's problems.
2. Don't try to investigate some of the world's problems.
3. Investigate one problem.

The Researcher Has the Knowledge, Time, and Resources Needed to Investigate the Problem

This requirement is pretty obvious, isn't it? A researcher lacking any of these criteria might cause the research to fail or, at best, add significantly to the length of time it would take to complete. For example, I was involved in a study that looked at the need for mental health counseling for families of soldiers returning from combat deployment. My initial literature search indicated that levels of posttraumatic stress disorder were, in many instances, as severe in family members as it was for the returning service members. I was applying for grant funding and needed a certified mental health counselor as part of my team. Since one of my best students is a nationally certified counselor, I assumed she had the knowledge, time, and resources needed to get involved with the project. I thought we had a "win–win" situation; I would have someone to help me, and she could write her dissertation as part of the study (Stevenson, 2014).

Unfortunately, my assumption that she had the knowledge, time, and resources didn't hold true. While she did ultimately finish her dissertation, despite her knowledge and experience as a counselor, I had put her into a situation where she did not have the specific knowledge needed to work within the military culture. Because of that, before she was able to move forward with writing her proposal, she had to spend time reading and talking to members of the military in order to understand the dynamics of military families. She also did not have the resources necessary to investigate the problem and it took her several months to find military families that were willing to participate in the counseling program. Again, she did finish her dissertation, but it took quite some time for her to overcome these obstacles.

Finally, many doctoral students underestimate the cost or availability of resources they might need to finish their dissertation. For example, one of my students focused on understanding the life experiences of single mothers returning to graduate school. Her plan seemed simple enough: she would record interviews with 12–15 students and then analyze transcripts of those interviews. Unfortunately, it didn't go as smoothly, financially, as she might have hoped. First, she needed recording equipment and software that cost several hundred dollars, and after the interviews, she quickly found out that accurately transcribing over 20 hours of interviews was a job best left for a professional; that wound up costing another $1,200 or so. While needing resources such as these might sound obvious, they can be easily overlooked while planning research. Costs for other things, such as travel, testing instrumentation, surveys, software, work–study assistance, or anything else that is required to finish your dissertation, should be identified and planned for while writing your proposal.

The Problem Can Be Researched through the Collection and Analysis of Data

This requirement is also quite obvious. When we are investigating a problem, we have to be able to collect data to help in our decision making. Depending on the problem, we might need numeric **quantitative data,** such as grades, miles per gallon, or medical measurements, such as weight or blood pressure. In other cases, we might need **qualitative data** from interviews, transcripts, or texts. Finally, there are problems we can address only by collecting both quantitative and qualitative data. We'll talk more in detail about different types of data and issues with data collection later when we get into the methodology chapters, but for now let's just accept the fact that data are required to investigate a problem and move forward.

Investigating the Problem Has Theoretical or Practical Significance

Simply put, whether a problem has theoretical or practical significance means that it can pass the "Who cares?" test. In looking back at the problems dealing with attrition rates from doctoral programs or high school dropout by students from inner-city schools, we can readily see that these are practical problems and investigating each problem is worthwhile.

In other cases, we might investigate a problem that has theoretical significance. In my dissertation, for example, I investigated the following problem:

Students in fifth-grade math classes have low levels of intrinsic motivation. Research has shown that low levels of intrinsic motivation lead to low levels of achievement.

I ultimately based my study on a theory that suggested achievement feedback that is timely and informational and would lead to higher levels of student intrinsic motivation (Deci & Ryan, 1985). In doing that, I looked at the differences between elementary school students receiving weekly graphical "cause-and-effect" report cards versus traditional report cards received every 6–9 weeks. Unfortunately, my intervention did not work as planned. We'll discuss this problem in more detail later, but now suffice it to say that sometimes there is value in showing what doesn't work.

Let's look at a few more examples and determine whether their investigation is either theoretically or practically significant:

Imported cars are better than domestically made cars.

At first glance, this seems like a practical problem, doesn't it? We want to find out whether foreign-built cars are better than those we make here in the United States. It seems, though, that there are too many issues here to make it a practical problem. First, what does "better" mean? Would we be comparing fuel mileage, crash test results, resale value, or one of the myriad characteristics that contribute to the definition of "better" in this context? Second, what does "imported" and "domestic" mean? Are we talking about companies whose headquarters are in foreign countries versus those that are based in the United States? While that may be something to look at, we have to keep in mind that, among others, Honda, Hyundai, and Mercedes-Benz have plants here in the United States. I'm sure there are other issues we should be worried about, but the bottom line is that this doesn't seem like a very good problem statement for a student to investigate.

Let's look at one last problem:

> *Emergency room physicians historically make more diagnostic mistakes*
> *than physicians in other specialties.*

This was an actual problem statement presented to me by one of my doctoral students. The authors of the original study (Berner & Graber, 2008) found that many physicians are overconfident in their diagnostic abilities, leading to a higher number of errors than might be expected. The authors noted that a key to addressing this issue might be teaching decision-making strategies to physicians in an effort to decrease the number of errors of this type.

At first, this seemed like a problem that might bear investigation. It stands to reason that, when the health of a patient is at stake, physicians would want to quickly make a diagnosis that is as accurate as possible. In this case, my student wanted to develop a software system that emergency room physicians could use during the examination of their patient. I told her to go ahead with the initial work on her dissertation based on her assertion that it could have both practical and theoretical significance. Unfortunately, her proposed study fell through very quickly as she learned that, while theoretically the diagnoses might be more accurate, in many instances, emergency room physicians simply do not have time to turn their back on their patients in order to enter data into a computer and wait for diagnostic help. It is best for the physicians to rely on the skills they were taught in school and that are reinforced by their training residencies, internships, and experience.

It Is Ethical to Investigate the Problem

There are many examples in the history of research of studies that were clearly unethical. Among others, these include withholding drugs from terminally ill patients in the Tuskegee Syphilis Studies (Jones, 1993), to Milgram's (1974) research focusing on the simulation of electric shock to investigate a person's reaction to authority. It's obvious to most researchers when a study is not ethical, but at most colleges and universities, institutional review boards (IRBs) have been established to ensure any study conducted within their venue meets prescribed organizational and legal standards. In most instances, approval is not an issue but when human or animal subjects are part of a research study, proposals are closely scrutinized to determine whether they should be approved. For example, do you think the study using computers to assist emergency room physicians would be considered **ethical research**? Probably not, since a patient's life is hanging in the balance. It's best to err on the side of caution; regardless of the type of study you are conducting, if you're not sure whether it's ethical, always ask. We discuss this issue in far greater detail later in the book.

Writing the Problem Statement

In the preceding sections, we defined and discussed the characteristics of a good problem statement. We now have to put those things together and learn how to actually write a good problem statement using the following criteria:

Problem Statements Must Be Clear and Concise

The most important thing to keep in mind as you write a problem statement is that the reader must understand what the problem is—it must be stated as clearly and concisely as possible. We alluded to this issue in an earlier section but let's look at another example to ensure we understand exactly what this means. It's common for me to receive a problem statement such as this:

> *Higher student engagement in courses using online learning management systems.*

What does this mean? Is what the author trying to say clear and concise? In this case, it is not; in order to state the problem more clearly, the author needs to establish the relationship between student engagement and learning management systems. It could be presented in this manner:

> *Observations indicate that there are low levels of student engagement when using online learning management systems in our school.*

Thinking back, does this statement meet our six criteria? First, we can only hope that it's interesting to the researcher and the necessary time, skills, and resources are available; if not, why would it be worth investigating the problem? Next, the problem can certainly be analyzed through the collection and analysis of data—numeric data from a survey designed to measure engagement, or interviews with students discussing their reaction to using online learning management systems. The results of the study would seem to have practical significance and while it appears it would be ethical to investigate the problem, it would be best to have an IRB confirm that for us. Finally, the scope of the problem is manageable because it is limited to our school.

Is this problem statement clear and concise?

> *Seizure disorders and diet.*

In this case, we don't know much about what the researcher is proposing to investigate, but it could be reworded to make it clearer:

Seizure disorders in children are a prevalent concern in the United States. There has been only limited research investigating the relationship between these disorders and children's diets.

Here again, we're assuming the researcher is interested in the problem and has the knowledge, skills, and time necessary to study it properly. Investigating this problem has both theoretical and practical significance, and numeric data can be collected. There is still an issue with the ethics of investigating this problem in that the participants are children and they are being treated for a medical condition; both of these issues raise a red flag with IRBs and would be closely examined to ensure the health and well-being of the children while in the study. The scope of the problem, however, seems to be our biggest concern. Who are the children the author wants to work with? All of those in the United States? The state where the children live? Who? In short, this problem statement should reflect a much narrower scope, one the researcher has access to and has the ability to work with.

The Problem Statement Must Include All Variables to Be Considered

The second criterion for writing a good problem statement is that each of the variables to be investigated must be included. For example, in the problem statement where we wanted to investigate the relationship between online learning management systems and student engagement, no other variables were included in the problem statement.

In another case, suppose we were notified that our insurance company would no longer cover a brand-name medicine that patients use to control cholesterol and triglycerides, and instead it would only cover a generic brand of the specific medication. Although the drug manufacturers have assured physicians that there is no difference in the efficacy of the drug, researchers could state:

Physicians are concerned that a generic version of a medication does not control cholesterol as well as the brand-name version of the same medication.

In this case, our problem statement is clear, but it does not include both variables. If the drug is advertised as controlling both cholesterol and triglycerides, in order to fully address the physicians' concerns, the problem statement could better be stated as:

Physicians are concerned that a generic version of a medication does not control cholesterol and triglycerides as well as the brand-name version of the same medication.

The Problem Statement Should Not Interject the Bias of the Researcher

Here again lies one of the biggest pitfalls that underlie research: far too many people want to "prove" things or conduct research that supports their personal beliefs or goals. For example, if I was arguing for the need for more technology in our public schools, I might write:

> *Students who do not use computers as part of their curriculum have lower achievement than students who use computers as part of their curriculum.*

That's a fairly large assumption on my part, isn't it? Suppose I do conduct research and show that there is increased achievement after obtaining new technology? Have I proven anything? Absolutely not! There are far too many things that affect achievement: the students themselves, a change in the curriculum, new teachers who work in a manner different from their predecessors, and the like. At the same time, what would occur if achievement went down? Would we go back to Apple, Dell, or Gateway and demand our money back? Of course not, we do not know whether the technology had any effect on student achievement. There are far too many factors that influence achievement to assume we can "prove" anything. Instead of the problem statement above, what about the following one?

> *Research has shown a clear positive relationship between the use of computers as part of a public school curriculum and achievement. The schools in our district do not have an ample number of computers to support student needs.*

In this case, we are clear and concise. We have included all variables to be considered—in this case, technology and achievement—and we have not interjected our personal bias. This seems to be a good problem statement.

Before we move forward, however, there is one caveat we need to discuss. When I said that the problem should not interject the bias of the researcher, this isn't to say that the researcher cannot use his or her personal judgment when identifying a problem or writing a problem statement. We see a great example of this in the next section.

The Problem Statement as Part of a Dissertation Proposal

Even though we're able to write a good problem statement, that is not enough for a dissertation proposal. We need to clearly tell the reader the genesis of the problem; we call this the **background** of the problem. We also need to tell the reader why investigating the problem is important; we call this the **significance** of the problem.

We touched on both ideas while discussing the characteristics of a good problem, but let's look at how we would actually include these in a dissertation proposal.

When a student approaches me with a potential dissertation idea, I tell him or her not to create a full proposal right from the outset; instead, I want a three- to five-page paper that tells me the background and significance of a potential problem. I insist that the background and significance are not just their own opinion and that they must include substantiating references from other related literature. By doing this, I am assured that the student is off to a good start on their dissertation proposal.

For example, let's use an actual problem statement from one of my former students. He works at an institution described as a historically Black college or university (HBCU). This is the problem he described to me (Poorandi, 2001):

> *African American students at ABC College fail entry-level algebra I classes at a rate higher (i.e., 22%) than the historical U.S. average of 15%.*

When I asked my student how he knew this, the answer was simple: faculty at the college knew they had a high failure rate but were astonished to find it was higher than the national average. When I asked him to provide me with the background of the problem, he presented me with something along the lines below. As I said earlier, including references from the problem area is important; for the sake of the example, I'm paraphrasing what he said and "inventing" the references he used:

The Background of the Problem

Many students enter college with weak math backgrounds (Bosley, 2009). In schools where general requirements include math classes, historically the failure rate for algebra I is approximately 15% (Alderman, 2011).

So far, this is looking good; my student has laid the groundwork by establishing a firm background for his problem. He followed up with the following section explaining why investigating the problem is important (i.e., the significance); again, he included references to the literature to help make his point:

The Significance of the Problem

Failure of classes early in a student's academic career not only extends their time in school for having to repeat a course but it is also a major predictor of dropping out of college (Schneider, 2006).

When my student put all of this together, it was a perfect introduction to his research proposal:

The Background, Problem, and Significance Together

Many students enter college with weak math backgrounds (Bosley, 2009). In schools where general requirements include math classes, historically the failure rate for algebra I is approximately 15% (Alderman, 2011). African American students at ABC College fail entry-level algebra I classes at a significantly higher rate (i.e., 22%). Failure of classes early in a student's academic career not only extends their time in school for having to repeat a course, it is also a major predictor of dropping out of college (Schneider, 2006).

This is a great example, but my students will tell you that in many instances writing the problem statement section isn't as easy as we've just demonstrated; it's often quite more extensive in terms of the material needed to write a meaningful and supportable problem statement. At the same time, in every case, the background/problem/significance model should be followed.

SUMMARY OF CHAPTER ONE

Understanding and clearly stating the problem you are investigating is the first step in writing a good proposal. Keep in mind, while formulating a good problem statement, that you must ensure you meet the following criteria:

1. You must be interested in the problem you are investigating.
2. The scope of the problem you want to investigate must be manageable.
3. You must be comfortable in terms of the knowledge, time, and resources necessary for you to investigate the problem.
4. You must be able to collect and analyze data.
5. There must be a practical or theoretical reason for you to investigate the problem.
6. It must be ethical for you to investigate the problem.

Once you are sure you have met these criteria and begin writing the actual problem statement, you must ensure that you are clear and concise, that all variables to be investigated are included, and that you do not interject your personal bias. Following all of these rules ensures that you have a viable problem statement. Keep in mind that stating a valid research problem is only the first step of the proposal. As I stated above, the problem statement is followed by the purpose statement, the research questions, hypotheses, a review of literature, and a detailed research method. We cover all of these topics in the following chapters but, for now, let's see how much we've learned up to this point.

Do You Understand These Key Words and Phrases?	
Background of the problem	Qualitative data
Ethical research	Quantitative data
Mixed methods data	Significance of the problem
Practical significance	Theoretical significance

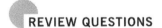

REVIEW QUESTIONS

Evaluate each of the problem statements below; are all six criteria for a good problem state-ment met? Are they clear and concise? Do they include all variables, and do they avoid inter-jecting personal bias? If the problem statement does not meet the criteria, what is wrong?

1. Birth weights of babies born to drug-addicted mothers.

2. Employees working in the older section of an industrial plant are concerned with the effects of asbestos used in building the plant.

3. Farmers in the United States are concerned that strict immigration laws will not allow them to hire enough farmhands to reap their annual harvests.

4. Publishers are concerned that the ever-increasing costs of printing traditional textbooks will cause decision makers in the elementary school market to opt for electronic text-books.

5. Subscriber feelings toward anonymous text messages used for advertising.

6. Is there a difference in recovery times among patients who receive medication for back injuries, patients who receive physical therapy for back injuries, and patients who receive a combination of medication and physical therapy for back injuries?

7. Engineering students at Wattsamatta University are concerned that changes in gravita-tional pull during the 28-day lunar cycle are affecting the structure of the microwave tower on their classroom building.

8. High-altitude climbers are concerned with hypoxia: the inability of the human body to perform due to a generalized lack of oxygen in the body.

9. Clients at an inner-city mental health facility who are suffering from depression and are working with therapists using a psychoanalytic approach are not responding to therapy as effectively and efficiently as those working with therapists using a cognitive-behavioral approach.

10. This study will investigate morale between soldiers wearing camouflage uniforms ver-sus those wearing khaki uniforms.

LET'S START WRITING OUR OWN PROPOSAL

I always tell my students that the key to learning to write a good dissertation is to just begin writing. Given that, I want you to start writing a proposal; you'll expand it as we move through each chapter by adding the material that was the focus of that chapter. Granted, by the end of this book, you probably won't have a dissertation proposal 100% ready for your dissertation supervisor and committee to approve, but you will have learned the process, and will be well on your way!

Given that, take a few minutes to think about a problem you would like to investigate. Reflect on articles you have read, classes you have taken, experts you may have talked to, or one of the myriad other sources for a good dissertation problem. Then, keeping in mind the six characteristics of a good problem, just start writing. Make sure that what you are writing is clear, includes the variables you are interested in, and does not interject your personal bias. As you are writing, ensure you reinforce the problem statement by using literature to develop sound background and significance sections.

Once you've finished, it's always a good idea to put your work aside for a day or so and then read it again with a "fresh set of eyes"; it never hurts to get someone else to read it and give you feedback. Chances are you won't get it right the first time but just keep trying; as trite as it sounds, practice does make perfect!

CHAPTER TWO

Writing Purpose Statements, Research Questions, and Hypotheses

Introduction

In the preceding chapter, our major goal was to learn how to write a sound problem statement; this included identifying the specific problem, as well as describing the background of the problem and explaining why investigating the problem is significant. In this chapter, we take this process a step further. We begin our investigation by learning to write **purpose statements**; this will tell the reader the overarching goal of your study.

We move from there into **research questions** based on our purpose statements. Within that section, we first need a general understanding of the different types of research methods. This will allow us to write research questions specific to the methodology dictated by our problem.

Following that, we'll get to a sticky spot in writing a proposal. We will focus on writing **hypotheses** for our study but will soon find that testing a hypothesis requires numeric data; this means they'll be included only in quantitative (i.e., when numeric data are collected) or mixed method studies where both quantitative and qualitative data are collected and integrated to help best answer the research question. We'll also find that the way we word our hypotheses is based partly on the ROL, which traditionally falls into Chapter 2 of a dissertation proposal. Despite all of that, once the hypotheses are written, most researchers include them in Chapter 1 of their study, mostly to improve readability. This may sound confusing, but hang in there; it will become clear as we move forward.

Once we've talked about all of these things, we'll see that the scope of each of these sections creates an inverted pyramid (see Figure 2.1): the purpose statement is very broad; the research questions narrow down our area of inquiry; and the hypotheses, when necessary, focus on exactly the variables we want to test. Keep in

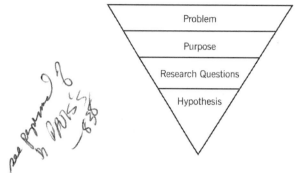

FIGURE 2.1. Narrowing down and focusing the problem statement.

mind that everything we discuss in this chapter, along with the problem statement discussed in the previous chapter, will be included in Chapter 1 of your dissertation proposal.

While this might seem like a lot of information to be included in only one chapter, remember to think of the proposal as a road map. A good proposal requires knowing, from the outset, where you want to go.

The Purpose Statement

The purpose statement defines the specific reason for your investigation. As the name implies, it tells the reader the overarching focus, goal, or intent of your study. While it is called a "statement," you'll find that the description of the purpose of your study will likely be longer than one sentence. Your goal is to create a precise statement that matches the reason for your work, the content of your paper, and its organization. Since the purpose statement does guide the reader, it should be included in all manners of studies (e.g., quantitative, qualitative, mixed methods; Creswell, 2014; Creswell & Guetterman, 2018).

Purpose Statements for Quantitative Studies

Generally speaking, purpose statements for quantitative studies (see Figure 2.2) should include or infer the following (Creswell & Creswell, 2020):

1. Include words that introduce the major focus of your study (e.g., "purpose," "intent," or "objective").
2. If your study is based on a theory, it should be included.
3. Identify the independent and dependent variables. We cover these in great detail later but, for now, we just consider our independent variable to be

The purpose of the proposed study is to test the theory of _____ that _____ (describe outcomes) or (compares? relates?) the _____ (independent variable) to _____ (dependent variable) controlling for _____ (control variables) for _____ (participants) at _____ (the research site). The independent variable(s) _____ will be defined as _____ (provide a definition). The dependent variable(s) will be defined as _____ (provide a definition) and the control and intervening variables will be defined as _____ (provide a definition).

FIGURE 2.2. Quantitative purpose statement script.

the "cause" we are investigating; the dependent variable can be described as the "effect" we want to measure. As you are writing, order these from left to right beginning with the independent variable. Follow these with any control, treatment, or moderating variables that might affect the results of the study.

4. Include words that connect the independent and dependent variables. These can include words or phrases such as "comparison," "relationship," and the like.

5. Identify the participants or **unit of analysis**. As explained by Babbie (2012), this is the "who" or "what" you are studying; it's the things we are examining that allow us to create summaries or make inferences based on them. These might include individuals, groups, organizations, and the like.

6. State the location where your study will be conducted.

Keep in mind that these are guidelines; not every entry is required for every study. For example, in my dissertation (Terrell, 1992), I wrote my purpose statement by carefully thinking through what I wanted to do and making sure I addressed the elements we just discussed. As I said, you'll see that I left out some of the elements simply because they weren't called for in my study:

The purpose (i.e., intent) of this proposed study will be to investigate the Cognitive Evaluation Theory (i.e., the theory) by comparing the effect of different types of achievement feedback on the motivation and achievement (i.e., the variables) of students at an elementary school in Dade County, Florida (i.e., the participants and research site). The independent variable will be defined as the type of weekly feedback a student receives, either a traditional or a graphical report card (i.e., the independent variable and two levels). The dependent variables are defined as levels of intrinsic motivation and fifth-grade math achievement (i.e., the dependent variables). There are no control or intervening variables that should be considered.

In this case, I accounted for all of the characteristics of a good quantitative purpose statement listed above. Just to make sure we have a good grasp of this, I've included more examples below:

Animal Therapy Quantitative Purpose Statement

Many senior citizens temporarily living in an assisted nursing facility due to health problems report high levels of depression. This can negatively affect their willingness to participate in wellness routines, interact with staff, and actively work toward being discharged back to their home and family. The purpose of this study is to investigate the effect of biweekly visits of pets from a local dog rescue ranch on senior citizens' levels of depression.

The purpose of this case is clear: the researchers want to investigate the relationship between patients' depression and contact with canine visitors. Notice that in this case, there is no independent variable because we are using only one group: the patients in their living facility, with no other group identified. Levels of self-reported depression before and after a series of visits would serve as our dependent variable. In this case, we are not basing our work on a theory and there isn't a need to. We have identified the research site and there are no other variables to be considered.

Productivity Quantitative Purpose Statement

The purpose of this study is to determine whether there are differences in productivity between employees of ABC Widget Manufacturing working a 4-day, 10-hour per-day work week and employees working a 5-day, 8-hour per-day work week.

The purpose of our study is to investigate the relationship between the type of work week and productivity. Our independent variable is the type of work week, and there are two levels: employees working a 4-day week and employees working a 5-day week. Our dependent variable is the number of widgets manufactured in a given week. We have clearly identified the location of our study; it is not theoretically based and there are no other variables we need to measure or control for.

Purpose Statements for Qualitative Studies

In qualitative studies, you will include many of the same elements as in the quantitative study but, instead of focusing on the relationship between a specific set of variables, your focus will be on the major issue; we call this the "central phenomenon." This is shown in Steps 1–4 below (see Figure 2.3):

1. The purpose (i.e., intent) of inquiry (e.g., Understand? Discover? Describe?).
2. The participants and the research site.

The purpose of this study will be to _____ (understand? explore? develop? discover?) the _____ (central phenomenon to be studied) for _____ (the participants, such as the individual, group, or organization) at _____ (the research site). At this stage in the research, the _____ (central phenomenon being studied) will be defined as _____ (provide a general definition).

FIGURE 2.3. Qualitative purpose statement script.

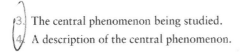

3. The central phenomenon being studied.
4. A description of the central phenomenon.

For example, if you were interested in better understanding why female undergraduate students choose to major in math, your purpose statement would read:

The Number of Female Undergraduate Math Majors Purpose Statement

The purpose of this study will be to understand the life experiences of female math majors at Pleasantville University in an effort to understand their decision to major in math.

Here, the component parts of our purpose statement are clear: we want to understand the reasons (i.e., our purpose) for female students' at Pleasantville University (i.e., participants and site) decision to major in math (i.e., the central phenomenon).

Just as we did above, let's identify the component parts of each of the following qualitative purpose statements:

Perceptions of Online Dating Purpose Statement

The purpose of this study is to better understand widowed or divorced senior citizens' perceptions of online relationship websites.

Our goal here is to better understand (i.e., our intent) the perceptions of online relationship websites (i.e., the central phenomenon) of widowed and divorced senior citizens (i.e., the participants). Notice that in this case since there is no clear research site identified, the study could be easily conducted face-to-face, over the phone, or online.

Teacher Preparedness Purpose Statement

The purpose of this study is to investigate how middle school teachers in traditional schools in Bowie County, Texas, responded to the sudden transition to online classrooms due to school closures caused by the COVID-19 pandemic.

In this case, our participants are middle school teachers, and for this example, we are investigating (i.e., our intent) their response to the COVID-19 crisis (i.e., the central phenomenon) in their individual classrooms in Bowie County, Texas (i.e., the site).

Purpose Statements for Mixed Methods Studies

Before we get into the detail of writing purpose statements for mixed methods studies, let's briefly discuss the idea of "mixing." We discuss this in great detail later in the book but, for now, let's just think of it as the point where we integrate the data to provide us with what we need to answer research questions or test hypotheses. In some cases, we will mix our data after sequentially collecting it; either quantitative first followed by qualitative, or qualitative first followed by quantitative. In other cases, we will collect and mix our data simultaneously. Again, we go into great detail about this later but, for now, let's get back to the elements that must be included in a good mixed methods purpose statement.

1. The purpose of the study (e.g., Understand? Discover? Describe?).
2. The central phenomenon being studied.
3. Qualitative data to be collected, including purpose and method.
4. Quantitative data to be collected, including purpose and method.
5. The participants and research site for both strands of data.
6. The point where mixing will occur.

For example, we could expand the study above where we compared productivity at the ABC Widget Manufacturing plant between employees working a 4-day week and those working a 5-day week. If, after collecting these quantitative data, we wanted to determine why or whether any differences in productivity existed, we could add a qualitative component. Based on this idea, we could state the following mixed methods purpose statement:

Work Week Productivity Mixed Methods Purpose Statement

The purpose of this study is to determine (i.e., intent) whether there are differences in productivity (i.e., the central phenomenon) between employees (i.e., participants) of ABC Widget Manufacturing (i.e., research site) working a 4-day, 10-hour per-day work week and employees working a 5-day, 8-hour per-day work week (i.e., participants). Quantitative data will represent actual productivity rates (i.e., a quantitative dependent variable) between the two groups (i.e., independent variable), with qualitative data collected from semistructured interviews focusing on employees' perceptions (i.e., a qualitative dependent variable) about their particular work week. These data will be analyzed sequentially in order to determine whether the employees' perceptions might explain any differences in productivity that might exist between the two groups (i.e., sequential mixing).

Equine Competition Evaluation Mixed Methods Purpose Statement

The purpose of this study is to develop an equine competition evaluation form that can be used to equitably grade horses and riders as they compete in different types of show competitions and exhibitions. Qualitative data will be collected from prior event judges, riders, and owners to determine which characteristics they consider to be important in these types of equine events. Once collected, each characteristic will be ranked on a scale of 1–5, with higher-ranked items included in the evaluation form.

Although I live in an equestrian area, I don't own a horse, and I don't ride. I do know, however, how valuable these show horses are, and the importance placed on winning by the owners and riders. An accepted tool that might help ensure equity in these evaluations could be useful and appreciated. In this case, the purpose of the *sequential–exploratory* study is to develop a rating instrument that could be used to equitably evaluate (i.e., the central phenomenon) both horses and riders (i.e., the participants) during competition. In developing the instrument, qualitative data will be collected from riders, event judges, and owners; the instrument developed from these data will be used to judge the competitions (i.e., quantitative data and sequential mixing).

Defining and Describing a Research Question

Research questions allow us to further narrow down the purpose of our study by focusing on exactly what we are trying to investigate or understand. I've found the best way to begin writing research questions is to start by asking myself a series of time-oriented screening questions:

- Past: What is already known about the problem area?
- Present: What specific questions do I want to answer about the problem area by conducting my research study?
- Future: What research is being called for in the problem area?

Following that, I then need to ensure that the following characteristics are met:

1. The research question is derived from the purpose statement.
2. The research question is clear and focused.
3. The research question adheres to the same criteria as that of the problem statement:
   a. It is interesting to the researcher.
   b. Its scope is manageable.
   c. The researcher has the time, knowledge, and resources necessary.
   d. Data can be collected and analyzed.

e. Investigating the problem has theoretical or practical significance.

f. It is ethical to investigate the problem.

By ensuring we follow these guidelines within the context of our problem statement and research purpose, we soon get a feel for exactly what we want to learn from our proposed study. Notice, again, that reading the literature relevant to the problem area is important in order to allow you to answer these questions; this is especially true for what is already known about the area (i.e., the past question) and what research is being called for in the field (i.e., the future question). As I've said before, some students get the idea that, just because Chapter 2 of a proposal is titled "The Review of Literature," all reading is limited to that area. Nothing could be farther from the truth: Understanding what has already been written that is relevant to the field underlies every aspect of the dissertation.

The Methodological Point of Departure

Because the research questions narrow down the focus of our study, many researchers consider them to be the methodological point of departure (Booth, 1995). A good research question will lead us through the literature with which we need to be familiar, and then point us toward a sound research method we can use to answer the research question. We go into this issue in much greater detail later, but by getting our feet wet now, we get a better understanding of the relationship between the research question and the research method.

Research Questions Ultimately Lead to the Study's Research Method

Up to this point in the book, we briefly mentioned the differences between qualitative data and quantitative data, and, even as I said, at this early point in your research study, you may already know the type of data you plan to collect. Whichever is the case, the data you collect determine the type of study you will conduct: quantitative studies use quantitative (i.e., numeric) data, qualitative studies use qualitative data (e.g., conversational, narrative), and **mixed methods research** uses both quantitative and qualitative data. Again, we expand on this topic later but, for now, let's discuss the overarching characteristics of each method.

Quantitative Methodologies

Quantitative studies (Babbie, 2012) are often described as "if" or "did" research. The researcher wants to determine "if something happened," "Did something happen?" "Did one event cause another to happen?" and "To what degree did something happen?" by collecting and analyzing numeric data. For example, during the 2016 elections, one of the major issues on the ballot in Florida was the expanded legalization of medical marijuana. Usage had been approved by voters in a prior election for terminally ill patients; the 2016 amendment proposed expanding the usage to persons with other serious conditions, such as Parkinson's disease, post-traumatic stress disorder, Crohn's disease, and other debilitating medical conditions. In this case, passage of the bill had to be by a "supermajority" of 60.00%; the results of this simple quantitative survey study showed that it did pass by 71.32%. While voting is a simple survey, by collecting numeric data (i.e., the number of votes in each category), it tells us that the amendment passed answering the "To what degree did something happen?" question.

Qualitative Methodologies

We all remember the interrogative pronouns "Who?", "What?", "When?", "Where?", "Why?", and "How?" that we learned during elementary, middle, and high school. Our teachers explained that understanding them is important because they are essential to information gathering. Unbeknown to them, they were setting the stage for us to become good qualitative researchers because those are exactly the questions we ask when we are trying to better understand an event or situation (Patton, 2001). Data collected from sources such as interviews and transcripts are analyzed inductively with the idea that the results can be used to better understand a specific event or scenario.

For example, one of the many issues we are dealing with during the COVID pandemic is the sudden closure of schools and, in many cases, a rapid transition to an online learning environment. Fortunately, some school districts and teachers were readily able to make these changes but, in other cases, students and teachers weren't as prepared. In order to better understand this concern, I created an online survey that asked teachers:

1. How well were you personally prepared to change from the traditional to the online environment?
2. What would you do differently if we start the next school year in an online environment?
3. What do students need in order to be successful in an online learning environment?

I collected data from over 100 science teachers. By analyzing the teachers' answers, we can identify common themes or issues that we can address by developing new tools, procedures, or policies to help them if they are called for in the future.

Mixed Methodologies

As I said earlier, mixed methods studies collect both quantitative and qualitative data in order to answer both quantitative and qualitative research questions taken together. The ideas described in the quantitative and qualitative sections above still hold true, but in different combinations (Creswell & Plano Clark, 2017). For example, I used one approach, called a *sequential–explanatory design*, when I wrote my dissertation. As I've said, I wanted to know whether different types of achievement feedback, such as graphical report cards, would increase student motivation in fifth-grade students. I collected quantitative motivation and achievement data at the beginning of the school year, and then worked each week with teachers for the remainder of the year helping them create the alternative graph-based report cards. When I collected motivation and achievement data at the end of the year, I was dismayed to find that my intervention had not worked: There was no significant difference in achievement and motivation between children receiving traditional achievement feedback and those receiving the alternative report cards.

Because of that finding, I interviewed students and tried to determine why what I had proposed didn't work. As you can see, the data were collected sequentially, quantitative (i.e., motivation and achievement scores) followed by qualitative (i.e., the interviews), with the latter data being used to explain or help understand the first. What I found is, when questioned, the students told me that they didn't actually understand the graphical report cards they were given; they knew their final grade, but all of the graphing leading up to that was not understandable or important. My first thought, when they told me this, was "They sure as heck waited a long time to tell me!" The good news is that the qualitative data did allow me to explain the results shown by the quantitative data and the lessons I learned were valuable.

Time Out: What Happens When Your Plan Doesn't Work?

As an aside, some of you might be thinking, "I'm reading a book written by a guy who has Dr. in front of his name but who just admitted that the intervention he planned and wrote about in his dissertation didn't work. How did his alma mater let him get by with that? If his study wasn't successful, why did they let him graduate?" If you are asking these questions, then you're in the same boat I was when I first finished analyzing my data and, with trepidation, approached my dissertation advisor to discuss the results. He was far calmer than I was and asked me two questions.

First, he asked, "Steve, did you design a good study?" I assured him that my proposal was sound. Second, he asked, "Steve, did you conduct your study without deviating from the sound proposal you had written?" Again, I assured him that I had. "That's good," he said, "you've just shown what does not work. Now, once you've graduated, take your results, make any modifications necessary, and replicate your study if you want to."

What was the key to what he said? First, I loved hearing the word "graduate" but, more importantly, it showed that writing a sound proposal is essential to a successful dissertation, irrespective of the results. Data collection, analysis, and the reporting of results is only as valid as your planned approach and that your study was conducted by closely following your planned approach. That's what this book is about: helping you write a proposal that leads to a good dissertation.

Getting Back to Stating Our Research Questions

That seemed like quite a detour, but it served a good purpose; we now know that a good research question ultimately leads to the research method we will use to answer it. Keep in mind, however, that before we can even consider the methodology, we must be familiar with what is already known about the field, the types of studies other researchers have conducted, and the type of research that is being called for in the literature we read. Knowing that, because we're familiar with it, let's look at one of my actual dissertation research questions:

Is a student's motivation level significantly affected by the use of graphical feedback to report the student's grades?

How would I answer this research question? First, I read the literature to familiarize myself with the topic, to see what research had been conducted, and to determine whether further research in the field had been called for. In this case, I found out there is research indicating that students who receive timely feedback have higher levels of intrinsic motivation (Deci & Ryan, 1985); my feeling that weekly report cards are certainly more timely than traditional report cards influenced me to move forward. I didn't find other research in the area, but there are always suggestions for research that lead to higher motivation and achievement. Taken together, I felt I had successfully answered the series of time-oriented screening questions listed earlier and I moved forward in writing my proposal.

Following that step, I had to ensure that this research question was valid. In this case, it was derived from the purpose statement and was clear and focused. It also met the characteristics of a good problem statement in that it was interesting to me, the scope was manageable, and I had the time, knowledge, and resources I needed for my investigation. Additionally, I could collect data to test my hypotheses, investigating whether it was ethical, and it allowed me the opportunity to add both practical and theoretical knowledge to the field via data collection and analysis. All of this taken together indicated to me that the research question was valid, and I could move forward.

A WORD OF CAUTION

As you might guess, other professors and authors might have a slightly differing approach to writing research questions. I have found my system offers a good set of guidelines and, using them, have successfully directed the research of my students, as well as guided the work I've done. In my case, I make sure each of the questions is answered appropriately; not doing so could lead to deleting or modifying the question.

Putting It Together: Problem Statements, Purpose Statements, and Research Questions

We're at a point where we can no longer think of each of these items individually. In order to evaluate a good research question, it's best to look at the big picture. Do the problem statement, purpose statement, and research questions flow together? Can we ultimately learn something about the research problem by answering our research questions? Having asked those questions, let's look at the following examples and try to determine whether we have stated a good research question.

Research Problem: Authors take too long to write textbooks.

Research Purpose: The purpose of this research is to investigate reasons authors take longer than expected to write a textbook.

Research Question: Does the availability and use of social media affect author productivity?

For the sake of the example, we have to assume that our problem statement meets all of the criteria for a good problem statement. The research purpose directly addresses the research problem and meets the criteria we discussed earlier, and the research question seems to be a direct extension of the purpose statement. Keep in mind that, before creating a research method to attempt to answer this research question, you would need to ensure that all of the criteria for a good research question are met. Following that, I could picture this being a qualitative study in which authors were interviewed and asked why they take so long to write their books.

Given this, how would you evaluate the following research problem, research purpose, and research question?

Research Problem: There are a large number of employees arriving late to work each day.

Research Purpose: The purpose of this research is to investigate reasons why employees at Tardy University arrive late to work.

Research Question: Do automobile problems cause employees to be late?

Assuming the problem and purpose are legitimate, let's focus on the research question. First, think of our screening questions. We probably already know from experience, from anecdotal evidence, and from the things we've read, that this is a problem that has been investigated or experienced many times. As far as it being current, we know that employees are tardy every day and there are many reasons for their tardiness. Because this is an ongoing problem, we can certainly ask the question—the literature we read will tell us whether there is any ongoing call for research in this area.

Assuming there is a call for research in this area, does this research question meet our other criteria? It's derived from the purpose statement, it seems clear and focused, but it is missing one of the criteria: We all know that automobile problems can cause workers to be late, so there doesn't seem to be any theoretical or practical significance to the project. Does this mean we should just do away with this research question, or should we consider other reasons, such as sleeping late, missing the bus, or getting the children ready for school? We certainly could pose those research questions, but my feeling is that, like car problems, we all know that these issues are fairly well documented.

Let's look at one last scenario:

Research Problem: There is a large gender gap between males and females with degrees in computer science.

Research Purpose: The purpose of this research is to investigate reasons why there are fewer females than males with degrees in computer science.

Research Question: Why are college-bound females less likely to major in computer science than their male classmates?

This is an actual problem statement that one of my current dissertation students is investigating. Let's check to make sure he wrote it right, and that I didn't miss anything.

First, this problem comes from data kept by universities, as well as from literature in the field: There is a disparity in the workforce between males and females with computer science degrees. Other research has been conducted and the literature calls for additional work to be conducted in the area. Based on this evidence, we're comfortable with the information asked for by our screening questions; now let's look at the characteristics.

The purpose statement tells the reader the focus of his study and identifies the variables and participants: he wants to know why fewer females major in computer science than males. Following that, his research question, which is derived from the purpose statement, is clear and focused, and adheres to all of the qualities of a good problem statement (e.g., it is interesting, the scope is manageable, data can be collected). This is great news for my student; he has asked a solid research question that is directly derived from the problem and purpose statements that will guide him in reviewing the literature, as well as ultimately designing a good study. In this case, he is collecting quantitative data, including numeric scores from a computer interest inventory, Scholastic Assessment Test (SAT) scores, and high school grade-point averages (GPAs). Based on this, it is easy to identify his as a quantitative study.

Problem Statements, Purpose Statements, and Research Questions in the Literature

Up to this point, we've looked at very basic examples of the introductory parts of a good research study. As you might imagine, although they exist, these same components might not be as clearly stated in a published article. For example, many authors imply these three components while not actually labeling them; you can see this in a paper I wrote several years back. While I won't include the entire passage from the article, the component parts will be evident (Terrell, 2014):

> A recent survey . . . reported a mean salary of slightly over $100,000 annually for terminally degreed persons working in the information technology research field. In order to advance their careers, many professionals desiring to earn a PhD elect to attend online or limited-residency programs. Unfortunately, the convenience of programs of this type brings with it a higher attrition rate than that from campus-based universities. . . . In particular, when discussing attrition from online or limited-residency programs, there is little consideration given to personality type, learning style or other constructs which have been shown to contribute to attrition in a traditional environment. The purpose of this study was to examine problems with the attrition of doctoral students in online programs through the lens of Kolb's (1984) work on experiential learning and the management process. (p. 1)

As you can see, our problem—attrition by doctoral students from online and limited-residency programs—is evident. The purpose of the study is to investigate learner constructs, in this case, experiential learning, and their effect on attrition by students in online or limited-residency programs. The research question asked, "Can a student's experiential learning style be used to predict attrition from a limited-residency doctoral program?"

In another case, Eide and Showalter (1998) investigated the effect of school quality on student performance:

> Studies which analyze the effectiveness of school quality on student performance have primarily relied on approaches which estimate the mean effect of school resource variables on student achievement. While estimating how "on average" school resources affect educational outcomes yields straightforward interpretations, the standard research method may miss what is crucial for policy purposes, namely, how school resources affect achievement differently at different points of the conditional test score distribution. For example, while increases in per pupil spending may not matter for average test scores, it would be useful to know if increased spending increases test scores at the bottom of the conditional distribution. In short, we not only address the question, "does money matter?" but we also ask the question, "for whom does money matter?" (p. 345)

While this may look somewhat complicated, the problem is clear: Eide and Showalter (1998) believe that the standard research method used in studies of this type may not identify issues that are crucial for organizational decision making. The purpose of their study, although it did not include the key words we outlined, was clear. The authors wanted to determine whether increased spending may increase test scores for students with the poorest performance; in this case, all of the characteristics of a good purpose statement are stated or implied. To paraphrase their research questions, they are asking, "Does spending money improve school quality and, if so, does it improve performance for lower-achieving students in particular?"

Finally, Skoe, Krizman, and Kraus (2013) were interested in investigating how differences in maternal education affect the neural development of the young child. In this case, they correlate maternal education with socioeconomic status (SES):

> Despite the prevalence of poverty worldwide, little is known about how early socioeconomic adversity affects auditory brain function. Socioeconomically dis-advantaged children are underexposed to linguistically and cognitively stimu-lating environments and overexposed to environmental toxins, including noise pollution. This kind of sensory impoverishment we theorize, has extensive reper-cussions on how the brain processes sound. . . . By studying SES within a neuro-scientific framework, we have the potential to expand our understanding of how experience molds the brain, in addition to informing intervention research aimed at closing the achievement gap between high-SES and low-SES children. (p. 17221)

The problem here is clear: The researchers state that little is known about the rela-tionship between a child's socioeconomic background and their auditory brain func-tion, a physiological operation closely tied to academic achievement. While not stated clearly, the purpose of Skoe et al.'s (2013) study was to investigate the relationship between a mother's level of education, highly correlated with SES, and a child's level of auditory brain function. The authors' investigation was driven by asking, "Is there a relationship between auditory brain function and socioeconomic background?"

Stating Hypotheses for Your Quantitative Research Study

Keep in mind, as we said earlier, that stating a research question is not enough for a quantitative study. In order to fully answer the "if" or "did" question, we need to state a hypothesis for investigation. We've all heard, seen, or used the word "hypothesis" but, despite this, when I ask my students what their hypothesis is for a proposed thesis or dissertation, they tell me two things. First, many understand that a hypothesis is an important part of a research study but, second, they can't exactly explain what that means. It's easy, I tell them (Terrell, 2012): "A hypothesis is noth-ing more than a statement expressing the researcher's beliefs about an event that has occurred or will occur. Once stated, hypotheses are tested by collecting and analyz-ing numeric data." While this is straightforward, there are several things we need to discuss before moving forward. First, there are different ways for stating hypotheses depending on the type of study we're conducting; we also need a good understand-ing of the direction of hypotheses, as well as learn why statisticians always test hypotheses stated in the null format. Let's get started with a few examples.

An Example of Stating Our Hypothesis

Let's suppose I am the principal of a high school and I have decided to spend the day reviewing scores from the most recent administration of a standardized science test called the ABC. Interestingly, as I am reviewing the science scores, a pattern seems to emerge. Students taking science in the morning appear to consistently score higher on the ABC than students taking science in the afternoon. Based on my observations, I surmise there is some type of meaningful relationship between the time of day a student takes science and how well he or she does on the ABC test; knowing that, I could conduct a research study to investigate it.

Before moving forward, what have I just identified? The problem, of course. Students taking science in the morning appear to score higher than students taking science in the afternoon, so let's write a problem statement based on that:

> *Science achievement scores of the morning students are higher than science achievement scores of the afternoon students.*

This statement meets all of the criteria listed above for a good problem statement; I am interested in the achievement of my students, I am certainly comfortable with the problem area, and the scope of the problem is manageable. The problem has practical significance, is ethical to investigate, and I can collect numeric data for analysis.

I can also deduce the purpose statement of the study:

> *The purpose of this study is to better understand whether the time of day a student takes classes in science has any effect on their performance on a standardized test in science.*

We can also write a research question:

> *Do students taking science classes in the morning score higher on the ABC standardized test than students taking science classes in the afternoon?*

While I seem to be on the right track, I decide to follow up on my observations by going to the library to review literature on the subject and try to determine whether there have been studies investigating the effect of time of day on achievement. Much to my surprise, I discovered quite a bit of information suggesting that students studying science in the morning seem to outperform students taking science in the afternoon. Based on this discovery, my observations are supported: The time of day a student takes science might have an effect on their class achievement.

Now, based on what I have observed and read, I can make a statement about what I believe is occurring in my school. In other words, I can state a hypothesis because it is nothing more than my beliefs about what is happening with science students' standardized test scores in my school.

Requirements of a Well-Stated Hypothesis

A well-stated hypothesis has four requirements:

1. It must provide a reasonable explanation for the event that has occurred or will occur.
2. It must be consistent with prior research or observations.

3. It must be stated clearly and concisely.
4. It must be testable via the collection and analysis of data.

Knowing these four things, I can state a formal hypothesis based on what I have seen:

Students taking science in the morning have higher levels of achievement than students taking science in the afternoon.

It is easy to see that our hypothesis meets the four requirements. First, it is stated clearly and is consistent with both our prior observations and reading. It is a reasonable explanation for what has occurred, and we are able to collect data for analysis. Given these things, it appears we have met the criteria: We have a well-stated hypothesis.

Understanding the Four Basic Requirements for Hypotheses

Before we move forward, we need to look more closely at how we state hypotheses and what we do once we state them. We just saw that there are four basic rules and we have looked at a good example that follows those rules. Some of these rules are straightforward, but there are nuances we should clear up to avoid possible misunderstandings later on.

The Direction of Hypotheses

As we just saw, both my observations and the research suggested that students studying science in the morning have higher achievement than those taking science in the afternoon. Because it would contradict both my observations and readings, it would not make sense to hypothesize that the time of day during which a student takes science has no effect on achievement.

Because hypotheses have to be stated to reflect our readings or observations, it is necessary to state either **directional** or **nondirectional hypotheses**. The use of a directional hypothesis shows we expect a "greater than" or "less than" relationship in our results. Nondirectional hypotheses indicate that we expect a difference in our results, but we do not know whether it will be a "greater than" or "less than" relationship. We can use both types of hypotheses to make comparisons between data we collect and an exact value (e.g., the average body temperature of a group of clients to 98.6°F), or we can use them to compare two or more groups of data we have collected (e.g., profits made by two or more divisions within a company).

Using Directional Hypotheses to Test a "Greater Than" Relationship

In many instances, we might be interested in hypothesizing that one variable about which we have collected data is greater than an exact value. For example, college football coaches are always interested in finding ways to improve the skills of their players. After implementing a new strengthening regime, a coach might be interested in comparing the range of his kickers to 42, the average range of kickers throughout the conference:

> *The average range of kickers following the new strength training regime*
> *will be greater than 42.*

When we are not comparing something against an exact value, we can state hypotheses that compare data collected from two or more groups. For example, with the hypothesis we stated concerning the difference in achievement between science students in the morning and afternoon, we expect the morning group to have higher scores than the afternoon group. We are not stating an exact value; we are just saying that one group will do better than the other:

> *Students taking science in the morning have higher levels of achievement*
> *than students taking science in the afternoon.*

Using Directional Hypotheses to Test a "Less Than" Relationship

We can do the same thing when we are looking at a "less than" scenario. For example, suppose state-level corrections administrators have introduced required rehabilitation programs focused on helping current inmates develop skills needed to help them lead more productive lives after their release. The administrators feel that these new programs will lower the recidivism rate below the national average of 22%. From this it's easy to state a testable hypothesis:

> *The recidivism rate at prisons where training programs are offered is less*
> *than the national average of 22%.*

In another case we might be concerned with the rising number of disciplinary problems in our school and have read studies showing that students who are required to wear uniforms to school have fewer disciplinary problems than students in schools where uniforms are not required. Before requiring our students to wear uniforms, we decide to test this assertion for ourselves. It would be easy to identify schools in our district where uniforms are required, and those where uniforms are not required. From that, it would be a simple matter to collect data to investigate the following hypothesis:

> *Schools where students are required to wear uniforms report fewer*
> *disciplinary problems than schools where students are not required*
> *to wear uniforms.*

Nondirectional Hypotheses

In the preceding examples, the hypotheses were consistent with the literature or our experience; it would not make sense to state them in any other manner. What happens, though, when the prior research or our observations are contradictory?

To answer this question, let's use the debate currently raging over block scheduling as an example. For anyone who hasn't heard of block scheduling, it is where students in middle and high schools attend classes every other day for extended periods. For example, a student might be enrolled in six classes, each of which meets in a traditional class for 1 hour each day. In a school with block scheduling, the student meets for three 2-hour classes one day and meets for 2 hours with each of the other three classes the next day. Proponents feel that longer periods allow teachers to go into more detail and make for more meaningful class sessions. Opponents of block scheduling criticize it because they believe many teachers do not know how to effectively use a longer class period or, as is the case with many math teachers, because they believe students need to be exposed to their subject matter every day.

Instead of both sides of the issue giving us their personal beliefs or feelings, wouldn't it be a good idea to see what the literature says? Interestingly enough, the reviews of block scheduling are just as mixed in the academic research journals. Some articles suggest that block scheduling negatively affects student achievement and others seem to show it increases student achievement. Knowing this, how do we write our hypothesis? Simple; we have to state a nondirectional hypothesis:

There will be a difference in achievement between students taking algebra in a block schedule and students taking algebra in a traditional schedule.

In this example, the hypothesis implies no direction; instead, we are stating that we believe a difference in algebra achievement will exist between the two groups. No "greater than" or "less than" direction is implied.

Just as was the case with the directional hypotheses, we can use a nondirectional hypothesis to make a comparison to an exact value. Suppose, for example, someone told me that the average age for doctoral students in the United States is 42, but I did not feel that accurately describes my students. In order to investigate my belief, I ask each student their age and then test the following hypothesis:

The average age of my students does not equal 42.

Notice here, again, I have not said "less than" and I have not said "greater than." All I care about is whether a difference exists. Later in the book we will see that different statistical tests are used when we compare data we have collected against a specific value or compare data we have collected from two or more groups.

Hypotheses Must Be Testable
via the Collection and Analysis of Data

Because hypotheses are based on problems we've identified, it follows that a good hypothesis is one about which we can collect numeric data. In order to analyze those data, we use **inferential statistics**, specialized mathematical tools developed to help us make decisions about our hypotheses. Because of that, it is imperative that we word our hypotheses in a way that reflects or infers the collection of some type of data.

For example, in our hypotheses involving football, it would be easy to collect the distances of the kicks made by our team and compare them to the national average. In our example about science achievement, we could simply compare the test scores of our morning students to those of our afternoon students. While these examples are straightforward, we need to "throw in a monkey wrench" at this point.

Research versus Null Hypotheses

In each of the preceding examples, we have stated what is called a **research hypothesis**, or as it is sometimes called, an **alternate hypothesis**. The logic behind the name is straightforward. First, it is stated based on prior research or observations and, second, it is what the researcher wants to investigate. In order to address these issues, which we will cover later, it is imperative that we state a **null hypothesis** for every research hypothesis we state. The null hypothesis is nothing more than the exact opposite of the research hypothesis and, like everything else, can best be explained with an example.

Stating Null Hypotheses for Directional Hypotheses

Let's suppose we administer the Law School Admission Test (LSAT) to students applying to our school. We know that scores on the LSAT range from 120 to 180 with an average of 150, and we want to make sure that our applicants score above average. In order to do that, we can state the following directional research hypothesis:

The average LSAT score of our students is greater than 150.

Obviously, if something is not greater than 150, it could be less than 150 or exactly equal to 150. In our research hypothesis, because we are interested only in the "greater than" scenario, we can state our null hypothesis in this manner:

The average LSAT score of our applicants is not greater than 150.

It is just as easy to develop a null hypothesis for comparing the achievement of students taking science in the morning to students taking science in the afternoon. Our directional research hypothesis was:

Students taking science in the morning have higher levels of achievement than students taking science in the afternoon.

In this case, the opposite of "higher levels" could either be less than or equal to:

Students taking science in the morning do not have higher levels of achievement than students taking science in the afternoon.

Finally, using our example concerning school uniforms, our research hypothesis was:

Children attending schools where uniforms are required have fewer disciplinary problems than children in schools where uniforms are not required.

Here we are doing exactly the opposite of the prior two research hypotheses: Now we are using a "less than" research hypothesis. Given that, we state our null hypothesis in the following manner:

Children attending schools where uniforms are required do not have fewer disciplinary problems than children in schools where uniforms are not required.

Issues Underlying the Null Hypothesis for Directional Research Hypotheses

Stating the null hypothesis for a directional hypothesis is a thorny issue. Although the manner we just used is technically correct, it is common practice to write the null hypothesis for a directional hypothesis to simply say that no difference exists. For example, we just stated the following research hypothesis:

Children attending schools where uniforms are required have fewer disciplinary problems than children in schools where uniforms are not required.

Its null counterpart was:

Children attending schools where uniforms are required do not have fewer disciplinary problems than children in schools where uniforms are not required.

In thinking about this null hypothesis, it is actually hypothesizing that one of two things will occur:

1. Children attending schools where uniforms are required will have exactly the same number of disciplinary problems as children in schools where uniforms are not required.

2. Children attending schools where uniforms are required will have a greater number of disciplinary problems than students in schools where uniforms are not required.

Given this, as well as other issues we will discuss shortly, it is better to state the null hypothesis for the directional hypothesis in the following manner:

There will be no difference in the number of disciplinary problems between children attending schools where uniforms are required and children attending schools where uniforms are not required.

Stating the null hypothesis in this manner ignores the "greater than" or "less than" condition stated in the research hypothesis by saying that no difference exists; doing so better reflects what we are actually trying to hypothesize. No difference would mean we have an equal number of disciplinary problems in the two groups. If we subtract the average of one group from the average of the other group, the answer will be zero or "null."

Stating Null Hypotheses for Nondirectional Hypotheses

In our example where we compared achievement between students in a block schedule to students in a regular schedule, we had the following research hypothesis:

There will be a difference in achievement between students taking algebra in a block schedule and students taking algebra in a traditional schedule.

Stating the null hypothesis for a nondirectional hypothesis is logical; the exact opposite of "there will be a difference" is "there will be no difference." Putting that into a null format, you would write:

There will be no difference in achievement between students taking algebra in a block schedule and students taking algebra in a traditional schedule.

We can do the same thing with the nondirectional research hypothesis where we want to compare the age of our students to a known value:

There will be a difference in the average age of my students and 42.

The null hypothesis would then be stated as:

There will be no difference in the average age of my students and 42.

In this case, if the average age of my students is 42, and the average age of the population I am comparing it to is 42, when I subtract one from the other, the answer is zero. Zero obviously corresponds to null, again, the name of the type of hypothesis.

All Hypotheses Must Include the Word "Significant"

I don't want to get too involved in the statistical tests that would be used to test our hypotheses, but I do want to bring up one issue that leads to a perfectly stated hypothesis. In the large majority of cases, when we're collecting data to test our hypothesis, we will be testing a **sample** or subgroup of the overall **population** of possible participants. For example, thinking back to our hypothesis investigating algebra achievement between students on a regular schedule and students on a block schedule, we might not be able to collect data for every student in a given school (i.e., the population of students). Instead, we might select one or two of each type of class, collect the achievement data from each of them, and compare the results. This creates a problem: Any time you use a sample of data rather than data from the entire population, you run the risk of making an error because chances are that the average of the sample will not be exactly equal to the average of the population it was taken from. To take this issue into consideration, all we do is include the word "significant" in our hypothesis—this means we're looking for a difference that is due to something other than chance. For our research hypothesis dealing with the difference between morning and afternoon students, we would write:

> *Students taking science in the morning have significantly higher levels of achievement than students taking science in the afternoon.*

Our null hypothesis would read:

> *There will be no significant difference in levels of achievement between students who take science in the morning and students who take science in the afternoon.*

For our example of those children wearing uniforms versus those children not wearing uniforms, our research hypothesis would be:

> *Children attending schools where uniforms are required have significantly fewer disciplinary problems than children in schools where uniforms are not required.*

Our null hypothesis would read:

There will be no significant difference in the number of disciplinary
problems between children attending schools where uniforms
are required and children attending schools where uniforms
are not required.

By adding the word "significant" to our hypotheses we are supporting our desire to ensure that any difference we find when we are analyzing data is "real" and not due to chance. Once the data for a study are collected, we use inferential statistics to sort out the differences. That, however, is a subject for another book.

Other Parts of Chapter 1 of the Dissertation

As we've just seen, there are parts of Chapter 1 that must always be included: A proposal without a problem statement, purpose statement, or research questions would be meaningless. At the same time, there are components of Chapter 1 that may only need to be included on an "as-needed" basis. The most common of these are the assumptions, limitations, delimitations, and definitions of terms.

Assumptions

Assumptions are just as they sound: things we believe to be true but cannot verify. For example, if I conducted a survey asking people their annual salary, I would assume they would tell me the truth. It's obvious that false assumptions could lead to spurious results. While we cannot control for it, we simply tell the reader that we know the possibility exists that some respondents would not tell us the truth, but there's nothing we can do about it.

Limitations

Limitations are constraints outside of the control of the researcher and inherent to the actual study that could affect the generalizability of the results. For example, in Chapter One, I stated a hypothesis that read:

Students in fifth-grade math classes have low levels of intrinsic
motivation. Research has shown that low levels of motivation lead to
low levels of achievement.

In this case, several limitations might exist: Things such as the location of the study or the socioeconomic status of the students may affect the generalizability of the results. There is a bit of good news, however. If you're interested in a given research area and find a similar study that has been limited to a specific population, it's quite common to replicate the study in an environment more in line with the focus of your study.

Delimitations

Delimitations are further limitations actively put into place by the researcher in order to control for factors that might affect the results, or to focus more specifically on a problem. For example, in the case above, the researcher might be interested in investigating intrinsic motivation in mainstream children; children in special needs or advanced classes would not be included. Again, by delimiting the study, the door is left open to replicate the study in different locations with a different population.

Definitions of Terms

The **definitions of terms** section includes terms the researcher might feel are specific to the study and may require additional clarification. In this case, if the authors were delimiting their study to include only mainstream children, they might want to define exactly what "mainstream" means in the context of their study. While it is fairly straightforward, a given school district may use a definition unlike other districts. By including the definition, the researcher is ensuring that the reader understands exactly what is being investigated.

SUMMARY OF CHAPTER TWO

We've covered a lot of material in this chapter, but it is fairly straightforward. Problem statements lead to purpose statements, followed by research questions and, in the case of quantitative studies, a hypothesis. Keep in mind, however, that all of this is still part of Chapter 1 of a dissertation proposal. We're moving on to the ROL, Chapter 2 of your dissertation proposal, in the next chapter. Before we do, let's see what we've learned.

Do You Understand These Key Words and Phrases?	
Alternate hypothesis	Null hypothesis
Assumptions	Population
Definitions of terms	Purpose statement
Delimitations	Qualitative methods
Directional hypothesis	Quantitative methods
Hypothesis	Research hypothesis
Inferential statistics	Research question
Limitations	Sample
Mixed methods research	Unit of analysis
Nondirectional hypothesis	

REVIEW QUESTIONS

Before we move forward, let's make sure we have a good handle on what we've covered by working on the problem and purpose statements, research questions, and hypotheses below. Once you are finished with both sections, you can check your work at the end of the book.

The Case of Distance Counseling

When a person feels he or she needs some type of counseling, he or she typically enlists the services of a local counselor. The therapist is able, by working directly with the client, to address the problems and concerns with which the client is trying to cope. What happens when a person has time or location constraints and cannot find a professional to work with?

Some people feel the answer to this dilemma is "distance counseling." Much like technology-based distance education, the therapist is able to work with a client using Internet-based chat sessions, phone consultations, and email. While many people debate the efficacy of this approach, very little research has been conducted; no one really knows whether either counseling method works better or worse than the other.

Given what we know, suppose we wanted to determine whether it takes therapists the same number of sessions to deal effectively with depression cases in a traditional versus a distance approach. How would we write our purpose statement? What would be a good research question to investigate? How would we state our research and null hypotheses?

The Case of the New Teacher

A new teacher, straight out of college, was complaining to one of her friends: "I have the hardest time with my classes. I send home notes asking for parent–teacher conferences and very few of the parents ever respond. I do not know what to do." Her friend, a teacher at a school in a very prominent area of town, told her, "Didn't you know that's to be expected? Your school is in an area of town with a lower socioeconomic base. There are many reasons why parents there do not have the time to come meet with you. Because we are in a higher socioeconomic area, we experience exactly the opposite. When we send out a note asking to meet with them, most of our parents contact us within a day or two." The young teacher then told her friend, "I can't believe that; parents are parents, and they should all want to hear what the teacher says about their child. I would like to collect data to help determine if there really are fewer parent–teacher conferences in my school than in yours." Based on this idea, what is our purpose statement? How would we write our purpose statement? What would be a good research question to investigate? How would we state our research and null hypotheses?

The Case of Being Exactly Right

A local chemical processing plant has been built to handle production waste from local industries. The purpose of the plant is to effectively clean the waste to ensure nothing hazardous is emitted into the atmosphere. Their equipment must run at exactly 155°F for the process to work correctly; anything significantly higher or lower will result in the inability to guarantee effective cleanliness. If engineers working at the plant were developing software to control the process, how would they write their purpose statement and research questions? What are the research and null hypotheses they would work with?

The Case of "Does It Really Work?"

With the rise of distance education, more courses are being offered in an Internet-based format. In addition to the traditional general studies courses, such as English and history, some colleges are starting to offer courses that have been traditionally lab based. Knowing that, the biological sciences faculty at one small college approached the dean about developing an online anatomy and physiology course. The dean was receptive but cautioned the teachers that they would have to ensure that the distance education students would have the same experiences and learn as much as their on-campus peers.

After developing and using the system for one semester, the faculty wanted to demonstrate to the dean that their efforts were successful. What is their purpose statement and research question? Using final exam scores as a measure of achievement, how would they state their null and research hypotheses?

The Case of Advertising

The superintendent of Pike County school district was worried about the low number of teachers applying for jobs within the system. "I can't understand it," she told a close friend, "we are spending several thousand dollars a month in advertising, and we are getting very few applicants." Her friend Wendy, the owner of a marketing consulting firm, asked several questions about the content of her advertisements and then asked where they were published. The superintendent quickly answered, "They are in the newspaper, of course. Isn't that where all job announcements are placed?" The consultant explained to the superintendent that many job applicants look for positions advertised on the Internet. Many young people, she explained, do not bother to read a newspaper and they certainly do not look for jobs there.

The superintendent decided it couldn't hurt to try advertising on the Internet and was interested in seeing whether the number of applicants really increased. If she wanted to test the effectiveness of the Internet advertisement by comparing the number of applicants in the month prior to the advertisement to the number of applicants in the month after the advertisement was placed on the Internet, how would she state her purpose statement, research questions, and research and null hypotheses?

The Case of Learning to Speak

Teachers of foreign languages in many universities seem to fall into two groups. The first group believes that a full understanding of the formal grammar of a language is important before even trying to speak it. The other group believes in "language immersion": Students naturally learn the grammar of a language when they are forced into a setting where they have no choice. If we wanted to compare the two methods to see whether there was a significant difference in language skills after 1 year of instruction, how would we state the purpose statement, research questions, and the null and research hypotheses?

✓ *Progress Check for Chapter 1 of the Dissertation Proposal: The Introduction*

As I said earlier, there are multiple ways to put together a dissertation proposal—probably the most common includes three chapters: an introduction, an ROL, and the methodology. Up to this point in the book, we've looked at the major components of the introduction: the problem statement, the purpose statement, the research questions, and the hypotheses. While these are the most important sections, there are other components, such as definitions of terms, limitations, and delimitations, that might be included if needed. In order to explain these, as well as to look at everything we've covered up to this point as a whole, I've included a complete, albeit brief, sample introduction in Appendix A. This example is a true story of an industrial waste plant in a small Alabama town.

LET'S CONTINUE WRITING OUR OWN DISSERTATION PROPOSAL

As I said in Chapter One, the key to writing a good proposal is to just start writing. Given that, think back to the problem statement you wrote at the end of Chapter 1 and write a purpose and research question, as well as a hypothesis if needed. Remember, once you've finished, put your work aside and read it again in a few days; as always, it's a good idea to have someone else read and comment on your work. I've said it before and I'll say it again: "The only way to get better is to keep trying!"

CHAPTER THREE

Writing the Review of Literature for Your Dissertation Proposal

It's not a paper on a topic. It is a paper on the research about a topic.
—JIM OLLHOFF

Introduction

For some reason, many students dread writing Chapter 2 of their proposal: the review of literature (ROL) for their dissertation. Some tell me they don't understand what it is, or its purpose, and many students aren't sure how to begin. I'm the first to admit that learning to write an ROL can be daunting and, although there are many guidelines you could follow, a magic formula doesn't exist. Knowing that, we focus on what has worked for my students throughout the years. We start by defining an ROL and then discuss its purpose. Once that is clear, you'll find that it is far easier to get into the actual process of writing.

What Is a Review of the Literature and What Is Its Purpose?

The ROL for your dissertation represents the major published works about your area of interest (Cooper, 1998; Creswell & Guetterman, 2018; Galvin, 2012; Jesson & Matheson, 2011; Machi & McEvoy, 2012; Pan, 2014). You won't use it to try to prove anything or support any preconceived ideas you might have—instead, it should be totally objective and be used to identify and present what is already known about the problem area you are investigating. While the term "review of literature" generally refers to the second chapter of a dissertation proposal, keep in mind what I said back in Chapter One: the ROL isn't the only time you need to refer to the literature as you write your dissertation proposal. For example, a large part of what you need to know about writing a good problem statement, with its supporting background and significance, will come from what you read. As you are writing your ROL, you'll also find that the literature is essential in guiding the research method of your study, planning your data analysis, analyzing your data, and presenting your results.

In this chapter, we see that the formalized ROL serves three purposes. First, it establishes the context of our study and is a prerequisite for establishing generativity, or the ability for your study to contribute back to the literature. Keep in mind that you're not conducting your research in a vacuum; you ultimately want what you find out about a given problem area to be part of the literature that future researchers can use to support their studies.

Second, as Ollhoff (2011) wrote, the ROL is a paper about what is already known about the research problem that you've identified and want to investigate. By reviewing the literature, you'll come to understand the history of your area of inquiry, be able to identify the key theories and researchers, identify ideas for new research, and build a strong theoretical foundation for your study; in short, you will become a subject-matter expert. Obviously, this requires a significant amount of reading, but you have to be selective; many beginning researchers try to include everything they read into their ROL and that can soon become problematic. In order to help avoid this issue, many professors have their students compose explicit statements describing the rules they will use while searching (e.g., the types of journals, a date range they might focus on, specific **key words** related to the topic they might use). This allows the student to help better focus the ROL before it begins. Further along in this chapter, we discuss how you can further identify, evaluate, and synthesize what you read. Doing these things allows you to develop a clear, relevant, and well-written literature review.

The third purpose of the ROL is for identifying appropriate research strategies, data collection instruments, and procedures. For example, one of our information systems students from the college of business just finished her dissertation wherein she focused on the lived experiences of managers in her organization and their perception of the use of project management software in the production of replacement parts for automobiles. As part of her literature review, she found a similar study in which the authors focused on the same topic, but in a manufacturing plant outside of the United States. While she couldn't replicate their study completely, she was able to get ideas for the general approach to such a study, ideas for interviewing participants, possible problems she might encounter, and suggestions for collecting and transcribing interview data.

In another study, one of my graduates focused on student anxiety in educational teleconferencing. As part of his ROL, he found several references to an anxiety survey that was easily accessible, administered, and scored. Since the characteristics of the students he was working with were similar to those in the reported studies, he was able to justify the use of the survey in his study. In other instances, I've had students who weren't able to locate a suitable test or survey to collect the data they needed; because of that, they used the literature to guide them in developing a sound, valid research tool. As I mentioned much earlier, because the research questions are the methodological point of departure, it is imperative that you use your ROL to identify the tools you'll need to develop a strong, valid research method that will help you answer those questions.

In short, the ROL should help us "present the results of similar studies, to relate the present study to the on-going dialogue in the literature, and to provide a framework for comparing the results of a study with other studies" (Creswell, 1994, p. 37).

There Isn't a Magic Formula for Writing a Review of Literature

As I said earlier, there is no one good way of writing an ROL. Different texts present different approaches, different professors may want their students to write the ROL in a specific manner, and different research methods may call for different formats. For example, quantitative studies are deductive; they call for extensive literature reviews because they are designed to test a theory developed from the review. Qualitative researchers take an inductive approach and do not require a hypothesis to guide their study. They tend to have much shorter ROLs so as to allow the literature to evolve from the interviews, recordings, documents, and other artifacts they rely on as data. Finally, if you are working with a mixed methods approach where you are collecting both quantitative and qualitative data, you will develop an ROL that supports both approaches, you will use the appropriate data collection tools for each type of data, and use both an inductive and deductive approach. All three of these different research methods are covered extensively later in this book.

Despite any differences, there is common ground. As we've talked about, we want to write an ROL that helps us become experts in our problem area, as well as one that guides us in the development of our research method, approaches to data analysis, and stating conclusions based on the data we've collected and analyzed. In order to help my students, I tell them to think of writing their ROL in two phases: getting ready to write, and actually writing.

In the second phase, students use the material from the first phase to write a strong, cogent, and focused ROL.

Phase 1: Getting Ready to Write a Review of the Literature

We want to ensure that the literature you ultimately include in your review is valid and firmly supports the background and significance of your research problem, the development of your methodology, and the data analysis approach you might take. Knowing that, how do we actually locate what we need? This requires several steps, with the ultimate goal of making sure that the literature included in the review is valid, relevant, and organized in a manner from which we can work. We talk about the specific material you'll use in Phase 2. For now, I've developed a set of six steps to guide us as we move forward.

Step 1: Recognize a Good Review of Literature When You See One

The first step in writing a good ROL is to know and understand what a good review should include. A really good place to start is by reading other literature reviews related to the problem area you are interested in investigating; while doing so, I suggest you first look at the study's problem statement, purpose statement, research questions, and, if quantitative data are being collected, the hypotheses. Following that, when you have finished reading the ROL, ask yourself:

1. Was what I read understandable?
2. Was the topic covered from a broad context and include both important historical and current research?
3. Was there a logical connection between the problem statement, the purpose statement, research questions, hypotheses, and the ROL?
4. Do I feel more like a subject-matter expert after reading it?
5. Would I feel comfortable developing a research method based on what I read, or is there something I feel is missing?

By reading reviews and asking these questions, it becomes apparent, very quickly, which reviews are good examples, and which are not. These experiences make it easier for students to write their own reviews.

Step 2: Create an Outline for Your Review of Literature Based on the Problem Statement, the Purpose Statement, and Research Questions

In order to set the stage for creating an outline for an ROL, let's look at a new example. In this case, my student was interested in investigating the effect of air traffic controllers' performance after training in a multimedia training environment (Mahoney, 1999). In her study, she identified a need to investigate ways by which controllers could be trained other than through older, less efficient, and costlier systems:

Research Problem: Current methods of training air traffic controllers are time-consuming, less efficient, and costly.

Research Purpose: To investigate the effect of air traffic controller training in a multimedia environment on air traffic controllers' performance.

Research Question: Are there differences in performance between air traffic controllers trained in a traditional environment and those trained in a multimedia environment?

Key Words: Air traffic controller, training, multimedia environment

We can begin with a high-level outline but, as we actually start reading the literature, we often find that additional subsections will be called for:

* Introduction: Here you want to acquaint the reader with the topic or issue you will be investigating by concisely restating the problem area and research questions. Describe the scope of your literature search and follow this by telling the reader how the review will be organized and presented.

* Body of the ROL: In this section, the author presents an in-depth review of the relevant literature in the field. Focused by the problem statement, the purpose statement, research questions, and key words, authors typically include journal articles, information from textbooks, conference presentations, and, in some instances, material from the popular press, such as newspapers and the like. The author groups the literature according to themes (e.g., theoretical articles, prior quantitative or qualitative research). In doing this, while writing your ROL, ensure that these themes do not emerge from one author—rather, they are representative of concepts often representing the work of several authors. These are then synthesized and written to "tell the story" of the current status of the problem area and support for further research in the field.

* Conclusion: This is a summarization and evaluation of what was read focusing on the contributions of studies that add to the body of knowledge related to the problem area and research questions. From that, you should point out calls for future research noted in those studies, gaps in the body of knowledge, papers that may demonstrate a need for new research because of methodological flaws, and conflicting studies in your given research area.

A Note about Hypotheses

As we said back in Chapter One, hypotheses in quantitative or mixed methods studies must be consistent with prior research or observations. Because of that, they naturally emerge from the ROL and should be placed at this point. However, as I mentioned earlier, many authors move them to follow the research questions in Chapter 1 of their proposal simply to improve readability. In either case, they are the focus of the research method we will use to test them in Chapter 3 of your proposal.

Step 3: Identify Key Words and Phrases to Help Identify the Literature You Need

We want to ensure that the literature you ultimately include in your review is valid and firmly supports the background and significance of your research problem, the development of your methodology, and the data analysis approach you might take. Knowing that, how do we actually locate what we need? Your problem statement and research questions will guide the start of your literature review. Based on those, you can identify key words that will guide you in identifying possible literature sources to include in your study. For example, in our recent research focusing on teaching STEM reference skills to middle school females, we used key words, such as "gender," "education," "STEM," "science," "engineering," "mathematics," and "technology." Using these, we were able to identify resources that we could possibly use in our work.

Step 4: From the Outset—Ensure the Validity of What You Read

Regardless of the resource you ultimately use, as you're reading, always keep in mind that one of the keys to a good literature review is the quality and validity of the material it is based on. As you read, ask yourself:

1. Does it seem accurate?
2. Does it come from a trustworthy source?
3. Does it seem to reflect valid research?

Granted, some of this may sound subjective but you will find quite a bit of literature that doesn't meet these standards. Fortunately, there are ways of avoiding problems such as these.

Examine the Impact Factor of a Journal

If you are reading an academic journal, a good way to help determine its validity is by looking at its impact factor. Without going into great detail about how it is calculated, the impact factor essentially reports the average number of citations of a journal over the preceding 2 years. This value, published yearly in *Journal Citation Reports*, is relative; one would like to think that the best journals have the highest impact factors. In the vast majority of cases, that is true; at the same time, always ensure you don't rely solely on a journal's impact factor when evaluating your resources.

Focus on the Well-Cited Authors and Other Research

As you read, also take note of the authors whose names appear in publications time and time again. For example, in a psychology article I recently read about student motivation, B. F. Skinner, Abraham Maslow, and Ivan Pavlov were mentioned repeatedly. Based on that repetition, I knew these were the key authors in the field and if I were to develop an ROL in motivational theory, I would rely heavily on their work.

Understand the Difference between Primary and Secondary Sources of Literature

Following up on the idea of identifying key authors in a field, we should also understand the difference and usage of **primary** and **secondary sources** of literature (Yale University, 2022):

> Primary sources provide firsthand testimony or direct evidence concerning a topic or question under investigation. They are usually created by witnesses or recorders

who experienced the events or conditions being documented. Often these sources are created at the time when the events or conditions are occurring, but primary sources can also include autobiographies, memoirs, and oral histories recorded later.

In most instances, researchers prefer to rely on primary resources simply because they describe the original research conducted, as written by the author. In some cases, however, it's necessary or desirable to reference secondary resources. Again, the experts at Yale University (2022) provide a good definition:

> Secondary sources analyze, interpret, and evaluate primary sources. Secondary sources typically reference or summarize primary sources and other secondary sources. Examples of secondary sources include scholarly works, textbooks, journal articles, histories, and biographies.

Remember—Just Because It's Published, Doesn't Mean It's Valid

Going back to the idea in Chapter Two of investigating different types of teacher feedback and its effect on student motivation, I could use the references shown in Figure 3.1.

As you can see, the student included material from respected authors in two solid resources: a well-known book publisher and an internationally known journal. An investigation would quickly show that each of these has high editorial standards, and material published by them is used as references across a number of disciplines. At the same time, while I certainly am not questioning the value or validity of Schneider's work, the requirements for having a document included in ERIC (Education Resources Information Center) are far less stringent than for the Deci and Ryan, and Gottfried sources. In this case, it is possible that my student researched other work by Schneider and found him to be a reliable source. If not, I would warn my student to be careful or eliminate the reference entirely. In any event, as you might guess from the ED report number of all zeroes, this is a fictitious example.

Beware of Personal Opinion

Keep an eye out for publications where authors use only literature that supports their personal opinion or where they are referring primarily to their own work. In other instances, you might find published authors who are not subject-matter

---

Deci, E. L., & Ryan, R. M. (1985). *Intrinsic motivation and self-determination in human behavior*. New York: Plenum Press.

Gottfried, A. E. (1983). Development of intrinsic motivation in young children. *Young Children, 39*, 64–73.

Schneider, B. (1993). *What I think about motivation and learning* (Report No. PSO-14-59-13). VA: Position paper. (ERIC Document Reproduction Service No. ED 000 000).

FIGURE 3.1. Example references.

experts or lack appropriate credentials. When issues such as these arise, you'll find that other authors are not citing their work—neither should you.

Rely on Peer-Reviewed Work

Material that has been "peer reviewed" means, prior to publication, it has been read and validated by subject-matter experts in the field. This helps ensure that the material you're reading is accurate and meets the high-level standards of a given discipline or research area. Basing your work on peer-reviewed material helps ensure that your dissertation is built on a solid foundation and increases the validity of your research and writing. The question then becomes "How do I know if the material I am reading is peer reviewed?" Obviously, there is no question with most of the well-known journals, but social media affords authors the opportunity to develop and publish online journals that might not meet our standards for validity. To help avoid these types of problems, there are guidelines you can follow.

The majority of your work will be based on academic journals in the field. Go to the journal's website—information will generally be included in a section labeled "Instructions for Authors," information about the journal itself, or something similar. In certain cases, particularly with older journals, you may not find information on a publisher's website, meaning that you might need to go to your library or media center to see if you can find a printed copy of the journal you're referencing. In other cases, the journal may not have a dedicated website. If this happens, check any **bibliographic databases** you have access to. Generally speaking, if you cannot find the material you want to reference on any of these sites, the validity is highly questionable!

Step 5: Locating the Literature You Need

At the risk of sounding like one of those old guys who starts a story with "Back in my day . . . ," locating the literature for your dissertation means something far different to you than it did when I was writing my dissertation over 30 years ago. Back in those prehistoric times, conducting a literature search meant going to the "stacks," that part of the library housing the academic journals, and spending many hours looking for what I needed. Thankfully, we've moved beyond that point!

Using Internet-Based Resources

All these years later, when most people hear the word "search," the first thing that comes to mind is the Internet; after all, one can find nearly anything they want somewhere on the web. Unfortunately, much of what you find on the Internet may not be directly related to your area of interest or, as demonstrated by the quote in Figure 3.2, might not be academically valid.

Fortunately, many publishers have recognized this problem and have developed web-based, discipline-specific bibliographic databases that house journal articles, conference proceedings, encyclopedias, historical documents, references to specific

It is sometimes difficult to verify the authenticity of information found on the Internet.

Abraham Lincoln, 1862

FIGURE 3.2. Verify your sources!

texts, or just about any other resource a scholar might need. Many are focused on a given discipline, thereby giving researchers a specific point at which to begin searching for the literature they need.

As you might imagine, the cost for individual access to these databases is usually somewhat prohibitive; because of that, most colleges and universities subscribe to these databases and make access freely available to their students. Of course, this brings with it good news and bad news. The good news is that it makes your search a lot easier; you can simply use your key words to search these databases and will usually be rewarded with page after page of publications related to your field of study. The bad news is that, again, you might find a lot of information you don't need; I can show you what I mean with an example.

I write a lot about student attrition from college, so let's suppose I want to find out what others have written. First, I just accessed one of the large educational databases and used "college" and "attrition" as key words to locate articles I might want to read. This initial search resulted in 28 full-text journal articles. Many of these articles also included the key word "dropout" and, when I changed my search to include it, the results showed 50 full-text articles that I might find helpful. Given this count, it's easy to see that someone interested in student attrition would easily be led to a trove of resources just by starting with one key word. Keep in mind, however, that just because an article contains those key words doesn't mean it is something you should use; there could be redundancy in the subject matter, the source of the article might be somewhat questionable, or it may simply not fit into the scope of your research. As we've said before, however, we probably won't use everything we find related to our research topic.

Besides these costly databases, there are free, readily available tools on the Internet, such as Google Scholar, that will help you identify works by primary authors, as well as other researchers. For example, I just typed "B. F. Skinner" into the search box of the Google website, and it showed that he had been cited over 128,000 times. This isn't unusual; results of searches for well-known authors often result in thousands of citations. This means that you may wind up reading more than you need to; you'll know this when you start finding redundancy in your reading—the same authors are cited time and time again. You might also find that other material you read just does not mesh well with your study. Remember, you must always avoid the temptation to include everything you find; most of the time there is no correlation between the length of your ROL and its worth. You're looking for themes, not individual authors!

Let's get into more detail about each of these resources.

Journal Articles and Professional Publications

Many disciplines and organizations publish academic journals and professional publications as a way for their members to share their work, as well as serve as a reference resource for others interested in, or conducting research in, their given field. For example, I'm interested in conducting and understanding research in a number of fields, so I subscribe to, among others, journals published by the American Educational Research Association and the American Counseling Association. This isn't to say that these are the only two sources I use—rather, they are two resources I can use where I feel comfortable with the validity of what is published.

In most instances, it's easiest to start locating the literature you need by identifying key words related to your problem area. For example, when my student was investigating training in a multimedia environment, she might have used "air traffic controller," "training," and "performance" as key words. Based on these, she would have been able to start identifying literature that helped with the initial development of her review.

When you do this, you'll soon find that the first articles you read will help you locate other literature that might contribute to your study by allowing you to identify other key words and topics. You'll soon discover that it's easy to become overwhelmed with the sheer volume of possible articles, conference presentations, and so on that you find but, as I said earlier, we'll talk about the validity of what you find later in this chapter.

 **A WORD OF CAUTION**

Just because you're reading a journal article, don't assume it is valid. For example, if you are reading an article published by the American Medical Association (AMA) or the Institute of Electrical and Electronics Engineers (IEEE), you can rest assured that the articles published therein have been reviewed and evaluated by a panel of experts in the field. In other cases, particularly in the case of "pay-per-publication" journals or articles from special interest groups (SIGs) focusing solely on the work of their members, the validity may be more questionable.

Using Books as Part of a Review of Literature

Whether or not to include books as part of your ROL is a contentious topic; there are those who frown upon it, and those who think they should be included as needed. I fall into the latter camp and know that there are literally thousands of texts you can work from, but there are several things to consider.

First, there are books we can use without question. If your research is focused on psychology, the primary work of Freud, Skinner, Jung, and many others is indisputable. If you are in the nursing field, authors including Carol Taylor, Pamela Lynn, Patricia Potter, Anne Griffin Perry, and many others are valid resources. Again, focus on the authors whose work is often referenced as you are reading other material in the field.

Second, ensure the publishing house and editor of the book you are reading are reputable; there are quite a few "vanity" publishers out there that charge authors a fee for publishing their work. In many instances, the quality of the work may be directly related to how much the author was willing to pay!

Following that, keep in mind that textbook authors write from their own "lens." For example, I wrote this book based on what I've learned both educationally and experientially; other authors may offer different perspectives. While I know that what I've written is valid and has been shown to be useful to students, other authors might disagree with my approach and guide their students differently. There is not a problem with that, just remember to keep in mind what we've discussed up to this point: rely on known authors, ensure the accuracy, trustworthiness, and validity of what you read—and don't forget that just because it's published, doesn't mean its valid!

The Popular Press—Steer Clear If Possible!

If you're in the checkout line at the grocery store and look to your right or left, you will most likely see scores of magazines and newspapers. Just like some of the journal articles discussed earlier, many of these can be considered valid (e.g., *Wall Street Journal* or *National Geographic*). In other cases, there are two concerns. First, some of these publications might include material solely focused on the author's perspective (e.g., the worst colleges in each of the 50 states); you would need to evaluate that source thoroughly before using it.

Second, if you were investigating a topic such as astronauts' perceptions of life on the space station and see a newspaper or magazine with a headline screaming "Adam and Eve Were from Outer Space," then you probably shouldn't include that one!

Don't Forget the Human Factor

While working on your dissertation, you have quite a few human resources to help you along the way. First, many colleges and universities have professional research librarians who are more than happy to help you identify the resources you need. They do this by assisting you in learning the various information resources available, as well as help students interpret and evaluate the material they have identified. You can also look for help from your dissertation chair; they are subject-matter experts with most having worked with numerous dissertation students over time. The same goes for other subject-matter experts in the field. As I've said, most authors are more than willing to help you identify what you need; personally, I can thank luminaries such as Robert Stake, John Creswell, Johnny Saldaña, Sharlene Hesse-Bieber, and others who have taken a few minutes to answer questions and give me their insight. At the same time, don't limit yourself to subject-matter experts within academia, look to those working directly in the discipline you are focusing on. I've had students reach out to an internationally known neurologist, retired FBI and Secret Service officers, an astronaut who had flown on two space shuttle missions, and others, all of whom were more than willing to spend time talking to them. Finally, look to other students working on their dissertations. While they may not be investigating exactly the same topic as you, they will be able to share with you their experience in locating and evaluating literature for their papers.

Step 6: Annotate and Save What You Read

As they're reading, some students try to keep full copies of journal articles or other material they have read, but that soon becomes very cumbersome. It's far easier to create an **annotated bibliography** for each article that includes the exact reference, as well as a synopsis of what was read; that way you can easily refresh your memory and locate the article again if needed. As you write each annotation, ensure that you include the following information in every reference:

1. Include a reference citation that is correctly formatted in the style your advisor expects. Papers requiring literature to be referenced generally have a specific formatting style that the publishers, the university, or the professors prefer. There are many such styles, including the Modern Language Association (MLA), the Chicago Manual of Style (CMS), and the American Psychological Association (APA). In this book, I am using APA formatting simply because it's what I was taught and what I am comfortable with. Before you start writing, be sure of the formatting style you are expected to use by your advisor and follow it exactly. While it sounds trite, first impressions are lasting impressions; nothing says, "This isn't very good" better than a paper with sloppy formatting.

2. Many professors, me included, tend to think that students are given exact instructions on formatting their papers; if they can't follow those, how good can the rest of the paper be? Get off to a great start and make your dissertation chair happy; ensure that your paper looks good.

3. Ensure that you're using a valid source, such as a refereed journal, text, or conference presentation.

4. Include a thorough summarization of what you read.

For example, in Figure 3.3, you can see what might be included in an annotated bibliography for someone writing a paper on administration in technology

Schrum, L., & Levin, B. (2013). Preparing future teacher leaders: Lessons
    from exemplary school systems. *Journal of Digital Learning in Teacher
    Education, 29*(3), 97–103.
The authors believe that teachers are qualified to assume leadership roles in
schools with rich technological environments. The authors collected qualitative
data in award-winning schools to understand lessons learned from leaders and
teachers; from these data they derived suggestions for teachers and leaders
to work together to foster school improvement and student achievement.
The authors focused on the need for teacher education programs to prepare
teachers to be leaders in technology use, training, and administration.

FIGURE 3.3. An example of an annotated bibliography.

education. By doing these three things, you're making it easier to synthesize what
you've read before you actually start writing. It also allows you to "cut and paste"
your references directly into your reference list at the end of your paper.

If you don't like the idea of manually creating an annotated bibliography, there
are software programs, such as EndNote and Reference Manager, that can actually
combine several of the steps we've covered. Many allow you to search online bibliographic databases, create databases on your personal computer to hold the material
you decide to keep, and then allow you to create searches within your personal
database using key words or phrases that you identify. In many instances, you'll be
allowed to print or save copies of the entire article as needed. An added advantage
of many of these software packages is that, once you've decided which references
you want to include in your paper, it will create a publication-ready reference list in
the style you prefer. In my opinion, just that alone is worth the price of the software.
Before you buy it, however, check with your university's information technology
department; in many cases universities have site licenses, meaning you can use the
software at no cost.

Step 7: Let's Add to the Advice of Ollhoff

Before we actually begin writing the ROL, let's keep in mind what Ollhoff (2011)
told us. We are not writing a paper on a topic—instead we're writing a paper on the
research about a topic. The literature you read is about work conducted by others,
and we have to make our writing reflect that. Plus (2013) helps us ensure that by
pointing out terms or phrases that should be avoided:

- Avoid words such as "should" or "ought." These reflect your personal opinion, not that of the authors.
- Do not personally evaluate what you read. Unless you are directly reporting what the author wrote, don't use words such as "better," "best," "bad,"
  "worse," and the like.

* Remember, you're using the work of other authors. Don't use personal pronouns, such as "I," "you," and "we."

* You should avoid writing that reflects your personal feelings. For example, unless it directly reflects the author's work, avoid using words such as "suspicious" or "questionable."

* Don't take sides. In many instances, authors contradict or disagree with one another. Your job is to describe what was written.

Phase 2: Writing the Review of Literature

At this point, we've covered the guidelines for writing a good ROL; now our job is just to put it all together. Believe it or not, that's the hardest part to get across to students. As I said from the outset of this chapter, the first step in writing a good ROL comes from recognizing one when you see it; you can only do that with experience. Following that, we've talked about all of the tools: formatting, synthesis, writing good introductory and concluding sections, and deciding what to include in the body of the ROL.

My final two steps are to summarize and synthesize what I've read, and then to write the actual review. In order to set the stage for this discussion, let's use the work of one of my prior students as an example to work from. Like another of my students we discussed earlier, he was interested in investigating causes for gender gaps between males and females pursuing undergraduate degrees in computer science. Based on literature suggesting that gender preferences for technology usage begin in about the fifth grade, he conducted a study based on the following outline (Ragsdale, 2013):

Research Problem: Females are underrepresented in technology-related careers and educational programs.

Research Purpose: The purpose of this study is to investigate reasons females are less interested in computing technology in elementary school when compared to their male classmates.

Research Question: What are the factors that may contribute to elementary school females and males displaying different degrees of interest in technology usage?

Key Words: Gender, technology use, computers in elementary school, technology acceptance

There are three things to note here. First, you can see that I've included only the problem statement, purpose statement, and one of the research questions at this point. As I've said, the hypothesis isn't included because it will be the result of what we learn in the ROL. Second, my student actually stated other research questions but, for the sake of example, we focus on just one. Finally, I've listed only a few of the annotated bibliography words he used.

Organize and Synthesize What You Have Read

Based on the literature my student identified, read, and annotated, we can demonstrate how he synthesized what he found, and then look at the ROL he wrote. In these examples of his annotated bibliographic references, you can see his sources are valid, he formatted the reference citations correctly, and provided thorough summaries of what he read:

1. Bhargava, A., Kirova-Petrova, A., & McNair, S. (1999). Computers, gender bias, and young children. *Information Technology in Childhood Education, 1,* 263–274.

Young children are intrinsically motivated to use computers, but a discrepancy exists between elementary school boys' and girls' ability to access technology. Differences in usage can be blamed on "gender-based classroom practices, lack of female role models, computer gender gap in homes, and the scarcity of bias-free software. . . ." The argument is made that a proactive approach to addressing these issues will prepare all students to use technology.

2. Butler, D. (2000). Gender, girls and computer technology: What's the status now? *The Clearing House, 73*(4), 225–229.

There is a gender gap in technology, but the argument is made that the current gender gap is not new; it is something educators have known about for a long time. This gap has been related to use of computers at home, course types taken, gender response to video games, a cultural bias that technology is a male domain, the relationship of computer usage to math ability, and so on. Boys have a more positive attitude than girls and are given more opportunities for technological mastery. Although young students start school with similar interests in technology, this changes from about the fifth through eighth grades.

3. Nicholson, J., Gelpi, A., Young, E., & Sulzby, E. (1998). Influences of gender and open-ended software on first graders' collaborative composing activities on computers. *Journal of Computing in Childhood Education, 9*(1), 3–42.

Using ethnographic methods, the researchers studied mixed-gender and same-gender groups of first graders using computers. Young boys and girls begin school with a similar interest in computers but that interest changes over time. Females tended to use "grouping" language, while males were more singular. Females had their work interrupted by males, but the reverse wasn't true. Males were quick to critique, laugh at, or criticize the work of female students.

When my student examined these annotations carefully, several clear themes emerged:

1. Young children begin school with similar enthusiasm, motivation, and willingness to use computers.
2. A gender gap in usage and interest begins early in their formal education.

3. Males often had more opportunities to use computers during class.
4. Differences in usage can be due to classroom practices or student preferences.

While I'm using only three of his references, as you might guess, these common themes held true in many more of the articles he read. Based on this information, he was able to write a strong introduction to his ROL (Ragsdale, 2013):

> A much larger percentage of men than women earn bachelors' degrees in the computer-related fields. This has been attributed to a number of reasons, but many researchers believe that differences in interest in the use of technology between males and females may start as early as elementary school. Males and females begin school with a similar interest in technology (Nicholson et al., 1998). Researchers have additionally noted ". . . computers are intrinsically compelling for young children" (Bhargava et al., 1999, p. 263). Somewhere between kindergarten and fifth grade, however, a trend begins to develop and peaks by the eighth grade (Butler, 2000); females lose interest in the subject, and it is reflected in their computer usage. The gender gap continues to grow with each successive grade level and may affect their choice of college major or career. This study investigates possible reasons for differences in interest in technology between young females and males by discussing various environmental, social, and pedagogical factors that may contribute to this problem.

If you look carefully, you'll see his introduction followed the guidelines stated earlier; he concisely restated his problem and research questions, and then discussed the scope and organization of the literature review. In fact, this paragraph is nothing more than a microcosm of what the entire ROL should be like—he wrote the paragraph in terms of a strong introduction, body, and conclusion.

Possible Content in the Review of Literature

At this point, I want to expand the overall idea of the ROL by discussing the flow of the review itself. As I said, there are different ways to approach a literature review, but I've never seen a good review that didn't present the chronology of the literature, a discussion of research methods, and, in most instances, readings that focus on theories underlying the topic of the ROL.

For example, in his reading, my student identified another key word—"self-efficacy"—and identified and read literature related to its relationship to computer usage. This allowed him to continue with the following paragraph:

> Earlier studies have examined the relationship between self-efficacy and technology acceptance (Emurian, 2004; Wang, Ertmer, & Newby, 2004) and report that computer self-efficacy increases when technology is utilized frequently as part of the curriculum. Unfortunately, the large majority of these studies have been conducted at the secondary or postsecondary level (Cheong, Pajares, & Oberman, 2004; Cole & Denzine, 2004; Elias & Loomis, 2002; Rugutt, Ellett, & Culross, 2003). Literature in the area of

self-efficacy and technology acceptance at the elementary level is scarce and research in this area is encouraged (Schunk & Pajares, 2001).

As you can see, his review spanned the history of the problem area; he started with a discussion of earlier studies related to self-efficacy and computer usage, and ended by noting a dearth of recent studies in the problem area. This meant, of course, that he needed to add to the literature in the field; his study was expected to extend what was known about self-efficacy and computer usage, thereby lengthening the chronology.

Mapping Out the Review of Literature

The example we just saw was fairly straightforward. My student identified the problem area and then found, in the literature, that one of the biggest reasons young females do not accept technology as readily as young males is lower self-efficacy; they simply don't think they can use it. What would happen, however, if my student found literature that supported more than one major theme predicting the use of technology by young boys and girls?

One easy way to address this is to graphically **map out the review of literature**, as shown in Figure 3.4. For example, in addition to self-efficacy, he may have identified intrinsic motivation, learning style, home environment, and SES as factors that may contribute to gender differences in an interest in technology. If this were the case, he would need to consider these as he wrote his ROL.

When this happens, I remind my students not to try to write a complete section for everything they find in the literature that might contribute to their discussion. "Synthesize your review," I tell them, "some of the constructs you've identified may not be unique unto themselves; instead, one may contribute to another." For

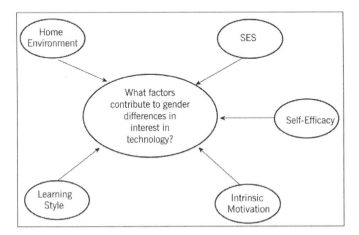

FIGURE 3.4. Literature map.

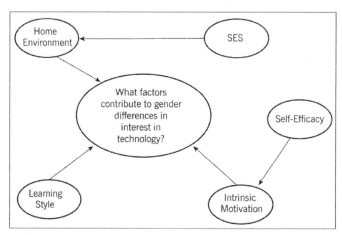

FIGURE 3.5. Synthesized literature map.

example, we know that the SES of a family certainly contributes to a student's home environment. At the same time, the literature shows us that self-efficacy contributes to levels of intrinsic motivation. That being the case, my student would need to rethink his outline and how he would write the literature review; see Figure 3.5.

Using this new map, he could synthesize each pair of constructs into one section each—for example, self-efficacy and intrinsic motivation could be discussed as part of a section titled "Motivation" and SES could be subsumed into "Home Environment." This means the body of his literature review would then comprise three sections instead of five:

1. Motivation
2. Home environment
3. Learning style

This would make for a more cogent ROL that would demonstrate his knowledge not only of the literature in general but of the themes within the literature.

Research Methods

Another important topic in the ROL is the presentation of research methods that have been used and published in similar studies. From those, you can get ideas for approaches you should consider, as well as pitfalls you should watch out for. Of course, this doesn't completely take the place of the material you've learned in your research and methodology classes, but it does allow for a better understanding of the topics from those classes. For example, Willging and Johnson (2004) published a straightforward descriptive study based on the following:

Research Problem: There is a high dropout rate in online programs.

Research Purpose: The purpose of this study is to investigate reasons why students leave online programs.

Research Questions:

1. Why did students drop out of the online program?
2. When did they drop out of the online program?
3. Are there factors that can predict the likelihood of a student dropping out of an online program?

Key Words: Attrition, online

In this case, Willging and Johnson (2004) used a simple descriptive design where they identified students who had dropped out of a program, sent them a survey, collected the responses, and analyzed them:

> This study utilized an electronic survey method to investigate the research questions. The electronic approach allowed data to be collected at low cost and relatively low response rate burden on the part of the participants. This was important for two reasons. First, the relatively high mobility of the dropout population was a big constraint, especially when trying to contact dropout students who left the program more than a year ago. Second, because the potential participants had decided to leave the educational program, they were unlikely to feel an allegiance to the program and may be more likely to refuse to respond. (p. 109)

A quick ROL finds that many studies have referenced this article, so it's clear that these other authors have learned from this approach and modeled their research method in the same manner. For similar studies, this would be a perfect addition to a researcher's ROL.

In another case, as an extension of my dissertation, a friend of mine and I were investigating the effects of technology on elementary student motivation (Terrell & Rendulic, 1995):

Research Problem: Elementary school students have low levels of motivation.

Research Purpose: To investigate the effects of instructional software on student motivation.

Research Question: Can instructional software increase levels of student motivation?

Key Words: Motivation, instructional software, elementary students

Herein, I've shortened the original text somewhat just to highlight what I'm talking about:

> In order to test these hypotheses, a quasi-experimental study was designed. Two classes of fifth-grade students, one designated the control group and the other the experimental group, participated for 27 weeks. Prior to the start of the study, all participants

completed the Children's Academic Intrinsic Motivation Inventory (CAIMI; Gottfried, 1983), an instrument explicitly designed to measure student intrinsic motivation. During the course of the study, the control group ($N = 31$) received no formal feedback other than the traditional report card delivered each 9 weeks. The experimental group ($N = 35$) received weekly graphic feedback in addition to their report cards. The study was divided into three 9-week periods that corresponded to the regular grading cycles of the fifth-grade class. At the end of the study, the participants again completed the CAIMI. Due to the nature of the construct being measured, as well as the frequency of measurement, an analysis of variance was used to determine whether there had been a significant motivational gain in either the control or experimental group during the school year.

This example is a bit more detailed than the descriptive study above. Here, because of the hypotheses we wanted to investigate and the student population we had to work with, we used what is known as a **quasi-experimental design**. As with the study above, we learned a lot about conducting studies of this type from reading other articles with this type of design, but we also had to rely on what we learned in our research methods classes. Other authors can do the same: read our work, include it in their ROL if necessary, and consider using our approach to their own study.

In this final example, let's look at a company where one of the floors in a recently remodeled building was designed with 50% of the offices having an exterior view; the remaining offices were enclosed within the building. Prior to assigning employees to their new offices, management wanted to ensure that feelings of being "closed in" by working in an interior office did not cause increased levels of anxiety.

Research Problem: Only half of all offices in a new corporate building were designed with an exterior view. Members of management are concerned that working in an enclosed office could lead to higher levels of anxiety. Many managers feel that higher levels of anxiety may lead to lower levels of productivity.

Research Purpose: To investigate the effects of office design on levels of anxiety.

Research Question: Is there a difference in levels of anxiety between employees working in interior offices compared to employees with a view outside of the building?

Key Words: Anxiety, working environment

In this case, 50 employees will be randomly assigned a new office on the recently renovated floor. This will result in half of the employees ($n = 25$) randomly assigned an interior office, with the remainder assigned an office with an exterior view. Prior to seeing the configuration of their new office, the employees will be administered the adult version of the State–Trait Anxiety Inventory (STAI-AD; Spielberger, 1983), a validated instrument shown to accurately measure levels of state and trait anxiety of persons taking the survey. After working in their new offices for 30 days, all employees will again complete the STAI-AD. Scores will be statistically compared to determine whether a significant difference in state anxiety exists between the groups.

In this case, we have described a pretest–posttest experimental study. Participants were randomly assigned to groups, and all were administered the measurement instrument both before and after the study. We talk about studies of this type in great detail later in the book. You'll find that there are many examples of experimental work in nearly every field imaginable and you can learn how to conduct research such as this as part of your ROL.

Data Collection Instruments

Another key role of the ROL is to help researchers identify tools they can use to collect data for their studies. As you saw above in the Willging and Johnson (2004) study, they simply created a survey and administered it via the Internet. In our study, we used the CAIMI; we first learned about it from reading other articles about children's motivation. Keep in mind, in the actual research method section in Chapter 3 of your proposal, you discuss the specific tools you will use to collect data for your study; in the ROL, you can identify instruments that have been validated and may be acceptable for your study.

Another commonly used way to identify instrumentation is through vendor publications and topic-specific databases. For example, the National Institutes of Health has developed and supports a database containing validated surveys from a broad range of fields: *The Mental Measurements Yearbook*, Health and Psychosocial Instruments, and many other topic-specific tools for your use. Vendors such as the Myers–Briggs Company, Consulting Psychologists Press, and others are also valuable resources for identifying and providing the instrumentation you might need.

Keep in mind, however, that you might not be able to find an instrument that meets your data collection needs. For example, in many qualitative studies, the instrumentation is composed of questions based on the topic at hand. For example, when the schools here in South Florida were closed due to the COVID pandemic, we immediately wanted to learn as much as possible about the teachers' feelings about how prepared they felt prior to the pandemic, their actions during the mandated school closure, and how they felt they could have been better prepared (Almeyda, 2020). While the actual development of any instrumentation will be discussed in Chapter 3, you should provide information in Chapter 2 about the constructs and content that might be meaningful as you attempt to answer your research question. This information will help you either identify, or develop, an instrument you can use as part of your study.

Writing the Conclusion

As I said earlier, the purpose of the conclusion is to recap what was presented in the body of the ROL. If needed, you can point out calls for further research in articles you've read, studies with obvious methodological flaws, and studies where an opportunity exists for replication with a new population or location. In the case where my student investigated gender differences in technology adoption, it's straightforward: females need to have strong feelings of self-efficacy in order to succeed in computer science.

> Margolis and Fisher (2002) advocate that a strong sense of self-efficacy is needed in order for young females to be successful in computer science courses. They state that positive self-efficacy beliefs are directly associated with persistence. If female students judge their computing abilities poorly, they are not likely to persevere in that field.

After having said all of that, if you look at the parts of my student's review of computer usage taken together, he's done a fine job:

Introduction

A much larger percentage of men than women earn bachelors' degrees in computer-oriented fields (Snyder & Willow, 2010). This has been attributed to a number of reasons, but many researchers believe that differences in interest in the use of technology between males and females may start as early as elementary school. Males and females begin school with a similar interest in technology (Nicholson et al., 1998). Researchers have additionally noted " . . . computers are intrinsically compelling for young children" (Bhargava et al., 1999, p. 263). Unfortunately, for many young females, a trend begins to develop as early as kindergarten, and peaks by the eighth grade, wherein they lose interest in computers and their usage drops (Butler, 2000). The gender gap continues to grow with each successive grade level and may affect their choice of college major or career. This study will investigate possible reasons for differences in interest in technology between young females and males by discussing various environmental, social, and pedagogical factors that may contribute to this problem.

Self-Efficacy

Earlier studies have examined the relationship between self-efficacy and technology acceptance (Emurian, 2004; Wang et al., 2004) and report that computer self-efficacy increases when technology is utilized frequently as part of the curriculum. Unfortunately, the large majority of these studies have been conducted at the secondary or postsecondary level (Cheong et al., 2004; Cole & Denzine, 2004; Elias & Loomis, 2002; Rugutt et al., 2003). Literature in the area of self-efficacy and technology acceptance at the elementary level is scarce and research in this area is encouraged (Schunk & Pajares, 2001).

Conclusion

Margolis and Fisher (2002) advocate that a strong sense of self-efficacy is needed in order for young women to be successful in computer science. They state that positive self-efficacy beliefs are directly associated with persistence. If female students judge their computing abilities poorly, they are not likely to persevere in that field.

Finally, after all of this, my student was able to state a testable hypothesis based on his problem statement and the literature he read:

Hypothesis

The computer self-efficacy of young female students in classrooms where computers are frequently utilized will be significantly higher than the computer self-efficacy of young females with less frequent classroom computer usage.

Before we move forward, note that my student met the guidelines for a good hypothesis that we talked about in Chapter 1 of the dissertation proposal:

1. It provides a reasonable explanation for the event that has or will occur.
2. It is consistent with prior research or observations.
3. It is stated clearly and concisely.
4. It is testable via the collection and analysis of data.

SUMMARY OF CHAPTER THREE

For many students, writing a good ROL is one of the most difficult parts of producing a good proposal. While it seems fairly straightforward, keep in mind what Ollhoff (2011) said in the epigraph to this chapter: "It's not a paper on a topic. It is a paper on the research about a topic." By becoming thoroughly familiar with the research on your topic, you become familiar with the research that has been conducted and identify gaps or opportunities in the prior research where you can focus your efforts.

Writing a good ROL first requires the ability to recognize a good literature review when you see one; that in turn comes from understanding what the components of a good literature review are. Keeping this in mind, you continue by reading the work of other researchers who came before you. Ultimately, you just have to start writing. There's a high probability that you won't get it right the first time; none of us do. Just keep on trying; with experience and time comes expertise.

Do You Understand These Key Words and Phrases?	
Annotated bibliography	Map out the review of literature
Bibliographic databases	Primary sources
Generativity	Quasi-experimental design
Key words	Secondary sources

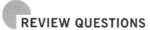

REVIEW QUESTIONS

Let's really ensure that you've got a good grasp of the material in this chapter by answering the following questions:

1. What do we mean when we describe a study as having "generativity"?

2. What are the three major components of the ROL? How do they relate to one another?

3. What is the purpose of key words?

4. Why is mapping so important in reviewing the literature? What is the relationship between mapping and synthesizing the literature?

5. What is the difference between primary sources of literature and secondary sources of literature?

6. What is the purpose of an annotated bibliography? How can writing one help us?

✓ Progress Check for Chapter 3 of the Dissertation Proposal: The Review of Literature

My mantra regarding an ROL is that, in order to write one, the first thing you need is to be able to recognize a good review when you see it. It has to have the requisite parts: an introduction, the body of literature reviewed, and a conclusion that summarizes what was read. In order to get a better feel for this, I've included a brief ROL in Appendix B that relates to the industrial waste proposal we began in Appendix A.

LET'S CONTINUE WRITING OUR OWN DISSERTATION PROPOSAL

In Chapters One and Two, we developed a problem statement, purpose statement, and research questions for a study you might want to conduct. Using those tools, begin writing an ROL of literature for your study:

1. Identify a set of key words.

2. Use those key words to locate, read, and annotate a minimum of five articles related to your study.

3. Analyze your annotations by looking for common themes.

4. While you will not have enough material to write an entire ROL, based on the common themes, write at least one paragraph or section that would belong in your ROL. As I said in Chapter Two of this book, once you've finished, put your work aside and read it again in a few days; as always, it's a good idea to have someone else read and comment on your work. I've said it before and I'll say it again: "The only way to get better is to keep trying!"

CHAPTER FOUR

The First Part of Your Dissertation Research Method

Introduction

As I said earlier, the research questions are your "methodological point of departure." Given that, you should consider Chapter 3 of your proposal as a road map, a plan for how you can get from your problem statement to your conclusions in a reliable, valid manner. Let me give you an example of what I mean.

I live in South Florida, but I love visiting the northwestern United States. If I identified my problem as wanting to go to Seattle, I could think of it along these lines:

1. **Research Problem:** I want to go to Seattle but don't know how to get there.
2. **Research Purpose:** To investigate ways I can travel to get to Seattle.
3. **Research Question:** What is the best way to go to Seattle?

Based on these statements, I could conduct an ROL and find I have many options: flying, driving, going by train, or even walking. Based on the review, I might decide that driving is my best option. Given that decision, my research method would focus on laying out the best route for me to drive, while at the same time making it so detailed that another person with the same problem would be able to follow my same path. If I'm careful to use all the knowledge I can gather, as well as identify the best route I can based on that knowledge, then if I wind up somewhere other than Seattle, the problem is probably with something I did wrong, not with the research method I developed.

The two key components of your research method chapter (Chapter 3 of your dissertation proposal) are the actual research design of your study and the procedures you will follow for conducting your study. We focus on three major designs: quantitative studies, where we collect numeric data; qualitative studies, where we collect interview, text, or recorded data; and mixed methods studies, where we collect both quantitative and qualitative data (Creswell & Poth, 2017; Neuman, 2011). Because of the detailed nature of each major design and the specific steps the procedure of each requires, we devote an entire chapter to each of the three.

Before we do that, there are two things we need to cover. First, we need to understand the basic philosophy underlying the different ways of conducting research and, second, we need to talk about elements common to Chapter 3 of a proposal regardless of your research design. In this chapter we talk about:

1. Identifying participants and samples of participants to work with.
2. Instruments to be used to collect data.
3. Plans for data analysis.
4. Ethical issues we may have to deal with.
5. Plans for presenting the results.
6. The summary of the chapter.

In the subsequent chapters, we focus on the research paradigm, the research design, and procedures for conducting our quantitative, qualitative, and mixed methods studies.

Philosophy 101

During my career as a doctoral student, I focused a lot on the third letter of PhD—the whole idea of being Dr. Terrell sounded good to me! At the same time, I paid little attention to the first two letters; I knew they were the abbreviation for "philosophy" but, up to that point, we hadn't talked about Socrates, Aristotle, Plato, or anyone else like them. As I began my dissertation, however, I quickly found out that the time for that had come; I had to pay attention to the "philosophy" part, or the "doctor" part wasn't going to happen. Keep in mind, however, that I'm describing my experience; these same ideas apply to students pursuing doctoral degrees in fields such as education (EdD) or one of the science disciplines (ScD).

Regardless of the degree you're pursuing, if you're automatically thinking back to a boring philosophy 101 class as an undergraduate student, let me set your mind at ease. This isn't going to be an extensive overview—rather, I'm going to try to explain, in a couple of paragraphs, why our research philosophy dictates which path we take at our methodological point of departure.

The Research Paradigm

Each time we plan a research study and begin writing Chapter 3, we start by stating our research paradigm; this is often called a research "lens." Much like the lens of a pair of glasses, depending upon the circumstances, we see things differently. For example, with bifocals we see one way, with reading glasses another way, and with a traditional pair of glasses yet another. The same happens with our research paradigm; the circumstances of our situation will point us in one direction or another. Each of these paradigms has four major components (Neuman, 2011):

1. **Axiology:** A researcher's beliefs about what is ethical and valuable.
2. **Ontology:** A researcher's beliefs about reality. Is there only one reality that we can identify and verify, or are there multiple realities that we can construct?
3. **Epistemology:** A researcher's beliefs about his or her role during the research process. Should he or she be actively involved or try to act as an observer?
4. **Methodology:** Based on the researcher's axiology, ontology, and epistemology, this is the methodological approach to answering research questions or testing hypotheses.

A combination of the first three components (i.e., a researcher's axiological, ontological, and epistemological beliefs about a given research project) identifies a specific paradigm (e.g., positivistic, constructivist, experimental) with each of these paradigms generally representative of either a quantitative method or a qualitative method. We discuss these terms in detail later in the text; for now, an overview is shown in Table 4.1.

Researchers using a quantitative method believe they must be objective and separate themselves from the problem they are investigating; this is termed dualism. Quantitative research is deductive; it begins with a specific research problem that is better understood with an extensive ROL. From that a hypothesis is formulated and tested using a quantitative research design. The results from data collection and analysis allow researchers to either support or fail to support their hypothesis. This, they feel, leads to the discovery of a truth that is objective, measurable, and real.

The qualitative method is inductive in nature. Researchers emphasize developing a research environment that is trusting, balanced, and ethical with all parties respecting the opinions and participation of others. Qualitative researchers begin

TABLE 4.1. Research Paradigms

Paradigm	Quantitative research method
1. Traditional	Surveys, correlational studies,
2. Positivistic	quasi-experiments, experiments,
3. Empirical	etc.
Paradigm	Qualitative research method
1. Constructivist	Ethnography, grounded theory,
2. Interpretive	case studies, phenomenology,
3. Historical	narratives
4. Postmodern	

with a broad area of interest or opportunity and actively work within the research space to interpret, create, or construct meaning. Emphasis is placed less on a solid literature foundation and more on working closely with the participants in the study to discover meaning or develop theories that could subsequently be tested quantitatively.

Finally, when we get to the idea of mixed methods research, we objectively collect and analyze both quantitative and qualitative data, and then blend (i.e., "mix") them to answer the study's overarching research question. While all of this may sound somewhat confusing right now, we'll discuss it throughout the following chapters; it will soon become abundantly clear why we need to understand the basic philosophy underlying each of these approaches.

Identifying the Population and a Sample for Your Study

This section of Chapter 3 in your proposal is where you identify the participants for your study and explain how they will be selected (Creswell & Poth, 2017; Gay, Mills, & Airasian, 2012; Henry, 1990). In most cases, this means people (e.g., students, voters, employees), but the ability to identify a valid sample is integral to many types of studies. For example, while developing the formula for the commonly used statistical t test, statistician William Gosset (Student, 1909) used small samples of ale to test the quality of larger quantities being produced at the Guinness Breweries.

The creation of a good sample involves first identifying the population you want to work with; this means you must consider everyone or everything that could possibly be used as a subject for your study. Following that, by using an appropriate strategy, you must select a sample that works best for the study you are conducting. The two major approaches are **random sampling** and **nonrandom sampling**. These are also known as **probabilistic** and **nonprobabilistic sampling**, respectively.

Random samples are generally used in quantitative studies where we are trying to identify a sample that represents, as closely as possible, the population it was selected from. In most instances, we use nonrandom sampling for qualitative studies; in those cases, the size of the sample and the manner by which it is created is defined by the objectives of the study and the characteristics of the population. We talk about these issues in each of the sections below.

Random (Probabilistic) Sampling

As we said, the first step in selecting a sample for a quantitative study is to identify the population we're working with; we sometimes call this the **sampling frame** (Henry, 1990). For example, if we're interested in looking at the effect of text messaging on the writing ability of middle school students (i.e., the population), it's obvious we couldn't work with all of the middle school students in a country, state, or perhaps even one school. Given that, in most instances where we conduct quantitative research, we want to identify a subset (i.e., a sample) that is representative of the population. For example, if we decided to continue with our study on text messaging, we would first look at the demographics of the population—in this case, middle school students—and ask questions, such as "What is the percentage of boys and girls in the population?", "How many students from each ethnic group are represented?", and "Are there clearly different groups based on socioeconomic status?" Because gender, ethnicity, or SES might affect your results (e.g., wealthier kids are more likely to have smartphones for texting), you want your sample to be as representative of these characteristics as possible; this is called the **generalizability** of the sample to the population (Henry, 1990). If the sample isn't generalizable, then the results based on the sample are likely not valid and will not reflect the true values in the population; we call this **sampling bias**.

To briefly explain this issue, Table 4.2 depicts gender for a group of 20 students, 16 males (i.e., 80%) and 4 females (i.e., 20%); just by chance the females occur at positions 4, 8, 13, and 17. If we wanted a 20% sample (i.e., 5 students), we could use a computer program developed to randomly generate numbers between 1 and 20. If, just by chance, we generated numbers for Students 3, 7, 11, 15, and 20, we would have a sample that is 100% male. We might use the same program a second time and it would select Students 4, 8, 13, 17, and 20; this sample is 80% female. We could continue randomly generating samples using this approach and, although most of the samples would be closely representative of the population, cases like the two we just saw could greatly affect the generalizability of our results; we call this **sampling error**. In the next section, we see how we can lower our chances of experiencing problems of this type using **simple random sampling, cluster sampling, stratified sampling**, and **systematic sampling** (Gay et al., 2012).

Simple Random Sampling

Simple random sampling is the best approach when you are trying to ensure that your sample is reflective of the population it is selected from and thereby minimizing sampling bias. For example, let's suppose we want to take a poll of voters in our city and interview them to determine their choice for a new mayor. If we have 20,000 eligible voters, there is no way we could interview all of them; given that reality, we have to devise a way to create a valid sample. Before we move forward, however, let's think about any factors in the population that might affect a person's choice: gender, age, ethnicity, and political party come to mind. That means a good

TABLE 4.2. Population Gender

Student	Gender	Student	Gender	Student	Gender	Student	Gender
1	M	6	M	11	M	16	M
2	M	7	M	12	M	17	F
3	M	8	F	13	F	18	M
4	F	9	M	14	M	19	M
5	M	10	M	15	M	20	M

representative sample will reflect percentages of each of these in the sample that are similar to those in the population. For the sake of discussion, let's look at the factor of political party, where we have the percentages shown in Figure 4.1.

The question then becomes "How can we create a good representative sample?" It's quite easy, actually. In this case, one good way might be to get a numbered list of all voters in the city and again use the random number software to help us select the members for our sample. We can see this idea illustrated in Figure 4.2.

A COUPLE OF CAVEATS

While this system is straightforward, you must be careful of two things. First, in order to lessen the chances of sampling error, your sample size should be large enough to allow for equal representation of the characteristics that you have identified as important. For example, if you selected a sample size of one, it wouldn't be representative of the population because it would only represent, in this case, one gender, age, ethnicity, and political party. Obviously, the larger the sample, the better it would represent the population it was drawn from. In order to determine the

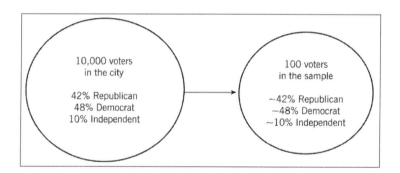

FIGURE 4.1. Population and sample.

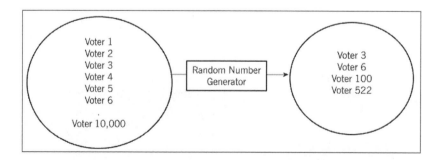

FIGURE 4.2. Selecting a sample with a random number generator.

sample size you need, there are specific guidelines in many statistics and research methods textbooks; there are also formulas that allow you to compute an adequate sample size based on the size of the population.

The second thing to keep in mind is that, in probabilistic sampling, every member of the population must have an equal chance of being selected. For example, if you're randomly drawing numbers from a hat to choose members from a population, every possible number in the population must be contained in the hat; not doing so means those people assigned to that number would have a zero chance of being selected.

Cluster Sampling

As you can guess, sometimes it is not possible to use true random sampling. For example, let's imagine that we want to investigate using e-readers in fourth-grade classrooms and we've already picked out a location for our study: a school with 400 fourth graders (i.e., our population) who are divided into 20 classrooms with 20 students per class. We might decide that we need a sample size of 80 and we could certainly use random sampling to identify those students. There are two problems with this approach, however. First, the school probably isn't going to allow us to randomly select 80 students and divide them into four new classrooms (i.e., 20 students × 4 classrooms = 80), especially if the school year has already started. Second, it would create havoc if you randomly assigned e-readers to students in existing classrooms where other students would be using traditional textbooks.

Because of these problems, we can use cluster sampling, or the selection of intact groups within the population in order to get the total number of participants we need. In this case, in order to get our 80 students, we could randomly select four classes (see Figure 4.3). While this is still a form of probabilistic sampling, we are creating a limitation to our study by running the risk of randomly choosing a classroom where students have characteristics that skew the results. For example, if two of the classes in the population represent honors students (i.e., 10% of the population) and were chosen as part of the sample of four classes (i.e., 50% of the sample), it is not likely the results based on the sample would be representative of the population.

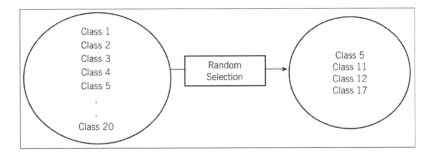

FIGURE 4.3. Cluster sampling four classrooms from 20 classrooms.

Stratified Sampling

In other cases, we might be faced with trying to select a sample that is representative of a population, but there are issues within the population itself that might affect our ability to do so. This is when we turn to stratified sampling. For example, let's suppose we are taking a political poll from a population of 1,000 registered voters but this time there are 690 Republicans (69%), 300 Democrats (30%), and 10 voters registered as Independent (1%). If we want to create a sample of 10% of the voters, that means we want a sample size of 100 that contains about 69 Republicans, 30 Democrats, and 1 Independent. The problem is, because the number of Independents is so small, just due to chance, it's likely it won't be represented in our sample.

In order to deal with this problem, we can stratify the population before we start the sampling process. By this I mean we can identify all Republicans and then randomly select 69 of them; we would do the same by randomly selecting 30 people from those identified as Democrats, and one from the group identified as Independents (see Figure 4.4). Stratified sampling is considered probabilistic because it does include a random selection component because the members of each stratified group are randomly chosen.

Systematic Sampling

Systematic sampling is the most problematic in terms of generalizability. Using it, the sample pool is identified and starting at a random point in the population, every nth subject is selected. For example, if we have a population of 250 participants and we want a sample size of 20, we would list the participants, pick a random starting spot, and then select every 20th subject. Notice in Figure 4.5, because of where we started in the list, we would have to start again at the top of the list in order to get the sample size we want. For example, we can see this happen. When we get to the 13th case where we choose Subject 245, we then have to count the last five positions in the table and then go to the start of the table and count the first 15. That gives us the range of 20 that we want and takes us to Subject 15, the next participant in our sample. While this is a simple way to select a sample, care must be taken. While it is possible that every participant has the chance to be selected, it depends upon the sample size and the point where you start selecting your participants in the table.

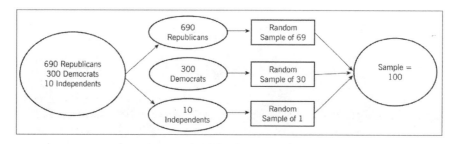

FIGURE 4.4. Stratified sampling of political parties.

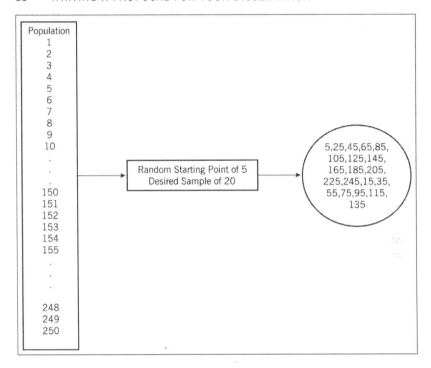

FIGURE 4.5. Systematic sampling.

Nonrandom (Nonprobabilistic) Sampling

In some cases, it is simply not feasible to obtain a random sample, and we have to resort to nonprobabilistic approaches. Because participant selection is not random, the **validity** and generalizability of the results can be negatively affected; sometimes this is unavoidable and sometimes it's not important. This will become evident as we look at the examples below.

Convenience Sampling

The **convenience sampling** technique is often called **accidental sampling** and uses participants who just happen to be in a given place at a given time. For example, imagine a pollster asking opinions of shoppers in a mall. The sample is convenient because they're already there, but the generalizability is limited because they just happened to be in the mall at a given time. I was shopping with my wife at a mall in Miami a couple of weekends ago; one large department store was conducting a sale aimed at local Hispanic youth and had one of the local radio stations broadcasting in Spanish from within the store. Imagine that a newspaper reporter was there asking shoppers their thoughts on ending the war in the Ukraine. The results probably wouldn't represent all shoppers in the other stores in the mall, much less the city in general. The argument could be made that they are generalizable to other Spanish-speaking youth, but are they really? What about the kids who were working, simply not interested, or didn't have enough money to go shopping that day? Aren't their opinions important too?

Quota Sampling

Quota sampling is very similar to quantitative stratified sampling; the difference lies in how the participants are chosen once the stratification takes place. For example, imagine that we wanted to know how our presidential candidate was faring with males and females in the United States. The first thing we would need to know is, percentage-wise, the distribution of gender in our country and then ensure our sample has the same distribution. In this case, I happen to know that approximately 51% of our citizens are female; given that, I would want a sample with the same characteristics: 51% female and 49% male. Unlike stratified sampling, where I would randomly select potential voters from the population, in this case, I would identify a population of potential voters and recruit participants until I had the sample size I wanted with the proportions called for.

Purposive Sampling

Purposive sampling, also called *intentional sampling*, is just as the name implies: It is a sample chosen "on purpose" because those sampled meet specific criteria. This type of sampling is used in many qualitative studies to allow the researcher to identify small, specific groups to work with. For example, I have written a lot about attrition from college, particularly doctoral students who complete their coursework but ultimately do not finish their dissertation. In the ROL for one article (Terrell, 2014), I found that most attrition occurs after students have been in their programs for 5 years or longer. Because I wanted to interview doctoral students who had dropped out after 5 years, I purposively chose 12 students who met my criteria and interviewed them. While I cannot be absolutely certain that the results of my student sample represent the population of students who left their doctoral programs, I do realize that this is probably the only way I could collect the data I wanted.

Snowball Sampling

This is a type of purposive sampling used by many qualitative researchers because of its ease of use in identifying a small number of participants. In order to get the general idea, imagine the researcher making a small snowball and then rolling it down a hill; as it goes along, it gets bigger and bigger. The same idea applies to this type of sampling: The researcher identifies a small number of participants, perhaps even one, and then asks those participants to recruit other potential participants for the study they are in.

For example, here in South Florida I see dog lovers walking their pets every day but it's rare to see large dogs, such as a Saint Bernard, a Great Dane, or a bullmastiff. If I wanted to learn more about raising this type of dog in this hot, humid climate, I could use **snowball sampling**. I would start by asking owners of these types of dogs to help me identify friends or neighbors who might also own large-breed dogs. Sampling of this type would help me find potential participants who might otherwise have been missed.

Summary of the Sampling Process

As you can see summarized in Table 4.3, there are clear instances where a given sampling technique was called for by the needs of either a quantitative or qualitative study. In reading through these, however, you would be correct in noting that some of the sampling approaches we discussed could be used in either a quantitative or qualitative study. For example, a quantitative researcher could certainly use

TABLE 4.3. Summary of Sampling Types

Type	Approach	Description
Simple random sampling	Random	Participants are randomly selected from a population using a tool such as a random number generator or a table of random numbers.
Cluster sampling	Random	Samples are created by randomly selecting preexisting groups from within a population.
Stratified sampling	Random	Subgroups within a population that must be proportionately represented in a sample are identified. Participants from each of the subgroups are then randomly chosen for inclusion in the sample.
Systematic sampling	Random	The sample is created by identifying a sampling pool (i.e., population) and then selecting every nth member to be part of the sample.
Convenience sampling	Nonrandom	A sample is created from members of a population who happen to be readily available.
Quota sampling	Nonrandom	Created by first defining percentages of the sample that must meet certain criteria (e.g., needing a sample of 60% females and 40% males). Members of the population are then identified by the criteria and invited to participate until the sample size is met.
Purposive sampling	Nonrandom	A sample is selected from a population based on defined inclusion criteria.
Snowball sampling	Nonrandom	An initial participant who meets the criteria for inclusion in the sample is selected from the population. The sample size is increased by that participant recruiting other like participants into the sample. All identified participants then, in turn, recruit additional participants.

a convenience sample for his or her work; he or she would just have to realize, and explain to the reader, that the results are limited due to the type of sampling used. It's also true that a qualitative researcher could use a random approach. Given the specificity needed for their sample, as well as smaller sample sizes, most qualitative researchers use nonrandom sampling. The key is this: Let your study design, as well as the circumstances you're working in, guide you in selecting your sample. Just keep in mind and report the benefits, or liabilities, of whichever approach you take.

Data Collection Instrumentation

In our research, there is always the need to collect data and, as was the case with sampling, there are different data collection tools for the types of studies we conduct. Quantitative research calls for numerically based methods, such as tests, surveys, opinion polls, sport rankings, and the like. Qualitative researchers generally use text-based observations or interviews to collect qualitative data. As we look at the different types of data collection instruments below, keep in mind that the key to selecting an appropriate instrument for your study is the type of data called for in your research questions and hypotheses (Billups, 2021; DeVellis, 2011; Fink, 2003).

Instrumentation for Quantitative Research

As we know, quantitative studies focus on the collection and analysis of numeric data to answer research questions and test hypotheses. Depending on the situation, tests or surveys can be used to measure a content area (e.g., customer satisfaction, preference rankings, or academic achievement) or a **construct** (e.g., intelligence, intrinsic motivation, or personality). Within each of these broad categories, there are different tools we can use to meet our specific needs.

Achievement Tests

We're all familiar with **achievement tests** that are developed to measure performance in a specific subject area. We also use them as standardized examinations for overall achievement (e.g., the Stanford Achievement Test), college credit (e.g., the College-Level Examination Program [CLEP]), and admissions purposes (e.g., the Graduate Record Examination [GRE]). Whether we develop an achievement test, use one that is provided by a publisher, or administer a standardized test, we must focus on the tests' validity (i.e., Do they measure what they're supposed to measure?) and **reliability** (i.e., Do they consistently measure what they're supposed to measure?). We cover these topics in detail later in this chapter.

Affective Tests

Affective tests are instruments that are used to numerically measure constructs—that is, values we know exist but aren't tangible. For example, I use the Strong

Interest Inventory to help students focus on the type of job or profession that meets their interests. Upon completion, my students' learning and vocational preferences are matched to careers or vocations that have shown to be enjoyed by workers with similar interests. In other cases, using a research question such as "What are the causes of attrition from graduate school?", I've used the Beck Depression Inventory and the STAI to determine whether there are common characteristics about students leaving graduate school. If these are identified as problematic, my goal is to develop teaching styles and tools that might meet the learning needs of these students. I have also used other common affective tools, including the Myers–Briggs Type Indicator (MBTI), and the Human Information Processing (HIP) survey in investigating the needs and characteristics of students I've worked with.

Behavioral Observation Scales

Teachers usually have to deal with disruptive students; it may be appropriate to track this with a **behavioral observation scale**. The administration and guidance counselors want to know such things as the identity of the student, the severity of the problem, and the particular classes where the student is being disruptive. To collect that information, teachers in all of the student's classes would be given one of the evaluation forms (shown in Table 4.4) and asked to put an "x" in the "Observations" box each time the undesired behavior is observed. At the end of the period, the teacher would count the number of observations and insert that value into the "Total Count" column. At the end of the day, the scales would be collected from all teachers, and decisions made based on the specific classes where the negative behaviors were observed, as well as the total number of occurrences.

Ranking Scales

Let's suppose we are at a wine tasting and the organizers ask us to rank our preference from seven different varieties; their goal is to determine the preference for each wine and then stock their stores accordingly. The person asking our opinion could certainly interview each of us, but if the idea was to get the opinions of everyone at the event, the use of a **ranking scale**, such as the one shown in Table 4.5, would be more appropriate.

Using this ranking scale would be easy. Each person would complete the survey by ranking the wines by their preference. The organizers of the festival could use the

TABLE 4.4. Behavioral Scale for Disruptive Behavior

Student: Lisa Bermudez

Behavior: Talking to classmates during math class

Date	Class Period		Observations	Total Count
12/18/14	8:00 A.M.	9:15	x x x x x	5

TABLE 4.5. Wine Rankings

Wine	Rank
Bordeaux	
Merlot	
Sauvignon	
Port	
Vermouth	
Marsala	
Zinfandel	

sum of all rankings and ensure wine lovers that they could find the wine they want the next time they're in the store.

Surveys

We've all filled out surveys and, with the growth of the Internet and email, it seems we're asked to fill them out more than ever. Surveys are used to gather information about people and can be used to measure almost anything. For example, at the end of each semester, my students receive an email wherein they are asked to evaluate my class and me. Using a survey such as the one shown in Table 4.6, they rate various aspects of my class using a scale; their ratings can range from 1 (i.e., the lowest level of satisfaction) to 5 (i.e., the highest level of satisfaction). The results can then be used by my dean and me to evaluate my overall performance and effectiveness. In this case, in addition to the scale rankings, the survey includes a comments section for students to better explain the results of the numeric ratings or to supply additional qualitative information. As you might guess, this could be used in a mixed methods study for quantitative and qualitative data.

TABLE 4.6. Course Satisfaction

Please rate your satisfaction with Dr. Terrell's class:	Low				High
Quality of the academic experience	1	2	3	4	5
Instructor feedback	1	2	3	4	5
Class notes	1	2	3	4	5
Textbook	1	2	3	4	5
Overall experience	1	2	3	4	5
Comments:					

Instrumentation for Qualitative Research

As I said earlier, we most often use interviews or observations to collect qualitative data. We have to be careful, however, as there are instruments that are used to collect both types of data (Billups, 2021; Hesse-Biber & Leavey, 2011; Merriam, 2009; Munhall & Chenail, 2008). For example, in the course satisfaction survey earlier, we saw that students were able to numerically evaluate five aspects of my course; at the end of the survey, however, it asked for their comments. Obviously, we won't analyze these with quantitative tools—instead, we would need to use a qualitative approach.

Interview Protocols

Whether it be for a job, as part of a jury pool, or admission to college, we've all been interviewed at some point in our lives. In order to ensure that interviewers capture the exact data they want, good interviewers use one of three approaches: a **structured interview,** a semistructured interview, or an **unstructured interview.** Each of these is approached differently and each is designed with a specific goal in mind.

An unstructured interview has a broad open-ended approach and allows the person being interviewed the freedom to answer questions according to what he or she believes relates to the topic. For example, during the current pandemic, we're interviewing teachers about their experiences moving from a traditional classroom to a virtual platform. If we wanted to use an unstructured approach, we could prompt interviewees to "Tell us about your experience as a teacher during the COVID-19 pandemic"; they could then tell us their story in their own words. In doing so, they might talk about topics such as how prepared they were to teach in an online format, the equipment they had to help them, administrative support, other personal issues, and so on. The key is, they would tell us about their experiences with no other guidance from us.

In certain instances, when we give teachers free rein to describe their experiences, they don't cover all of the specific topics we are interested in. For example, it's not unusual for the teachers being interviewed to tell us, in general terms, stories about coursework, student achievement in the online classroom, and technology problems. Without additional prompting, however, sometimes they don't get into the specifics of issues we want to learn more about. Because of that, we've taken a semistructured approach and added probing and follow-up questions we can ask during the interview itself.

For example, if a teacher begins talking about moving into a virtual classroom, we might ask questions such as:

- "What could have been done to help make you feel prepared to start teaching in an online classroom?"
- "What could administrators have done to support teachers and students in the virtual environment?"
- "Looking forward, how can you apply what you've learned this year, in case we need to continue in a virtual environment next year?", etc.

These types of ad hoc questions allow us to expand the type and amount of information we collect.

We could also use a structured approach in which we ask specific questions, trying to prevent the person being interviewed from straying too far in their answers. In this case, I might ask:

- "What percentage of students showed up for class each day?"
- "Did students remain engaged during in-class sessions?"
- "What percentage of your time was taken up with technical issues?"
- "Do you feel prepared to move into another school year online?"

We could certainly collect a lot of good information by using a structured approach but there are issues we would need to avoid, primarily those of scope. In order to collect the data we wanted, we would have to ask questions specifically focusing on that area. For example, if we wanted to know whether teachers felt they had the technical skills necessary to work in an online environment and didn't ask that question, we would not collect the data we needed.

Knowing that, it is best to use a structured approach when we're very familiar with the field about which we're collecting data; this allows us to develop clear, focused questions aimed at collecting data in the area of interest. In order to further increase the validity of the data you collect, the questions must be standardized and asked in the same order with no changes in the manner they are asked.

Demographic Data Forms

Almost every type of study we conduct requires us to collect demographic data. Information such as gender, ethnicity, age, and race are collected and saved on a demographic data form. This allows us to describe the characteristics of a group we're working with, and demographic data can also be used to better understand other data we've collected. For example, if I administered an achievement test, I could also collect gender information that would allow me to make comparisons between males and females. If I found that a difference in achievement existed between my male and female students, I could then focus on helping lower-performing students by developing new instructional tools or practices.

Projective Tests

In the field of psychology, we use **projective tests** to measure constructs or ideas that we know exist, but we are not able to collect the data in a standard manner. For example, we have all seen the famous Rorschach test (i.e., the inkblot) that mental health professionals use to help better understand issues their client is experiencing. Another less commonly used tool is Buck's (1992) house–tree–person projective drawing technique (see Figure 4.6). By asking a client to draw each of these figures (i.e., "project" their beliefs or feelings), a trained professional can use both the

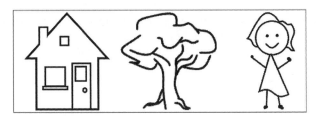

FIGURE 4.6. House–tree–person.

drawing and the client's interpretation of the drawing to assist in his or her diagnosis.

Reliability and Validity

Throughout this book, you'll see that we discuss the ideas of reliability and validity in several places. It's important to point out that these terms don't mean the same thing in all instances. For example, when we discuss the reliability and validity of a research method, we're talking about whether the results were caused by an intervention, and whether they are generalizable to different locations or populations. In this section, we discuss the reliability and validity of data collection instruments. Let's cover each of these concepts individually and use examples to fully explain what we need to know.

Reliability

A well-developed test must consistently measure what it's intended to measure; in short, it must be *reliable* (Skaggs, 2022). For example, imagine you develop a test for a college math exam and administer it to a group of students. Later in the term, if you gave the same test to the same group of students, you would expect the two sets of scores to be correlated. This means that students who made higher scores the first time they took the test would tend to make higher scores the second time; students who had lower scores on the first test would also have low scores on the second test. Although we'll talk a great deal about correlational research later in the book, let's touch briefly on it now, so as to better explain instrument reliability.

As I said, scores from both iterations of a test can be numerically compared to see how well they are correlated. In order to be precise, we can use a formula to measure this correlation by computing a **reliability coefficient**. Depending upon the type of test being developed and the reliability approach being used, this coefficient can be generated by formulas, such as the Spearman–Brown prophecy formula, the Küder–Richardson formula, or **Cronbach's alpha**. Values of these coefficients range from zero (i.e., low reliability) to 1.0 (i.e., high reliability). In short, the larger the reliability coefficient, the more comfortable you would feel about having consistent results regardless of when the test was taken or who administered it. We use the coefficient to look at four types of instrument reliability: test–retest, equivalent forms, interrater, and split-half.

Test–Retest Reliability

Imagine working as a prison psychologist and giving an IQ test to a group of inmates and, after a month, administering the same IQ test to the same group of inmates. Because IQ won't change much over a short period, if you computed a reliability coefficient using the two sets of test scores, you would expect a high reliability coefficient (**test–retest reliability**); inmates who demonstrated a low IQ on the first iteration of the test would tend to have low scores the second time it was taken. The same would hold true for prisoners with high IQs; a high score the first time would predict a high score the second time. If this were the case, you would expect to compute a reliability coefficient close to 1.0. If you computed a reliability coefficient closer to zero, chances are there is a problem with the way the instrument was developed; in short, there would be poor instrument reliability. This concept can be seen in Figure 4.7.

Equivalent Forms Reliability

At some point in our lives, most of us have taken a test that's labeled Form A, Form B, Form C, and so on. Test developers create different versions of a test to help prevent dishonesty, or to keep students from researching and memorizing the answers in case the same test is administered again. This is accomplished by assembling a pool of test questions and then randomly selecting an equal number of them for each form of the test. To ensure that all forms of a test measure the same knowledge, researchers would administer one form of the test to a group of students and administer the other form of the test to the *same* students. If a large reliability coefficient is computed between the resulting sets of test scores, the forms of the test are said to have **equivalent forms reliability** and can therefore be used interchangeably in a testing situation.

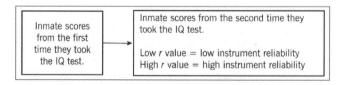

FIGURE 4.7. Instrument reliability.

Interrater Reliability

We saw earlier that my students have used a survey to rate my performance as a teacher. In order to judge the reliability of their rankings, my dean could measure the **interrater reliability** of the survey form by compiling all of the ranking forms and computing a reliability coefficient. If the reliability coefficient is large, the dean can rest assured that the survey is valid; that way I can point out that the one really low evaluation I got was an aberration and really not indicative of what the rest of the class thinks!

Split-Half Reliability

We can wrap up our discussion of reliability by looking at the concept of **split-half reliability**. This is simply where we take the questions from an exam, divide them equally, and make two exams from the original set of questions. For example, if we had an exam with 40 items, we could include the 20 even-numbered items in one of the new exams, and the 20 odd-numbered questions in the second exam. This is shown in Figure 4.8.

We could then administer both exams to a group of students and, after grading, determine how well the sets of scores are correlated. A large reliability coefficient would indicate consistency and suggest that test takers would do equally well on either of the 20-question tests.

Keep in mind, however, that by using the odd- and even-numbered questions from the 40-question test to create our two new exams, we've compared only one possible way of selecting the 20 questions for each of the new tests. Instead of using the odd- and even-numbered questions, we might decide to include Questions 1–20 in the first new test, with the remainder comprising the second new test (see Figure 4.9).

We could again administer the two exams and correlate the scores, but there's a real possibility that a reliability coefficient computed from these two 20-question

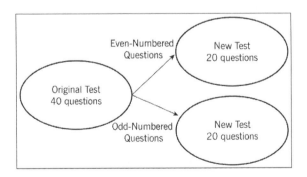

FIGURE 4.8. Even and odd questions.

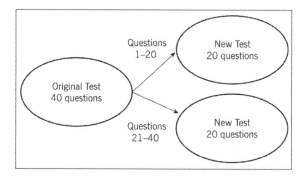

FIGURE 4.9. Questions in sequence.

tests would not be exactly equal to the reliability coefficient we computed from the exams created using the even and odd questions. This could be problematic because, as you might expect, there are many other ways to create the two 20-item tests (e.g., Test 1 might contain Questions 1–10 and Questions 31–40; Test 2 would contain Questions 11–30), and a split-half reliability coefficient could be computed for each of them.

Although many of the reliability coefficients would be equal, others would differ, some only slightly, others more so. In order to control for the differences between each of these values, we can use Cronbach's alpha to estimate the correlation of all possible halves on each of the new exams taken together. As in the earlier cases, the closer the alpha value is to 1.0, the higher the split-half reliability, meaning the more likely it will consistently measure what it's supposed to measure.

A summary of the different types of reliability is shown in Table 4.7.

TABLE 4.7. Different Forms of Reliability

Test–retest reliability	The degree to which scores from the first iteration of a test or evaluation are correlated to subsequent iterations of the same test or evaluation.
Equivalent forms reliability	The degree to which two tests in a given subject area, given to one group of test takers, are correlated.
Interrater reliability	The degree to which scores or evaluations from two or more people are correlated. A large reliability coefficient suggests higher interrater reliability.
Split-half reliability	The degree to which scores from one-half of a test or evaluation are correlated to scores or evaluations from the second half.

Validity

Obviously, even though a test consistently measures what it is supposed to measure, it's even more important that it is valid, or that it measures what it's supposed to measure. For example, given the importance placed on standardized testing by our schools, we want to make sure that any results we report accurately reflect student achievement. If we used a test that covers basic arithmetic to report ninth-grade algebra achievement, our students might score amazingly high, but the results would reflect what they know about basic math, and not necessarily what they know about algebra. There are many sources for tests of this type: publishing companies, textbooks, teachers' manuals, or perhaps one you create specifically for your class. Our goal here isn't to learn to create our own exams, or to use specific publishers—rather, we want to talk about the different types of validity measures we might encounter while conducting our research.

Construct Validity

As was mentioned earlier, constructs are values such as IQ and personality that we know exist but are not tangible. When we focus specifically on **construct validity**, we're investigating the degree to which an instrument measures what it claims to measure. This is the most important type of validity because it attempts to answer the question "What is this test really measuring?" As you can imagine, establishing construct validity of a test you've written requires verification from many sources and is not easy to establish. Unless you do establish validity, however, the data you collect using the instrument may be inaccurate.

For example, as I said earlier, I've written quite a few papers and presentations on the causes of attrition from graduate school. In several instances, I've talked about the need for doctoral students to interact with one another outside of the classroom. This idea, called "connectivity," is something I know exists because, purely by observation, it seems that students who keep in close contact with one another are generally more successful in class than those who don't. My colleagues and I hypothesized that a construct named connectivity exists and developed the Doctoral Student Connectedness Scale (DSCS; Terrell, Dringus, & Snyder, 2009) to measure it.

Establishing the validity of our instrument wasn't easy. First, we talked to our students and asked them if they believed being in contact with their colleagues during their program was meaningful. Most of them agreed it is important, so when scores from the DSCS matched their opinion (i.e., persons who scored higher on the connectivity scale were those who indicated that connectivity was important), we felt a degree of validity had been established. We followed this by having students take both the DSCS and Rovai's (2002) Classroom Community Scale (CCS). Because Rovai's instrument had already been shown to be a valid measure of connectivity at lower levels, we felt that a high degree of correlation between students' scores from both exams supported our claims for the validity of the DSCS. Finally, we collected grade information for each of our students and correlated those with scores from the

DSCS. A meaningful positive reliability coefficient between these two values helped substantiate our belief that our instrument is indeed valid and does measure the construct called connectivity. Only by establishing the validity of our instrument could we feel comfortable in interpreting any results based on its use.

A NOTE ABOUT CONVERGENT AND DISCRIMINANT VALIDITY

These two types of validity are subsumed under construct validity. **Convergent validity** investigates whether the construct you're measuring is highly correlated with a similar construct. We saw this when we helped establish the validity of the DSCS by showing a strong correlation between connectivity and classroom community (i.e., the scores converged). At the same time, we would not want our instrument to highly correlate with other constructs, such as anxiety, depression, or anything else that might negatively affect our results (i.e., we want our scores to diverge from one another). This idea of **discriminant validity**, taken together with convergent validity, demonstrates the construct validity of the instrument we are evaluating.

Content Validity

Content validity asks the question "Is the entire content area I want to measure covered?" We ensure content validity by looking at each of the items (i.e., *item validity*), as well as the scope of the exam (i.e., *sampling validity*). For example, if I wanted to evaluate the sampling and item validity of a test designed to cover my students' knowledge of the first manned landing on the moon, I would ask two questions:

1. Does my test cover the entire flight, from launch to landing?
2. Is each question on the exam pertinent to the content area?

The first question above relates to **sampling validity**; I would need to make sure my questions covered all of the major events relative to the lunar landing: the names of the astronauts, the first person who stepped on the moon, the name of the mission, and the like. If I didn't cover this material, I couldn't be sure that my students had mastered the subject area.

The second question refers to the **item validity** of each question. It would be necessary to evaluate each question to make sure it is relevant to the subject matter taught. A question asking the name of the first person to stand on the moon is relevant and has good item validity; a question asking the name of the first astronaut from Russia into space would not be valid for this exam.

Criterion Validity

Criterion validity is concerned with how well the results of a survey or test you develop correlate with a previously validated instrument (i.e., the criterion). Depending on the purpose of your instrument (i.e., its criterion), you must establish concurrent or **predictive validity**.

For example, psychologists have historically relied on the Beck Depression Inventory to help in diagnosing depression (Beck, Ward, Mendelson, Mock, & Erbaugh, 1961). Clients answer a set of 21 questions; the scores calculated from their answers are highly correlated with the depression construct (i.e., a reliability coefficient of zero indicates no depression, with increasingly greater values indicating higher levels of depression). Since then, a shorter form of the inventory, consisting of 13 questions, has been published (Beck, Steer, & Brown, 1996). In order to ensure that the second version of the instrument measured the same construct as the original (i.e., the criterion), **concurrent validity** had to be established. This was done by asking clients to take both forms of the inventory at the same time (i.e., concurrently); a high degree of correlation between the two sets of scores assured that both forms could be used in diagnosing depression equally well.

Predictive Validity

Predictive validity is somewhat similar, but its use may be more familiar to most of us. For example, each year thousands of young children throughout the United States take placement exams; the results can be used to identify children for advanced academic programs, specialty programs in the arts, selection of a college major, and so on. We can think of predictive ability as the degree to which the examination accurately places a child in a given program. If a child is placed into an advanced program and can't keep up with the curriculum, we would have to question the predictive validity of the exam he or she took.

Plans for Data Analysis

Much like the way your research method guides your study, this section is your "road map" for analyzing your data (Gibbs, 2007). Keep in mind that our experience and research classes have prepared us to feel comfortable in writing this section but, as we have in other parts of the proposal, we also have to rely on the ROL to guide us in analyzing our data. I've found that, in many instances, student researchers will go into great detail in their plan to analyze their data but then problems arise. Issues such as the inability to collect enough data, data distributions that are problematic, and statistical tests that prove to be invalid or unreliable in a particular situation can change their plans dramatically. In order to help avoid issues of this type, you should develop a detailed discussion of the different descriptive and inferential statistical tests that will be used to answer your research questions and test your hypotheses (Terrell, 2021). This, of course, will be up to you and your professor to decide.

Ethical Considerations

As we talked about in Chapter One when discussing the characteristics of a good problem, when we conduct research with human participants, it must be ethical.

This idea is straightforward and makes common sense but that's not always been the case. The literature is replete with research such as the Tuskegee syphilis experiment (Tuskegee University, 2015), where ethical violations were clearly obvious. In that case, U.S. public health doctors, starting in 1932, began investigating the long-term effects of syphilis using a purposive sample of impoverished sharecroppers in rural Alabama. The health of these participants, who had contracted the disease prior to the start of the study, was compared to that of syphilis-free participants in a study lasting from 1932 to 1972, despite the fact that penicillin was developed in the mid-1920s and could be used to cure the affected patients.

Studies such as these led to the U.S. government empaneling the Belmont Committee to investigate these improprieties. Their resultant publication, the Belmont Report (1979), mandates three overarching principles for conducting research using human subjects:

1. Beneficence: Participants in a research study must be treated ethically by having their decisions respected, being protected from harm, and having their well-being ensured.

2. Respect for persons: Participants in a research study should be treated as individuals capable of making decisions affecting their well-being. Participants incapable of acting autonomously are entitled to protection.

3. Justice: Participants in a research study should receive all benefits to which they are entitled, with no burdens imposed unduly.

In particular, three specific areas are focused on:

1. Informed consent: Researchers must ensure that participants in a study are made aware of the purpose of the study and of their rights as a participant. Following that, participants must provide written acknowledgment of and their agreement to participate.

2. Assessment of risks and benefits: Researchers must conduct a thorough investigation of the nature and scope of the risks and benefits inherent to the study. This allows an institution to make the judgment as to whether any risks to participants are minimized and justifiable, as well as to provide participants with the information they need to decide whether to participate in the study.

3. Selection of subjects: Researchers must establish and follow fair procedures for identifying and selecting participants for a research study. Participants should not be purposefully included or excluded for reasons of risk or reward.

The publication of the Belmont Report (1979) led to the development of institutional review boards (IRBs) at many colleges and universities. These boards require researchers who desire to work with human participants to file an application describing their proposed research. The application is closely scrutinized for adherence to the principles set forth by the Belmont Commission. Following that, the IRB will either approve your proposal, ask for modifications to your proposal, or reject your proposal outright.

Plans for Presenting the Results

This section is straightforward. First, you will always tell the reader that you plan on presenting your results in Chapters 4 and 5 of your dissertation. Second, in cases where you're conducting research in a "real-world" environment, you will also indicate any reports and the like that you will supply to interested parties.

SUMMARY OF CHAPTER THREE: THE FIRST PART OF YOUR DISSERTATION RESEARCH METHOD

As I said at the outset, Chapter 3 of a dissertation proposal details the research method for your study. The title "Summary" speaks for itself. Briefly tell the reader the research questions and hypotheses you will be investigating, how you will conduct the study, how data will be analyzed, and how you will present the results of your statistical tests. Try to make the summary of your proposal inclusive but succinct enough to get the point across without rewriting the entire chapter.

Although the research design is included as part of Chapter 3, we leave the discussion of the three major research approaches—quantitative, qualitative, and mixed methods—until later in this book. In this chapter, we've focused only on content that is generally common to all three of the research designs. Because a good research methodology includes these, as well as the design and procedures, we'll wait to add to our case study about the industrial waste site, as well as continue our own writing, until after those chapters. As for now, let's wrap this up by looking at the key words and phrases, taking a quiz, and continuing to write.

Do You Understand These Key Words and Phrases?	
Accidental sampling	Convenience sampling
Achievement tests	Convergent validity
Affective tests	Criterion validity
Behavioral observation scale	Cronbach's alpha
Cluster sampling	Demographic data forms
Concurrent validity	Discriminant validity
Construct	Dualism
Construct validity	Equivalent forms reliability
Content validity	Generalizability

Interrater reliability	Sampling error
Item validity	Sampling frame
Nonprobabilistic sampling	Sampling validity
Nonrandom sampling	Semistructured interview
Predictive validity	Simple random sampling
Probabilistic sampling	Snowball sampling
Projective test	Split-half reliability
Purposive sampling	Stratified sampling
Quota sampling	Structured interview
Random sampling	Survey
Ranking scales	Systematic sampling
Reliability	Test–retest reliability
Reliability coefficient	Unstructured interview
Sampling bias	Validity

REVIEW QUESTIONS

Mark each of the answers true or false. If false, explain why.

1. ____ Constructs are measured using an affective test and specific content is measured using an achievement test.

2. ____ Probabilistic sampling gives all members of a population the least chance of being selected for a sample.

3. ____ Purposive sampling and intentional sampling mean the same thing.

4. ____ Constructs are values that are known to exist but are not tangible.

5. ____ It is always better to use a structured interview rather than a semistructured or unstructured interview.

6. ____ Demographic data forms are needed for all studies.

7. ____ The Spearman–Brown, Küder–Richardson, and Cronbach's alpha reliability coefficients are all strong measures of validity.

8. ____ Projective tests should be used when measuring a specific content area.

9. ____ Content validity includes item and sampling validity.

10. ____ Researchers should be aware of ethical concerns in every type of study.

11. ____ Dualism refers to the establishment of validity by having at least two people review your data collection and analysis.

Provide a short answer to each of these questions:

12. What is the difference between nonprobabilistic and random sampling?

13. What is the difference between cluster sampling and stratified sampling?

14. What is the difference between validity and reliability?

15. What is the relationship among samples, populations, and sampling bias?

16. How do convergent validity and discriminant validity differ?

17. What are the differences between convenience sampling and systematic sampling?

18. What is the difference between equivalent forms reliability and test–retest reliability?

19. Describe the relationship among a population, the sampling frame, and a sample.

20. When assessing reliability, when should Cronbach's alpha be used?

CHAPTER FIVE

Quantitative Research Methods

Introduction

In the previous chapter, we talked about components of the different research methodologies that are common to most research studies. At this point, we need to focus our efforts and only look at studies that use a quantitative design. In this chapter, we discuss four different designs: survey research, correlational studies, quasi-experimental research, and true experimental studies. The design you use will be based on the research questions you ask and any hypotheses you want to test.

Different Types of Data

Before we move further, we need to discuss the different types of numeric data we might collect in a quantitative study; this is important because it affects the type of design and data analysis you will propose. There are four distinct types of numeric data: nominal, ordinal, interval, and ratio. Each of these types of data has a unique set of properties and understanding them is imperative (Terrell, 2021).

Nominal Data

Nominal data or, as it is sometimes called, categorical or discrete data, is simply a value that we count. For example, if we are interested in determining the number of males and females we work with, the data value "gender" is nominal in nature. To analyze these data, we could start by simply counting the number of persons falling into each category. The important thing to remember is that the categories are mutually exclusive because the items being counted can only fall into one category or another. For example, a person cannot be counted as both a male and a female. Other examples of nominal data include ethnicity, college class, or just about any other construct used to group persons or things. In Table 5.1, we can see where we have asked 100 people the political party to which they belong. Each of the parties represents a distinct category; a person cannot belong to more than one.

In Table 5.2, we have asked 500 students to tell us the primary method they use to get to school. There are five possible choices and, because we have asked for only the primary method of transportation, a student could choose only one. Because all we want to know is how many students fall into each group, this meets the definition of nominal data.

Ordinal Data

The second type of data is called **ordinal data** or, as it is sometimes called, *rank* data. When we use ordinal data, we are interested in determining what is important or significant while investigating non-numeric concepts, such as happiness, discomfort, or agreement. For example, I recently took my car to the dealership for scheduled maintenance. Within a day of picking it up, I received an email asking me to rank their service using a form like the one in Table 5.3. You can see that a scale ranging from "very dissatisfied (1)" to "very satisfied (5)" was used. I was asked to assign a ranking to each of the statements shown therein.

There are things about ordinal data that are essential to remember. First, the answers are subjective; there is no one standard for the choices. You could have the

TABLE 5.1. Distribution of Political Party Preference

Republican	Democrat	Independent	Other
40	35	20	5

TABLE 5.2. Primary Transportation to School

Drive	Carpool	Public transportation	Walk	Bike
210	105	85	62	38

TABLE 5.3. Ordinal Scale: "Please Rate the Quality of the Service You Received"

	Very dissatisfied	Dissatisfied	Neutral	Satisfied	Very satisfied
Explanation of services needed					
Price					
Staff helpfulness					
Time needed for service					

same service performed, and pay the same cost, as another customer. The rank you give is your opinion; you might be satisfied with the price you paid while another customer is very dissatisfied. Because of that, even if we assign numeric values to the scores (e.g., very dissatisfied = 1 and satisfied = 4), we can't compute an average level of satisfaction for the service performed simply because the scores might not be relative to one another. Again, all the answers are subjective. In short, the properties of the actual variable are not known. You will see, later in the book, that we can use other statistical tools to look at the midpoint of the data distribution.

Interval Data

Interval data is the first of two types of data that are called quantitative or continuous data. By this, we mean that a data value can hypothetically fall anywhere on a number line within the range of a given data set. Test scores are a perfect example of this type of data because we know, from experience, that test scores generally range from 0 to 100 and a student taking a test could score anywhere in that range.

As suggested by its name, the number line shown in Table 5.4 represents the possible range of test scores and is divided into equal increments of 10. Given that, the 10-point difference between a grade of 70 and a grade of 80 is the same as the difference between a grade of 10 and a grade of 20. The differences they represent, however, are not relative to each other.

For example, if a person scores 80 on the exam, his or her grade is four times larger than a person who scores 20 on the exam. We cannot say, however, that the person who scores 80 knows four times more than the person who scores 20; we can only say that the person with the 80 answered 80% of the questions correctly and the person scoring 20 answered 20% of the questions correctly. We also cannot say that a score of zero means that the unfortunate student knows nothing about the subject matter nor does a score of 100 indicate absolute mastery. These scores only indicate a complete mastery or lack of knowledge of the questions on the examination.

The point is, even though the score data are measured in equal intervals on this type of scale, the scale itself is only a handy way of presenting the scores without indicating that the scores are in any way related to one another. Other examples of interval-level data include temperature, aptitude scores, and intelligence quotients. These ideas, using temperature as an example, are shown in Table 5.5.

Ratio Data

Ratio data is also classified as quantitative or continuous data. Ratio data differs from interval data because it does have an absolute zero point and the various points on the scale can be used to make comparisons between one another. For

TABLE 5.4. Range of Test Scores

0	10	20	30	40	50	60	70	80	90	100

TABLE 5.5. Temperatures at Different Locales

School	Fahrenheit temperature	Comment
University of Alaska	0	This doesn't mean there is no temperature in Alaska; this is just an arbitrary value where the temperature in Alaska falls on the scale. There could be a value below zero.
University of Virginia	25	This doesn't mean that Virginia has a temperature and Alaska doesn't. The two temperatures are relative to the scale and nothing else.
Troy University	50	Troy is not twice as warm as Virginia. Just like above, this is just where the temperature for Troy falls on the scale.
University of Texas at El Paso	100	El Paso is not four times as hot as Virginia nor is it twice as hot as Troy. Having lived there, 100 is actually not that hot!

example, weight could be measured using an interval scale because we know that the relative difference between 20 pounds and 40 pounds is the same as the relative difference between 150 pounds and 300 pounds: in both cases, the second value is twice as large as the first. There are, however, three important distinctions between interval and ratio data.

First, a value of zero on a ratio scale means that whatever you are trying to measure doesn't exist—for example, a bank account with a zero balance means that there is no money in the account. Second, ratio data allows us to establish a true ratio between the different points on a scale. For example, a person who owns 600 shares of a company has twice as many shares as a person owning 300 shares; the same person would own six times as many shares as a person owning 100 shares. This added degree of precision allows us to use ratio scales to measure data more accurately than any of the other previously mentioned scales. Other examples of ratio-level data include distance and elapsed time; one of my favorite examples, annual income, is shown in Table 5.6.

Having said all of this, you might be asking why we spent so much time talking about different types of data. It's simple: like I said at the outset, the type of research design, and particularly the type of data analysis you propose, depends somewhat on the type of data you collect.

 **A WORD OF CAUTION**

As you just read, interval and ratio data are referred to together as quantitative data. This doesn't mean that we can't use nominal and ordinal data in a quantitative

TABLE 5.6. Income for Different Professions

Job	Annual income	Comment
Student	$0.00	This student is making absolutely nothing—he has a lack of income. That's OK; he can study now and earn money later.
Textbook author	$25,000	Believe me, we are only in this for the love of writing. This is a very optimistic estimate.
College professor	$50,000	This is another profession where you had better not be in it for the money. At the same time, look at the bright side; you're making twice as much as a textbook author.
Medical doctor	$250,000	This is better. Ten times as much as the author and five times as much as the college professor. Did I mention it takes longer to get a PhD than it does to get an MD?
Chairperson of Microsoft	$1,000,000,000	This is where we want to be, a billion dollars. The college professor's salary times 20,000! It is even 4,000 times what the medical doctor makes! For those of you majoring in education and psychology, forget it. It is probably too much trouble keeping up with that much money anyway.

research design. This is simply an adjective we use to describe values that fall on a number line. As you have learned in your statistics classes, you generally use certain statistical tests to analyze nominal and ordinal data, and another set of tests to analyze quantitative data.

Quantitative Research Designs

The research design is the plan you will use to describe the groups you collect data from, how often you collect the data, and at what point the data are analyzed. The design is only part of the overall research method of your study wherein you describe how the population is identified, the manner in which the sample will be selected, when the data will be collected, and so on. In short, Chapter 3 of your proposal will include the material discussed in the previous chapter of this book; it will all be tied together within the design and research method itself. As I said earlier, in this chapter, we discuss the four major quantitative research designs: survey research, correlational research, causal–comparative research, and experimental research. As we talk about each of these designs, I'll include an example of each type either within the text or in the appendices at the end of this chapter. Throughout the section I've synthesized the work of a lot of great authors (e.g., Creswell & Creswell, 2020; Gay et al., 2012; Salkind, 2012; Sekaran & Bougie, 2013) to provide as inclusive a perspective of quantitative research as possible.

Survey Research

Survey research is just as its name suggests: It investigates and reports on the current status of a population based on numeric data you've collected (Fink, 2016; Fowler, 2013). As you would expect, choosing a descriptive research approach starts with the problem statement, the purpose statement, and the research questions but doesn't include a hypothesis; we discuss why shortly. Let's start with a scenario where we're supporting a particular candidate for governor, and are interested in determining voter intentions prior to an election. We would do this in order to identify cities within our state where our candidate has strong support, thereby allowing us to allocate our resources in cities where support for our candidate is weaker.

> **Problem Statement:** In order to effectively allocate human and capital resources, politicians want to identify areas within the state where voter support is lacking.
>
> **Purpose Statement:** The purpose of this study is to identify areas with low voter support; this will allow the expenditure of human and capital resources to increase support for our candidate in those areas.
>
> **Research Question:** Are there areas in our state where our candidate for governor has the support of less than 50% of the voters in that district?

Obviously, this type of study is very simple: We would poll registered voters in an area and ask who they support for governor (see Table 5.7).

Answering our research question is easy: our candidate has a comfortable lead in four of the five cities polled, but he definitely needs to focus on building up support in Delta Junction. Keep in mind that, just as the name suggests, all we're doing is describing the current status of voter intent; our procedure is straightforward. We simply need to identify the sample we need, develop or locate a data collection instrument, collect our data, and then compute the necessary **descriptive statistics** (e.g., the average or mean) to answer your research questions (see Figure 5.1).

Obviously, the **instruments** you would use, how you would identify and select your sample, and the exact steps you would go through to collect your data would be straightforward for a study of this type. Knowing that, I've included a brief example of a descriptive research method in Appendix 5.1 at the end of this chapter.

TABLE 5.7. Survey Data

City	Registered voters	Voters supporting our candidate	Percentage
Ableville	7,640	6,000	78.5%
Bakertown	12,393	8,939	72.1%
Charleston	22,991	15,786	68.7%
Delta Junction	9,312	3,076	33.0%
Echoton	15,982	13,326	83.4%

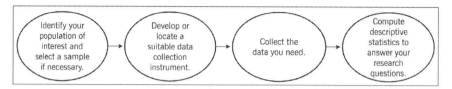

FIGURE 5.1. The survey research approach.

Why Isn't There a Hypothesis for Survey Research?

As we noted earlier, you do not include a hypothesis in a descriptive design simply because you are not examining the relationship between variables or testing for cause and effect. Instead, you're answering your research questions by using descriptive statistics, such as the mean or range of values in your data set, and **graphical descriptive statistics**, such as a bar chart showing the number of occurrences of a value in your data. More advanced research designs call for inferential statistics, tools such as *t* tests, **analysis of variance (ANOVA)**, and regression analysis that allow us to make decisions about the data we have collected and the hypotheses we've stated. While computing and interpreting statistical tests isn't the focus of this text, we look at examples later in the chapter.

Correlational Research

Quite often in life we're interested in knowing the relationship between two variables; in **correlational research** we ask questions, such as:

1. Is there a relationship between years of education and salary?
2. Does ice cream consumption change depending on the outside temperature?
3. Does a larger police presence lead to lower crime rates?

As we briefly discussed earlier in this book, each of these questions asks whether a correlational relationship exists (Chen & Krauss, 2004); this generally means one of three things.

First, if values in one data set get larger, so do values in the second data set. We would expect that type of relationship between years of education and salary; generally speaking, the longer you go to school, the more money you'll make. Since both values are getting larger (i.e., moving in the same direction), we say the type of correlation they have is a **positive correlation**.

Second, in the question regarding ice cream consumption and outside temperature, we might find that people tend to eat less ice cream when it's cold outside. That means, when one value (i.e., temperature) goes down, so does the other (i.e., ice cream consumption). Contrary to what seems logical, this is also called a positive correlation because, just like the first example, the data values move together in the same direction.

Finally, there are situations where when one value gets larger, the other gets smaller. That could certainly be the case with the number of police officers and the amount of crime; it seems logical that a larger number of police officers on patrol would lead to lower levels of crime. In this case, we have a **negative correlation:** When one value gets larger, the other value gets smaller. You can see examples of all of these ideas in Table 5.8.

In the two leftmost columns, you can see a set of values for the average speed driven, as well as miles per gallon. As you might expect, as the speed goes up, the number of miles per gallon goes down. As we've just discussed, this means there is a negative correlation; we can verify this with the *r* value at the bottom of the column. This value, called **Pearson's *r*,** is a **correlation coefficient** showing the strength of the relationship between the two sets of quantitative data. Values approaching +1 indicate a strong positive correlation, values nearing –1 mean a strong negative correlation exists, and values closer to zero indicate a weak or lack of correlation. In this case, our *r* value is –.975, meaning that a strong negative correlation does exist, just as we expected.

In the middle two columns of Table 5.8, it appears that we have a moderate positive correlation between height and weight in that, generally speaking, when a person's height goes up, so does their weight. Not only is this positive correlation intuitive, it is also supported by a Pearson *r* value of .679. Finally, in the two right-most columns, when we look at the relationship between the time spent studying and grade-point average (GPA), we see a very strong positive correlation: Pearson's *r* = .928. This is strong evidence that the less a student studies, the lower their GPA will be. Remember, just because both values are getting smaller, it's still a positive correlation simply because both values are moving in the same direction. These ideas are summarized in Table 5.9.

A WORD OF CAUTION

In each of the statements below, a strong correlation exists:

There is a negative correlation between the amount of hair on a man's head and his salary (i.e., the less hair, the more money).

There is a positive correlation between the number of churches in a town and the number of drug addicts in a town (i.e., the more churches, the more drug addicts).

By looking at this, it seems the best way for me to make more money is to shave my head (actually, it wouldn't take a lot of shaving). At the same time, cities could be free of drug problems if they tore down their churches. Obviously, although a strong correlation exists, these statements are nonsense. Why? It's simple: Although both variables in each statement are correlated, they are also correlated to another variable that explains the relationship; we call this a **confounding variable.** For

TABLE 5.8. Correlation Coefficients

Speed driven	Miles per gallon	Height (in inches)	Weight (in pounds)	Time studying (in minutes)	Grade point average
50	30	60	130	180	3.59
55	29	62	135	170	3.40
59	25	64	140	150	3.20
60	24	66	145	145	3.10
65	20	68	130	120	2.80
66	18	70	200	120	2.30
$r = -.975$		$r = .679$		$r = .928$	

TABLE 5.9. Negative and Positive Correlations

⇅	⇊	⇈
Negative correlation	Positive correlation	Positive correlation
One value goes up, the other value goes down	Both values go down	Both values go up
Pearson's r is between zero and –1.	Pearson's r is between zero and +1.	Pearson's r is between zero and +1.

example, it's not the amount of hair that's related to salary, it's a man's age. Generally speaking, the older a man gets, the less hair he has; at the same time, a man's salary tends to get larger as he gets older. The same goes for churches; the real correlation lies between each of these values and the size of the city; larger cities have more drug addicts and churches, smaller cities have fewer churches and fewer drug addicts. This is similar to the stories showing a strong correlation between the number of cell phone towers in an area and the birth rate: More towers equal more babies. Again, there's nothing out of the ordinary going on; it's just that larger populations have both of each, smaller towns have fewer of each.

We have to always keep in mind that correlation doesn't necessarily mean causation—two values can be correlated and not have anything to do with the other. We can see quite a few of these noncausal correlations presented in newspapers, on television, and from other sources; in many of these cases, people are trying to use them to sell us something or bolster their point of view. What's the lesson? Simple: Always look at the big picture!

Let's go through a couple of examples to make sure we completely understand what we're doing.

Problem Statement: Researchers in the 1950s were astonished to find that the number of children born to teenage parents was directly proportional to the number of drive-in theaters in their communities. This led many governmental officials to determine that tearing down these theaters, thereby eliminating places where young lovers could be alone, would help address this problem.

Purpose Statement: The purpose of this study is to determine whether there is a direct relationship between the number of drive-in theaters and the number of children born to teenage parents.

Research Question: Is there a correlation between the number of children born to teenage parents and the number of drive-in theaters in a community?

In this case, conducting the study would be easy; we would count the number of drive-in theaters in a number of cities, determine the number of children born to teenage parents in those same cities, and correlate the two sets of data. We could then answer our research question based on the correlation coefficient. Unlike the earlier correlation coefficients, such as Pearson's r that we discussed earlier, if it's close to +1, we need to tear down the drive-in theaters and if it's close to zero, we don't have to worry. This makes sense, right?

No, it doesn't. Obviously, this is an example of a poor use of correlational research because the size of the community is a confounding variable; larger communities have more drive-ins and teenage births, smaller communities have fewer of each. In other cases, interested parties may try to use the confounding variable in a more insidious manner.

For example, by the late 1940s, scientists had determined a strong correlation between smoking and cancer rates. Obviously, the tobacco industry tried to explain this away by saying that cancer was actually more prevalent in blue collar workers, people in lower socioeconomic groups, and so on. Each of these groups had been shown to have higher rates of cancer to begin with; the fact that smoking was more prevalent in those populations had nothing to do with it. Again, always look at the big picture!

As you can see, a correlational study is straightforward; everything we've talked about can be seen in Figure 5.2.

Before We Move Forward . . .

As I said, we'll talk extensively about each of the experimental designs later in the chapter but, before we do, let's make sure we know where we're going by tying together some of the terms we've discussed up to this point.

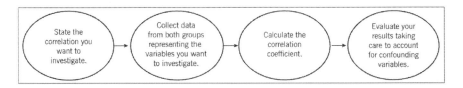

FIGURE 5.2. The correlational research approach.

For example, in the remainder of the chapter, when we state a hypothesis, it means our study calls for us to examine the effect of an **independent variable** (i.e., the cause) on a **dependent variable** (i.e., the effect)—if measured, this may be the **effect size**. Simply put, this means that we have an independent variable with one or more levels (e.g., categories such as male and female, or dogs and cats) and we look at the different effects of those levels on our dependent variable. For example, let's suppose we have a new incentive program that we want to try out with our employees. We are hoping that the new program will lead to fewer people leaving our company for "greener pastures." In this case, our independent variable would be "incentive program" and it would have only one level: Every employee is part of the incentive group. In this case, we would test our hypothesis by comparing resignation levels (i.e., our dependent variable) to a historical average.

> *The number of resignations after the new incentive program will be significantly lower than the historical average.*

In another case, we might be implementing the results of our incentive program by introducing it to your employees in the Seattle office, and not to your employees in your Denver office. In this case, your independent variable would have two levels: a group of employees who received the incentive program and a group who didn't. This split would lead to the following hypothesis:

> *Groups of employees receiving the new incentive plan will have significantly fewer resignations than groups of employees not receiving the new incentive plan.*

Keep in mind, in both of these examples, that your data collection is simple: You're counting the number of resignations. In other cases, you might need to find a specific data collection test or survey to collect your data. We would then test our hypothesis by implementing the program and then comparing the resignations at one office to that at the other.

Causal–Comparative Research

I love talking about learning theory and I've taught it for many years. While they're in my class, students complete a series of surveys that measure their level of intrinsic motivation, whether they suffer learner anxiety, and their personality type. Over the years, I've collected data from over 300 students. Recently, using those data, I've tried to determine whether any of those constructs predicted leaving the doctoral program in which I teach. I chose intrinsic motivation as my first measure (i.e., my dependent variable) because high levels of intrinsic motivation have been shown to be predictive of success in many endeavors. In this case, my independent variable is "graduate" and there are two levels: "yes" and "no." At this point, we have to decide based on what we know so far. We begin by asking ourselves, "How were the **levels of the independent variable** established? Did we assign people to the groups, or did they exist before I became interested in this investigation?" In this case, students had already either dropped out of the program or they had graduated; I had nothing to do with that. We then must decide whether we did anything to cause either group to act differently from the other; we are asking whether we *manipulated* the variable. Again, in this case, I did nothing to the groups; the students fell into one group or the other based on their own actions.

Simply put, these are the criteria for a **causal–comparative research** study (Shadish, Cook, & Campbell, 2001). I have two or more groups that differ in the variable of interest—in this case, graduation status—and I want to determine whether the levels of intrinsic motivation are different. This idea is shown in Figure 5.3.

Let's break these data down and look at the specific case we just discussed.

> **Problem Statement:** Students are leaving the doctoral program prior to graduation.
>
> **Purpose Statement:** The purpose of this study is to determine whether there is a relationship between a student's level of intrinsic motivation and whether or not they graduated from the doctoral program at their university.
>
> **Research Question:** Is intrinsic motivation a predictor of success in a doctoral program?
>
> **Research Hypothesis:** Students who graduate from a doctoral program will have significantly higher intrinsic motivation than students who do not graduate from a doctoral program.
>
> **Null Hypothesis:** There will be no significant difference in intrinsic motivation between students who graduate from a doctoral program and students who do not graduate.

Notice here that my research hypothesis is directional. My literature review has indicated that successful students should have significantly higher levels of intrinsic motivation than students who drop out. As expected, our null hypothesis simply says that no significant difference exists.

Hypothesis Testing

The null hypothesis is easy to test. From our statistics classes we know that in most cases where we have one independent variable with two levels, and one dependent variable representing quantitative data, we are going to use a *t* test. In this case, because being in one group precludes membership in the other group (i.e., the levels are independent of each other), we will use an independent sample *t* test (Terrell, 2021).

FIGURE 5.3. The causal–comparative research approach.

Keep in mind that this text focuses on writing a dissertation proposal, and data analysis occurs only after we have conducted a study; the results of our data analysis are then presented in Chapters 4 and 5 of the dissertation. Given that, while we won't get into a great amount of detail here, let's not leave ourselves hanging. Was there a significant difference in intrinsic motivation or not?

Interpreting the results of statistical software is essentially the same for all basic statistical tests. We use the software to analyze the data and compute a *p* **value**: This tells us the probability that our results are due to chance. We must then decide on an **alpha value**: the acceptable probability of making an error in testing our hypothesis based on differences in our data that are due to chance. We then compare our *p* value to our alpha value. If the computed *p* value is greater than or equal to alpha, we fail to **reject the null hypothesis** and fail to support the research hypothesis. If *p* is less than the stated alpha value, we will reject our null hypothesis and support our research hypothesis.

Let's use the data in Table 5.10 to test our null and research hypotheses as stated above. Note that I've set the alpha value to .05; this is the most common value used in statistical decision making.

Let's look closely at these results. In the first scenario, graduates have an average intrinsic motivation score of 75, nongraduates average 60. The *p* value is less than alpha, so we reject the null hypothesis and support the research hypothesis; it does appear that graduates have higher levels of intrinsic motivation than do nongraduates. In the other two cases, the averages are so close that the *p* value is very large and greater than the alpha value; in both instances we would have to **fail to reject the null hypothesis** and we can't support the research hypothesis.

 **A WORD OF CAUTION**

As you can see, in the first scenario, the graduates' average level of intrinsic motivation was 75, 15 points higher than students who did not graduate. Again, the

TABLE 5.10. Comparison of *p* and Alpha Values

Graduate	Average intrinsic motivation	*p*	Alpha	Decision
Yes	75	.04	.05	Reject the null hypothesis.
No	60			Support the research hypothesis.
Yes	65	.95	.05	Fail to reject the null hypothesis.
No	65			Fail to support the research hypothesis.
Yes	65	.66	.05	Fail to reject the null hypothesis.
No	64			Fail to support the research hypothesis.

resultant *p* value caused us to reject the null hypothesis. Be careful with your interpretation, however! The statistical formula works with the data you have; if the mean scores were reversed (i.e., 75 for the nongraduates and 60 for the graduates), the same *p* value would be computed. In that case, you would still reject the null hypothesis but would fail to support the research hypothesis. Always be careful: Look at your average scores before you make any decisions.

ANOTHER WORD OF CAUTION

Remember, with a causal–comparative study you're comparing data from two preexisting groups. There may be a true significant difference, or the difference may be due to a reason other than that you've hypothesized. For example, suppose the level of motivation was highly correlated to age; older people are more intrinsically motivated. In that case, would it be the students' motivation that predicted success or failure, or was it their age? We see in the next section, when we talk about experimental research, that there are several issues such as this that we have to consider.

Experimental Research

There are three groups of experimental designs that we'll discuss: pre-experimental designs, quasi-experimental designs, and true experimental designs (Creswell & Creswell, 2020; Gay et al., 2012; Shadish et al., 2001). Each of these groups has specific types of studies within it, but there are overarching characteristics of **experimental research** that we have to consider before getting into detail.

Regardless of which of the experimental designs you use, there are common characteristics that underlie each of these approaches. First, unlike descriptive and correlational research, you always test a hypothesis in experimental research. Following that, you continue by creating a research plan to guide you. This plan will include:

1. Stating your hypothesis.
2. Identifying appropriate data collection instruments.
3. Identifying your population and sample selection procedures.
4. Determining the design you will use to test your hypothesis.
5. Developing a detailed set of procedures you will follow while conducting your study.

We've already learned that the hypothesis is generally based on literature from Chapter 2 but is placed in Chapter 1. We've also seen how to find instruments to use in our study, as well as how to identify a population and select a sample. Before we move forward with selecting the appropriate research method, we need to talk about the validity of any research we conduct.

The Validity of Your Study

We discussed validity earlier when we discussed instruments for our study; in that case, we were simply concerned with whether our test or survey measured what it was designed to measure. At this point we refer to the validity of a study as the trustworthiness of your results (Gay et al., 2012; Newton & Shaw, 2014). Are they the accurate results of a carefully planned, written, and conducted study, or did something interfere and negatively affect your results? To address this issue, we have to concern ourselves with both the internal and external validity of our results. We can think of threats to **internal validity** as anything that might affect the accuracy of our results, while threats to **external validity** are issues that may affect the generalizability of our results. In this section, we see an overview of these topics, but I've included a reference guide, based on the work of Gay et al., in Appendix 5.5 at the end of this chapter.

Threats to the Internal Validity of a Study

As we are testing hypotheses as part of our research studies, we need to establish internal validity to the highest degree possible by controlling for factors, other than our independent variable, that might affect the accuracy of our intervention. There are several threats to internal validity that we need to be aware of (Campbell & Stanley, 1963).

HISTORY

During the 2019–2020 school year, I had a dissertation student working with sixth-grade females participating in a STEM club offered at an inner-city middle school (Almeyda, 2020). The goal of his study was to increase the STEM interest and awareness of these young students. His proposal was approved, and in September of 2019, he began by using a widely known STEM survey developed by the Friday Institute for Educational Innovation (2012) to collect information measuring these same constructs. Following that, the young girls participated in biweekly sessions, offered by local scientists who introduced hands-on lessons covering various science topics. I'll be the first to admit, these sessions really caught my attention. Really, how many of you have ever learned to build and launch your own model rocket to help understand Newton's third law of equal and opposite reactions?

My student planned on collecting data in April but, as we all know, schools were closed throughout the United States in March due to the COVID-19 pandemic. The students all participated in online classroom sessions for the remainder of the school year—however, it would be unrealistic to think that the results of any study conducted with students at that point in time would be meaningful. Simply put, the circumstances of the study changed dramatically; this more than likely affected his intervention, thereby putting into question the results of his study. This phenomenon is called an effect of **history**. In his case, we completely changed directions and he was able to finish in a timely manner.

MATURATION

We generally think of maturation in terms of physical, social, and personality changes over time. For example, if we're training high school athletes, we probably could not totally attribute all changes in strength or speed directly to our workout regimen; the student athletes' growth spurt during high school has to be taken into consideration. We can expand the idea of **maturation** in this context to mean anything that happens directly to a subject during the course of a study. For example, let's suppose we are investigating two approaches to teaching language arts to children in elementary school. Because of their rapid cognitive growth during those years, there's a strong possibility that, in addition to the independent variable we're investigating, it would also affect the dependent variable. Because this is a threat to the internal validity of the study, we can't be sure whether any results are attributable to the intervention we were investigating (i.e., the approaches to language arts learning), or its interaction with natural cognitive growth.

TESTING

Testing refers to the fact that when a person knows they are being tested, this fact can change his or her performance on an exam. For example, we all remember "cramming" for an exam the night before we had to take it. We knew we were being tested and, while we might score higher on the exam, the knowledge we gained just for the test probably didn't stay with us too long. In other cases, the **pretest–treatment interaction** might lead to higher scores, simply because the person taking the test remembers the questions, or perhaps has studied that area specifically, since the last time the exam was taken. Again, in both cases, the score on the exam was influenced by more than just the knowledge gained in the class.

INSTRUMENTATION

Instruments, or tools we use to measure knowledge or skill, should demonstrate two types of instrument-specific validity. While this is different from the external and internal validity of the overall study, the idea remains somewhat the same: We want to make sure that the tool we're using is right for the job. We talked about this earlier, but I want to expand it just a bit to make sure we know how it fits in with the idea of external validity.

Item validity means we're asking ourselves, "Does each item in the test or survey I've developed relate to the subject area I want to measure?" Sampling validity then asks, "Have I covered the entire range of the subject area I want to cover?" For example, I teach an introduction to statistics class twice a year to our students pursuing a master's degree. I could easily put together a final exam right off the top of my head:

1. What is the most common measure of central tendency?
2. Which *t* test would you use if you had two independent samples measuring quantitative data?
3. What is the capital city of Norway?

Right away, you can see we have problems. First, Items 1 and 2 are valid items, but knowing that Oslo is the capital of Norway doesn't demonstrate knowledge gained in my introductory statistics class. This means that Question 3 does not have item validity. Second, as you know, an introductory course in statistics involves knowing about more than *t* tests and measures of central tendency. Because of this, the exam doesn't cover the breadth of the topic, thereby it is not demonstrating adequate sampling validity.

As you might guess, the idea of developing or evaluating instruments involves much more than this; in fact, I once took a course devoted exclusively to that topic. For most instruments, however, item and sampling validity are the two biggest concerns we face. Problems with either can negatively affect the internal validity of our study.

STATISTICAL REGRESSION TO THE MEAN

This is an easy concept to understand. Simply put, **statistical regression to the mean** means that when an event is measured twice, extreme scores on the second attempt will tend to be closer to the average score of the group than extreme scores on the first attempt. For example, I teach an introductory statistics class twice a year. In order to better understand the gain in knowledge my students make, I always give a pretest the first week of class and a posttest the last week of class. As you might expect, the pretest scores are very low, and the posttest scores are radically higher.

To demonstrate this phenomenon, let's imagine I have a class of 50 students, and I select the bottom 10 (i.e., 20%) as a sample. Following that selection, I could compute the overall mean of the class, as well as the average of the sample of 10 students; obviously, the average score of the students in my sample would tend to be lower than the overall average. For our discussion, let's imagine having a pretest overall average score of 25 and a sample average score of 10. This means that the average score of the sample is 10/25, or 40%, of the overall average score.

At the end of the term, I could administer the same exam and the scores would again cluster around one another. More than likely the overall average would improve greatly, as would that of my 10-student sample. In this case, let's say our mean score for the overall group was 90 and the mean score for the same 10 students in our pretest sample was 72; in this case, the sample's score is 72/90 or 80%. Because of this change, we can say that the average score of the sample group has regressed, or gotten closer, to the mean score of the population.

The reasoning behind this is simple. Although the scores from the same 10 students on the posttest would hover around the same average, it's possible that some of them scored proportionately higher on the posttest than they did on the pretest.

When that happens, the mean score of the sample tends to move closer to the overall average. Obviously, this is something we need to concern ourselves with as we begin testing hypotheses, but we'll see in our quantitative research designs that we have ways of controlling for this type of validity problem.

DIFFERENTIAL SELECTION OF PARTICIPANTS

Differential selection of participants is a threat that happens when you select groups that are different to begin with; this difference may affect the dependent variable. For example, let's imagine a scenario where a civic action group is complaining about the indifference shown by many police officers toward homeless people. In order to appease their concerns, the chief agrees to study the effect of a new type of sensitivity training on police officers' attitudes. Just for convenience, the chief selects police officers from two stations: one group will receive the new training and the other will not. At the end of the study, our job would be to collect and analyze data to determine whether the intervention was successful.

After analyzing our data, suppose we found that the training didn't work; police officers still demonstrated the same levels of indifference. A lot of people would consider the training a failure and move on to something different. Before I did that, I would suggest that, because we used preexisting groups, we should look closely at the officers we worked with. It's possible that the station receiving the training was in an upper-middle-class suburban neighborhood. Sensitivity training might not have an effect on these officers simply because many of them did not deal with homeless people on a daily basis; their training would not be in a context they would understand. The other police officers, however, might work in a less prosperous part of town and see homeless people on a day-to-day basis. Their attitudes wouldn't change simply because they didn't receive the new training.

MORTALITY

Mortality in everyday use refers to passing away, but this doesn't necessarily mean that a person must pass away in order to negatively affect the results of your study; it can mean anything that causes a member of your population to leave the study, thereby affecting your results. For example, if you're looking at the effect of a new incentive program on sales, your results would be dramatically affected if your best salesperson resigned while you were implementing the program. That being said, we could no longer look at the independent variable (i.e., your incentive program) as the sole cause for any change in the number of sales (i.e., your dependent variable).

Threats to the External Validity of a Study

External validity asks the question, "Are my results generalizable to other groups or situations outside of the sample itself?" (Bracht & Glass, 1968). For example, if I conducted a study about employee incentives and found that my new plan decreased the number of resignations, would my same plan work at other companies? Would it work for a local insurance firm's employees or for an industry giant such as Apple or Google?

Threats to generalizability tend to be caused by the actions of participants involved in the study, problems with the sample or how it was created, or issues beyond the control of the person conducting the study. In some cases, if you recognize the threats to external validity, you can design your study to control for them; in many cases, however, a particular research design will not control for a given threat. In those cases, researchers must recognize the threat and decide whether its severity is such that it completely invalidates the results of the proposed study. In either event, the researcher needs to acknowledge the threat and its potential effect on the generalizability of the results.

SELECTION–TREATMENT INTERACTION

Many of the threats to the external validity of your study (i.e., whether your results can be generalized to other groups or situations) depend upon who your participants are. For example, imagine that you're investigating the effect of software to teach a foreign language to elementary school children. You could ask the school administration to choose two existing classes for you: One would use the software and one would receive traditional instruction. At the end of the study, your results might show that the software group greatly outperformed the traditional group. Does that mean that we can advise the school to teach foreign languages only by using computers? No, we can't, simply because the two classes may have been different to start with.

In this case, suppose you were teaching Spanish using the two methods. Given the large growth of the Hispanic population in the United States, just by chance there could be more native Spanish speakers in the experimental group than in the control group; this could affect achievement. We call this threat to external validity **selection–treatment interaction**; unfortunately, because it directly reflects the actions of the researcher, we aren't able to control for it with an experimental design. As we said, the researcher has to be aware of the potential of this threat and make decisions based on the results by taking this into consideration.

PRETEST–TREATMENT INTERACTION

The first of the two threats that can be controlled with an effective research design is called pretest–treatment interaction. This interaction simply means that a pretest at the start of a study may directly affect the way in which a participant acts toward the intervention.

For example, I'm thinking back to the introductory statistics pretest given to the doctoral students in my research classes each term. This lets me know whether there are topics I can rapidly move through, thereby giving me more time for advanced topics. Given that, it's quite possible that the test could affect the way students study, and what they focus on in class. For example, if I asked questions about an ANOVA on the pretest, it's highly likely that, when I talked about it during the term, my students might think back to the pretest and think "Dr. Terrell asked questions about this at the start of the term, and now he's covering it in class. This must be something he thinks is very important, so I better pay attention!" Because of the extra amount of time the students spent focusing on the ANOVA, it's likely that their scores would be higher than would be expected from students in other classes who didn't take a pretest. This could lead to results that would not be generalizable to groups outside of my study.

In either event, when we discuss the various experimental designs, we'll see that there are ways we can control for this threat by designing a valid study.

MULTIPLE TREATMENT INTERFERENCE

This is the second of the two threats to external validity that can be controlled for by a valid research design. In **multiple treatment interference**, a subject in one study may be participating in another study simultaneously where both are designed to test the effect of an intervention on the same dependent variable. For example, let's envision two randomly formed groups where we want to test the efficacy of a new antiseizure drug. The control group is using Dilantin, a medication that has been on the market for many years and has proven to be very effective; our experimental group will be using a new medication to see how it compares to Dilantin. Obviously, we would hope that the new drug works even better, but we will only know if we compare the two. Knowing that, we could conduct our study and, after several months, we might find that the frequency of seizures of the experimental group dropped dramatically! While that seems like we're successful, we have to consider everything that may have happened. What if we found that several of the participants in the experimental group were, at the same time, trying a new type of diet that has also been hypothesized to lower seizure frequency? Could we then say our success is because of the medication, or could it be a combination of the medication and the diet? What about the diet alone? Because of this interaction, we wouldn't be sure unless we conducted the study again and ensured that the only difference in treatment is the two drugs the participants are taking.

Multiple treatment interference can also be caused by conducting interventions sequentially. Let's imagine a scenario where we're interested in building up the red blood cell count of high-altitude climbers. The higher red cell count will allow for more oxygen to be carried through the bloodstream, thereby increasing the probability of climbing success. We could begin our study by having our climbers run sprints during training; this type of anaerobic exercise has been shown to increase red blood cell counts. We could measure its efficacy by comparing the cell counts of climbers before and after the sprint training. If the training was successful, we could try to get the cell counts even higher by stopping the sprint exercises and having our athletes take large amounts of B complex vitamins every day. At the end of the treatment period, we might find that the red cell count is exactly the same as it was after the sprint training. Does this mean that the vitamins are not useful? Of course it doesn't, it simply means they didn't increase the cell count when the athletes followed the training. It's possible that the vitamins would have worked, and reached the same level of efficacy, had they been used before, or instead of, the sprint training. Luckily, like the pretest–treatment interaction, we can design our studies to control for this threat.

TREATMENT DIFFUSION

I've taught a lot of online classes throughout the years. While doing that, one thing I've learned is that students interacting among themselves contributes greatly to their satisfaction and success. As I reflected back on my days in graduate school, I realized the same had been true for me: I learned as much from studying with my friends as I did sitting in the classroom for 3 hours a night. This phenomenon is called **treatment diffusion**. My job as an online instructor might be to create a learning environment conducive to this type of interaction.

Knowing that most of my students probably use social media on a daily basis, I have created a Facebook page dedicated to use by a class. In order to test the effect of this brainstorm, I first created the page for one of my research courses, but not for the others. My idea was that at the end of the term, the students using the Facebook page would report higher levels of connectivity with one another and greater interaction and achievement in the course overall.

At the end of the term, I was excited to see what the results would tell me—to my astonishment, both groups' results were about the same. I was disappointed that my idea didn't work, but then I found out the probable cause. Students from the class not using Facebook found out about the page the other class was using and, thinking it was a good idea, created one for their own use. In short, the effect of my treatment was diffused by one group adopting what was supposed to be unique to the other group. Because this is based on the actions of the participants within the groups, I can't control for it with a particular experimental design.

There's a key point to remember here: If you're working with something new or different in one section of a class, it's not surprising that students in other sections find out. In many cases, this will cause them to replicate what is going on in the class using the Facebook page, or do something even more different! Either way could diffuse the results of our intervention.

EXPERIMENTER EFFECTS

Friends of mine recently adopted two elementary school-age children from a third world country. Although they spoke limited English when they arrived here, the children have both eagerly learned to read and write English. Their daughter, especially, has become a voracious reader, finishing books well above what is expected of her in the fifth grade. Given that, my friend was puzzled by her daughter's low scores on the school's reading diagnostic test; the results indicated she was at a reading level expected of second graders. Interested in what I would think, she called me to ask my opinion.

I explained to her that it seemed clear-cut: Her daughter was performing differently because she was being tested by someone she didn't know, someone who might have expectations different from her mom. In short, she was acting differently because someone was watching her. Unfortunately, this same thing happens when we're conducting research, except we call it an **experimenter effect**. Participants in our studies may act differently than they normally would just because they know we're observing them. As you might guess, we can't control for this threat with the design of our study. We simply must keep in mind that we may not be able to generalize our results.

SPECIFICITY OF VARIABLES

Earlier in the book, when we talked about writing problem statements, I emphasized that the scope of a study must be manageable by the researcher. In doing that, however, sometimes we create a threat to our external validity by so tightly defining what we're investigating that the results may not be generalizable to other populations. This problem is called **specificity of variables**. For example, I'm currently involved in a study where we're offering mental health counseling but, instead of traditional face-to-face sessions, we've created a virtual office where we meet with our clients. Our hope is that counseling in this manner will be just as effective as counseling in a traditional environment. If so, we feel this allows clients who might not otherwise be able to seek counseling to get the help they need. While this sounds great, there are a couple of things that could possibly affect the generalizability of our results.

In this case, we're using an approach called solution-focused brief therapy; on average, a client should see their therapist only three to five times. If our results are positive, can we say without a doubt that all counseling approaches work in a virtual world? No. What we can say is that solution-focused brief therapy works in a virtual world. In this case, we've also limited our clients to family members of military personnel returning from an overseas deployment. If we find that our efforts are in vain, does that mean we've failed and should give up? No. What it means is that this type of counseling did not work for this specific population. In either case, we might find that another therapeutic approach or another client base may produce different results.

These two examples show problems with the specificity of our variables: In order to keep the study within our scope, we've defined our counseling approach and population specifically. That means our outcomes, good or bad, are limited to one particular definition of counseling and one particular client base. Because we cannot control for this threat with a particular research design, in most studies researchers acknowledge these types of problems by stating the limitations of their studies, usually in Chapter 1 of the dissertation proposal. In this case, the researcher would say something like "The results of this study are limited to family members of returning veterans receiving solution-focused brief therapy in a virtual environment." This can bring with it some good news: Problems of this type lead researchers to conceptualize and conduct new research by acknowledging these limitations and conducting a study with a new set of variables (e.g., psychodynamic therapy offered in a virtual world to persons with addiction problems). We talk more about this whole idea of limitations later in the chapter.

REACTIVE ARRANGEMENTS

Our son, Andy, who's now 38, was like most kids when it came to breakfast cereal—the taste didn't matter as much as the prize in the box! At one point, I remember one cereal company including small figurines representing figures in American folklore: Paul Bunyan, Daniel Boone, and Davy Crockett were just a few of the heroes that a child might find buried in their breakfast bowl. In one particular case, Andy's cereal contained a figure of a large, well-muscled African American man holding a sledgehammer above his head. When Andy asked me about it, I told him it was John Henry, the legendary steel-driving man.

For those who might not know the story, John Henry was a folk hero who worked for a railroad company: His job was to use his pick to make holes in large rocks wherein dynamite could be placed, so that the rocks could be removed, and railroad tracks laid. Legend has it that he was so good that he entered into a competition with a steam engine designed to do the same thing, which would eventually take his job. John Henry took on the challenge, worked as hard as he could and ultimately beat the machine; unfortunately, he then fell over dead, with his pick in his hand.

John Henry's demise was caused by a **reactive arrangement** that has come to be called the **John Henry effect**: he was challenged and acted differently than he would have in a normal workday. This same type of phenomenon, very similar to an experimenter effect, can easily be provoked in a classroom or work environment just because the participants believe they are being compared to another group, or to a standard that has been consistently reinforced (e.g., an expected score on a standardized test). In the latter case, if standardized test scores did increase, we have to consider whether it was due to the results we might normally expect, or whether they were caused by a reactive arrangement. Knowing that, we would have to be careful about generalizing our results. Interestingly, some of the most disturbing research in psychology, such as the Milgram studies, wherein perceived electro-shock was used to investigate obedience to authority figures, demonstrates just how serious the effects of a reactive arrangement can be. As an aside, if you ever visit one of my research classes and listen to me talk about reactive arrangements, don't be surprised if I pull out the figure of John Henry that was in Andy's cereal bowl all those years ago. Even then I realized the importance of a good visual aid!

Another reactive arrangement, called a **novelty effect**, sometimes caused by the timing of an intervention or measurement, can affect your results. For example, the first time I went to college, I majored in music: My primary instrument was piano. I'll admit that it was very easy to slack off and not practice the required 10 hours per week, and my lack of effort was evident in my recitals at the end of each semester. My enthusiasm was bolstered one fall when I went back to school and found that the music department had bought new pianos for each of the practice rooms; they were so beautiful, and sounded so great, that practicing was a pleasure. Of course, you know what happened next. My new enthusiasm lasted for a few weeks, and I then gradually went back to my old ways: In short, at first I practiced more because of the novelty of the new pianos, not because I had found a new desire to practice and perform. That's probably just one of the reasons I recently sold my piano, which had not been played in several years.

The last reactive arrangement we need to discuss is called a **placebo** effect. Probably the best way to describe it is to refer to an episode from the old *Andy Griffith Show*. In the episode, a new druggist comes to town to take over the business from her uncle. On her first day, an elderly woman comes into the store, places a dime on the counter, and asks for her pills. The druggist asks for her prescription and, when the lady cannot produce it, the pharmacist refuses to give her the medicine. This immediately causes the elderly customer to take to her sick bed; she's afraid she won't make it! The town was up in arms until the druggist explained to the sheriff that the elderly lady wasn't really sick and that the pills she has been taking for years are nothing but sugar pills, a placebo that made the customer feel better simply because she was taking them.

While this sounds funny, the same situation arises in research all the time. For example, let's continue our medical example by examining the results of a fictitious study investigating the effects of a new antidepressant. There are a total of 200 participants in the study: an experimental group of 100 clients was randomly chosen to receive the new drug and the remainder received a placebo. Both prior to and after the study, patients were asked to rate their personal symptoms related to depression, as shown in Table 5.11.

As you can see, the results are interesting. It seems that the groups have approximately the same number of clients reporting each symptom at the outset of the study (i.e., the "Placebo Before" and the "New Drug Before" categories are approximately equal); we would expect this result with a random sample. At the end of the study, we can see the values for both groups have changed. For example, there are seven fewer people in the placebo group reporting loneliness and two fewer people taking the new drug reporting a loss of appetite.

TABLE 5.11. Results of Controlled Drug Trial

Symptom	Placebo before	Placebo after	Change	New drug before	New drug after	Change	Change between groups
Loneliness	26	19	−7	25	20	−5	2
Difficulty sleeping	16	17	+1	18	19	+1	0
Fatigue	11	7	−4	12	8	−4	0
Loss of appetite	6	8	+2	5	3	−2	4
Feelings of helplessness	8	8	0	7	6	−1	1

Despite this finding, when you look closely, it's apparent that the results are very similar between the two groups for all symptoms. The number of people reporting fatigue as a symptom dropped by four in each group, while the number of clients having difficulty sleeping rose by one in each group. In fact, the greatest change was in the "Loss-of-Appetite" category with a combined total of four participants reporting a change.

Two things could cause this. First, since the changes are so small, the new drug simply may not be effective. Second, at the same time, the group taking the placebo may have reacted differently simply because they knew they were taking a medication that reportedly helped depression. We would obviously investigate this further as part of our data analysis.

Good News!

Unfortunately, there are other, more minor **threats to validity** but those I've just discussed are the ones most often experienced; keep in mind that I've included an overview of this entire topic in Appendix 5.5. In other instances, the threats may interact with one another (e.g., selection and maturation), causing their combination to affect your validity even more negatively. The good news is that we can control for most of these threats to a great degree depending on the type of research design we choose. We have talked about three of the four types of quantitative designs: descriptive, correlational, and causal–comparative. Now let's move on to the experimental designs (Creswell & Creswell, 2020; Gay et al., 2012; Terrell, 2021).

Experimental Research Designs

At this point, we begin to look at cause and effect using pre-experimental, quasi-experimental, and true experimental designs. Each of these allows us to test hypotheses but brings with them varying degrees of control over threats to the validity of our results: The **pre-experimental designs** have the lowest control, the **true experimental designs** demonstrate the highest control, and the quasi-experimental designs fall somewhere in the middle. Obviously, more control over the threats to validity leads to a greater ability to generalize the results of your study to the population your sample is taken from, as well as other populations.

In discussing experimental research, we use diagrams and the following nomenclature, as we discuss each design:

- R means that membership in a group is randomized.
- O represents a point where data are collected (i.e., a pretest, posttest, or survey representing the dependent variable).
- X indicates an independent variable. When there is more than one level, they will be numbered. For example, an independent variable with two levels would be shown as X_1 and X_2.

Pre-Experimental Designs

When we say we're conducting a pre-experimental study, it simply means we're conducting a study with only one group. For example, if your teacher decides to use this book for a term, and then looks at class achievement, you have one independent variable, the teacher, with one level: the same teacher. This may sound a little confusing, so let's go into more detail.

THE ONE-SHOT CASE STUDY

This is the simplest, and least valid, of all the experimental designs. As you can see below, a **one-shot case study** simply means that you have one independent variable. Because there is no number beside it means there is only one level, and you're measuring quantitative data following whatever your intervention is, represented by X.

$$X \rightarrow O$$

In many instances, this design is used as an exploratory tool. Suppose, for example, I wanted to determine whether being a veteran affected performance in graduate school. All I would need to do is collect grades from all veterans and compute an average. In this case, most of the threats to validity are not controlled for, or do not apply. For your convenience, a reference table showing all research designs and how they control for threats to validity is shown in Appendix 5.5. For example, because you don't know the achievement of these students before you collected the data, the threats of history, mortality, and maturation are not controlled for. The only thing that can be said for these results is that you know the achievement of one group and, perhaps anecdotally, you can think of how they compare to other groups of students over time.

THE ONE-GROUP PRETEST–POSTTEST DESIGN

Using that example, let's move one step higher by using a **one-group pretest–posttest design:**

$$O \rightarrow X \rightarrow O$$

If we're still interested in looking at the achievement of veterans, over the course of a term we could collect both pretest and posttest data and compare the results. Using this design, we're able to control for mortality (i.e., Did anyone drop out of the class or fail to complete the posttest?). The remainder of the threats to validity are either not controlled or, because you only have one level of the independent variable (i.e., only looking at one group), the threats are not applicable. This would lead us to be able to say whether the veterans' achievement went up, but not much else.

THE STATIC GROUP COMPARISON

The last of the pre-experimental designs, the **static group comparison**, is similar to the one-shot case study, with the exception that you're comparing the posttest performance of two groups, with no pretest information available:

$$X_1 \rightarrow O$$
$$X_2 \rightarrow O$$

We can use this design to continue our veterans' example by determining whether there are differences in achievement between male veterans and female veterans. We've labeled the first group with a 1; whether this represents the males or the females is up to the discretion of the researcher. By using this design, all the results would tell us is whether the scores from the males and females are different. This design does control for history, but the other threats are either not applicable or not controlled for. Again, a table showing all of the threats to validity, and how they are controlled for by the different experimental designs, is shown in Appendix 5.5.

Quasi-Experimental Designs

At the heart of experimental research is the ability to randomly assign membership to a group, as well as treatment to a specific group. Unfortunately, as you might imagine, sometimes this isn't possible. For example, if we're interested in comparison, we can't assign membership to a city, a class, or an organization; we have to work with the groups we have. Keeping that in mind, we have to do the best we can to control for threats to validity rising from these types of studies. You may be thinking, "This sounds like the problem may be related to differential sections of participants." If you are, you're exactly right; the researcher, for reasons beyond his or her control, is using preexisting groups with a treatment randomly assigned to one of the groups. Unfortunately, we see this much too often, but there are ways to control for it, as we see in upcoming sections.

THE NONEQUIVALENT CONTROL GROUP DESIGN

Nonequivalent control group design is an improved version of a one-group pretest–posttest design in that it compares results from two preexisting groups:

$$O \rightarrow X_1 \rightarrow O$$
$$O \rightarrow X_2 \rightarrow O$$

In this case, let's imagine we're interested in looking at the effect of workweek scheduling on the morale of employees at each of the two of our company's locations. We could randomly assign employees at one of the offices to start working four 10-hour days, allowing for a 3-day weekend each week; the key here is that the employees already worked at the particular location, but the treatment (i.e., the modified workweek) was randomly assigned to them. Employees at the other location would continue working the traditional 8 hours per day, 5-day week.

The addition of the pretest and the random assignment of the treatment to an existing group goes a long way in helping control for threats to validity. In this case, we've controlled for everything affecting validity except for regression to the mean, selection interaction, and pretest–treatment interaction. The results from studies of this type are certainly more meaningful than the pre-experimental designs but care has to be taken in generalizing what you find.

THE TIME-SERIES DESIGN

A **time-series design** is one of my favorite studies to conduct. In it, you measure your dependent variable several times before your intervention, and then several times after:

$$OOOOOXOOOOO$$

For example, I worked in a counseling center for several years and saw a lot of clients describing themselves as being depressed. A common scenario was for me to meet with the clients several times, usually on a weekly basis. As we worked together, I also evaluated their level of depression using a quickly scored survey, such as the Beck Depression Inventory (Beck et al., 1996). In some cases, I found that the counseling alone helped the client greatly; in other cases, I had to refer the client to our physician to be evaluated for an antidepressant medication. If the doctor prescribed some type of antidepressant drug, my job was then to evaluate its efficacy. Taken together, this means the first series of O, shown in the diagram above, represent my weekly evaluations of a client's mental health using the Beck Depression Inventory. The treatment, shown as X, is the point where medication was prescribed; this is followed by another series of weekly sessions where I evaluated the client's progress. This approach doesn't control for history, instruments, or pretest–treatment interaction; the remaining threats to validity are either controlled for or are not applicable to this design.

COUNTERBALANCED DESIGNS

The final quasi-experimental design we need to discuss is the **counterbalanced design**. It is used to test a treatment on two or more groups when we want to determine whether the order of the treatment makes any difference:

$$X_1 \rightarrow O \rightarrow X_2 \rightarrow O$$
$$X_2 \rightarrow O \rightarrow X_1 \rightarrow O$$

As you can see, in this case we have two groups, with two treatments. Each of the groups will receive both treatments, but in reverse order. In order to explain this design, let's suppose we're interested in looking at the cumulative effect of sleep deprivation on agility. In this study, I would use two groups. On the first night of the study, the first group would sleep 8 hours and the second group would sleep 4 hours. At 8:30 the next morning, all participants would take a timed agility test. On the second night of the study the sleeping arrangement would be reversed; the first group would sleep 4 hours and the second group would sleep 8 hours. Again, at 8:30 the next morning, the participants would be timed on the agility test. The average score for each participant would then be computed, followed by the overall average score for each group. By comparing the mean scores of the two groups, the researchers could determine whether there is any difference in agility between the two different patterns of sleep. In this case, because the design is so simple, you might be thinking, "This is so trivial. Who cares?" Believe it or not, the military, in preparing soldiers for deployment, has conducted many studies of this type. They want to get as much information as possible to help their troops perform optimally.

In this case, we had a simple design: two groups with two treatments. It gets tricky, though, when you get into larger numbers of groups; sometimes it can also be difficult to analyze data from studies of this type. Making matters worse, regardless of the number of groups or treatments, the design doesn't control for threats to external validity.

True Experimental Designs

When we use a true experimental design, we are getting as close to testing cause and effect as we are able. Being purely experimental means that we are able to randomly assign members to a group, and we're able to randomly assign groups to a specific treatment.

THE PRETEST–POSTTEST CONTROL GROUP DESIGN

The first of these, the **pretest–posttest control group design**, is similar to the non-equivalent control group design:

$$R\ O \rightarrow X_1 \rightarrow O$$
$$R\ O \rightarrow X_2 \rightarrow O$$

Unlike the nonequivalent design, however, we can see, from the uppercase R, that randomization has taken place, meaning participants have been randomly assigned to one group or the other. For example, I just received a telemarketing call where the agent was trying to sell me life insurance. I politely listened, explained that I had coverage through my employer, we exchanged pleasantries, and said goodbye. Unfortunately for her, she didn't sell me insurance, but her call did get me to thinking.

It was purely by happenstance that I was working at home today; I could have just as easily been working at the university, at the library, or out attempting to play golf. Suppose cold callers waited and focused on calls in the evening when more people should be at home. Would that cause their sales to go up? The insurance company could easily investigate this.

Let's envision a company where 50 of their employees worked all day making calls of this type. We could randomly divide these employees into two groups, and then randomly select one of the groups to start making their calls in the evening; the other group would continue working during the day. By using each employee's sales before the change of schedule as a pretest measure, followed by the number of sales after the new schedule had been implemented as a posttest measure, we could set up the following design:

Random Assignment of Employees to Day Group → Sales Before → Calls → Sales After

Random Assignment of Employees to Evening Group → Sales Before → Calls → Sales After

Once the data have been collected, it would be easy for the company's administration to determine whether there was a significant difference between the two approaches. This true experimental design controls for all threats to internal validity, but external validity is threatened by pretest–treatment interactions.

A WORD OF CAUTION

Many beginning researchers get the pretest–posttest control group design confused with the quasi-experimental nonequivalent control group design. In order to avoid this confusion, keep in mind that, in an experimental study, participants are randomly assigned to groups, whereas they are not randomly assigned in a quasi-experimental study.

THE POSTTEST-ONLY CONTROL GROUP DESIGN

Many researchers believe the pretest in the pretest–posttest design can lead to a pretest–treatment interaction. Because of that belief, as well as a belief that random assignment to a group causes an equal distribution of the value being measured within the groups, many researchers do not use a pretest. Instead, they use a **posttest-only control group design** to test hypotheses:

$$R \, X_1 \to O$$
$$R \, X_2 \to O$$

We can use this design to investigate the effect of short-term therapy versus cognitive-behavioral therapy, on levels of client hope. In this case, we might have a population of clients who have recently suffered through or witnessed some sort of tragic event. In many instances, this leads to a lack of hope that things will get better; it becomes the therapist's job to work with the client to "see the light at the end of the tunnel."

Let's imagine we started with 100 new clients. We could randomly assign 50 of them to the short-term group; the remaining 50 would fall into the cognitive-behavioral group. With this design, we're assuming that levels of hope are about equal between the two groups simply because we've randomly assigned each client to one of the groups. After a number of counseling sessions, we could administer a survey designed to measure hope, and statistically compare the results to determine whether a significant difference exists. In this case, all threats to validity, with the exception of mortality, are either controlled for or are not applicable. Again, keep in mind that Appendix 5.5 includes a table showing all of the designs, as well as their ability to control for threats to both internal and external validity.

THE SOLOMON FOUR-GROUP DESIGN

Sometimes I think that statisticians and researchers love to argue about which experimental approach is best; in short, they are the Democrats and Republicans of the academic world. In order to control for the threats to validity rising from the pretest–posttest design, and the mortality issue caused by the posttest-only design, many researchers call for using a **Solomon four-group design**, if possible. It is basically a combination of the pretest–posttest and the posttest-only designs:

$$R\,O \to X_1 \to O$$
$$R\,O \to X_2 \to O$$
$$R \to X_3 \to O$$
$$R \to X_4 \to O$$

In this case, members are still randomly assigned to one of two groups but only half of the members of each group are randomly selected to be pretested. This means, in the prior case, the clients would still be randomly assigned to either the cognitive-behavioral or the short-term group; this would be followed by randomly evaluating half of the clients in each group before treatment begins. Finally, we have a design that controls for all threats to external and internal validity!

Putting This All Together
for the Quantitative Dissertation Proposal

At this point we've discussed most of the component parts of a quantitative dissertation proposal. Now let's look at how we put them all together. As you can see, in Table 5.12, I've included an outline of a three-chapter quantitative proposal. We've already covered most of the material, so now let's put it all together in a logical

TABLE 5.12. A Three-Chapter Quantitative Dissertation Proposal

Chapter 1: Introduction

- Background
- Statement of the problem
- Significance of the study
- Purpose of the study (i.e., the central purpose)
- Research questions
- Hypothesis
- Definitions of terms
- Assumptions
- Limitations
- Delimitations
- Conclusion

Chapter 2: Review of the Literature

This chapter serves three purposes: it establishes the context of our study; it tells us what is already known about the problem area we want to investigate; and helps us identify research strategies, instruments, and procedures. The ROL for a quantitative study is very thorough, thereby allowing the development of hypotheses firmly grounded in theory.

Chapter 3: Research Methods

- The quantitative paradigm
- Research design
- Participants and sampling
- Instruments
- Research procedures
- Plans for data analysis
- Ethical considerations
- Plans for presenting the results
- Summary

fashion. Because we've already covered the components of Chapters 1 and 2, let's move directly into Chapter 3, Research Methods. Keep in mind, however, that in this book we're focusing on the three-chapter dissertation proposal. As I said earlier, an example of a four-chapter proposal, used by a limited number of disciplines, can be found in the appendices at the end of the book.

Chapter 3 of a Quantitative Research Dissertation Proposal

We've already discussed many of the component parts of Chapter 3: how to identify a population and select a sample for our study, instruments for data collection, ethical considerations, and plans for data analysis. Obviously, the manner in which they are written will reflect the research problem, research questions, and hypotheses stated in Chapter 1. At this point, however, we're missing three major sections for our proposal:

1. The quantitative paradigm.
2. The research design.
3. The research procedures.

Let's look at an overview of these three topics and then put them together in the form of a case study.

The Quantitative Paradigm

Thinking back to our section labeled philosophy 101, in this section we must support the reason we chose to use a quantitative **paradigm**. This starts with stating our beliefs about the project (i.e., axiology), the reality of our research environment (i.e., **ontology**), and our role as the researcher (i.e., epistemology). Don't forget: We want our results to reflect the effect of the intervention (i.e., the independent variable) on the results (i.e., the dependent variable); any interference by the researcher conducting the study may affect the validity of the results. Because of this problem, we often say that quantitative research is approached from an **etic**, or outsider, **perspective**. In doing so, we will collect quantitative data using valid and reliable instruments, and statistically analyze our results to test the hypotheses we've stated. As you'll see in our examples at the end of the chapter, while each design is different, the idea of eliminating or minimizing researcher interference remains the same.

The Research Design

Based on our hypotheses and research questions, and knowing the type of data we'll collect, the groups we'll need, and how they'll be formed, we can easily determine which design we should use. For example, if we have a hypothesis where we want to collect quantitative data where students have been randomly assigned to a group or treatment, we'll use some form of experimental design. In this section, you'll simply state the design you'll use, and your reasoning for doing so.

The Research Procedures

Here we need to lay out a painstakingly clear, step-by-step outline of how we will conduct our research. In the best of all possible worlds, by following our procedures, we could then conduct our study and be assured that our results are as close to 100% accurate as possible. As you can imagine, this doesn't always happen. For example, when we talked about using an experimental pretest–posttest control group design, I pointed out that a pretest–treatment interaction could affect the external validity of your results. Knowing that, it's always wise to recognize the possibility of that threat and state, before the study beings, that it may affect your results. As noted earlier, we do this by stating a limitation to our results and presenting it in Chapter 1. For example, in a case where we used a pretest–posttest control group design, we could include a section that might read like this:

Research Limitation

> The results of the study may be affected by students being tested before the treatment (i.e., pretest–treatment interaction).

In other cases, we might need to recognize an event that actually occurred during the study. For example, I once had a student whose participants went on strike while he was conducting his study; that problem led him to state:

> The effect of history may have affected the results in that participants went on strike against their employer during the course of the study.

Finally, you might simply acknowledge that the participants you studied may have characteristics different from other groups that may have affected your results. I've conducted a lot of work in inner-city schools; based on that, I might state a limitation, such as:

> These results are based on research conducted in a school in a lower socioeconomic section of the city. The results might not be generalizable to students in more affluent school districts.

As we're writing our research procedures, we have to keep in mind that our goal is to develop a sound, well-thought-out research plan. When we do that, it allows us to control for any foreseeable threats to the validity of our results once we actually conduct our study. Unfortunately, we can't anticipate everything that might go wrong, but, as I've said before, regardless of the results, if our plan and its implementation are sound, we've met our goals as a researcher.

Our First Example of Chapter 3 of a Proposal

Using what we discussed in earlier chapters and the topics above, below you'll find an example of Chapter 3 for a descriptive study. Notice that I've included the research problem, purpose statement, and research question from Chapter 1 in order to understand the purpose for the procedures presented; I have included an example of another descriptive study in Appendix 5.1 at the end of the chapter. Rather than including specific examples for correlational, quasi-experimental, and true experimental designs within the chapter, I've also included examples of each of those in Appendices 5.2, 5.3, and 5.4, respectively, at the end of this chapter. As you will see, they are brief and straightforward, but do demonstrate the requirements of each design.

For the following example, you've been hired as the principal of a high school with historically low scores on statewide tests. You've recently read literature that suggests that high school-age children learn better by starting school later in the morning. Because your school day begins at 8:00 A.M., you decide a change may be called for. Before you do, however, you figure it's best to get input from the parents regarding changing the start of the school day from 8:00 A.M. to 10:00 A.M.

Research Problem from Chapter 1 of the Proposal: Literature has shown that high school-age children perform better when school starts later in the morning. The principal of a high school, whose students historically score below average on state achievement tests, is interested in changing the school start time from 8:00 A.M. to 10:00 A.M. but wants to get the input of parents before instituting the change.

Purpose Statement from Chapter 1 of the Proposal: The purpose of this study is to collect data regarding a change in school start times from parents of children in the affected school.

Research Question from Chapter 1 of the Proposal: How do the parents of children in the school feel about changing the start time from 8:00 A.M. to 10:00 A.M.?

Hypothesis: Because this is a descriptive study, there is no hypothesis.

Chapter 3 of the Proposal: Research Methods

Following are the key components of Chapter 3. As you'll see, due to the relative simplicity of this type of study, some of the sections are quite brief. While this will happen from time to time, make sure you include all of the material you need. Remember, Chapter 3 guides your study; make sure you include everything needed to ensure the validity of your results.

The Quantitative Paradigm

In this study, the researcher functions as an objective observer and is independent from the actual study. The research process will be deductive and value-free, and the results will be used to explain the feelings of the parents. Based on this, the use of a quantitative approach is appropriate.

Research Design

This study employs a descriptive survey approach wherein all parents of students within the school will be surveyed to determine whether they believe the school's start time should be changed.

Participants and Sampling

All parents with children in the school will serve as the population for the study. Because the entire population is readily accessible, there will be no formal sample taken.

Instrumentation

There are no formal instruments for this study; all students will take home a form asking their parents' opinion on changing the school's starting time to 10:00 A.M. Parents will be given three options: (1) continue starting school at 8:00 A.M., (2) change to starting school at 10:00 A.M., or (3) either time is acceptable.

Research Procedures

Teachers will give a copy of the survey form to each student and ask their parents to complete it. Students will be given 1 week to return the form. If, at the end of the week, at least 70% of the forms have not been returned, students will be reminded to have their parents complete and return it. Those students whose parents have not returned the form will be given another form and asked to remind their parents to complete it. This will continue until the desired return rate is reached.

Plans for Data Analysis

Prior to analysis, the researcher must ensure that all returned forms are complete, and the desired number of responses has been collected. The data will be analyzed using a simple frequency count; results will be tabulated twice in order to ensure the accuracy of the results.

Ethical Considerations

Data from all participants will be anonymized, and no participants will be identified by name or by any other manner during or after the course of the study. All data will be kept in a locked filing cabinet and destroyed after 1 year.

Plans for Presenting the Results

Based on the completed analysis, all results will be presented in Chapters 4 and 5 of the full dissertation and a follow up report will be written and delivered to the principal. Based on that, a final decision will be made.

Summary

This proposed study will address questions posed regarding changes to the school's starting time. Completed parental survey forms will be scored and the data descriptively analyzed. The results will be included in the dissertation report and provided to the principal, who will make the ultimate decision regarding the school's starting time.

SUMMARY OF CHAPTER FIVE

This chapter is packed with a lot of good information but there is one major thing to keep in mind: the problem statement, research purpose, research questions, and hypotheses from Chapter 1 drive the process; you'll choose your design and research method based on what they call for. Chapter 3 will then be a step-by-step "road map" for testing your hypotheses or answering your research questions. Remember, the validity of your entire study rests on developing and following a research plan. Keep in mind that there are examples of each of these designs in the appendices of this chapter; for now, let's see just how much we've learned.

Do You Understand These Key Words and Phrases?

Alpha value	Nonequivalent control group design
Analysis of variance (ANOVA)	Novelty effect
Causal–comparative research	One-group pretest–posttest design
Confounding variable	One-shot case study
Correlation coefficient	Ontology
Correlational research	Ordinal (rank) data
Counterbalanced design	p value
Dependent variable	Paradigm
Descriptive statistics	Pearson's r
Differential selection of participants	Placebo
Effect size	Positive correlation
Etic perspective	Posttest-only control group design
Experimental research	Pre-experimental design
Experimenter effect	Pretest–posttest control group design
External validity	Pretest–treatment interaction
Fail to reject the null hypothesis	Ratio data
Graphical descriptive statistics	Reactive arrangement
History	Reject the null hypothesis
Independent variable	Selection–treatment interaction
Instruments	Solomon four-group design
Internal validity	Specificity of variables
Interval data	Static group comparison
John Henry effect	Statistical regression to the mean
Levels of the independent variable	Survey research
Maturation	Testing
Mortality	Threat to validity
Multiple treatment interference	Time-series design
Negative correlation	Treatment diffusion
Nominal (categorical) data	True experimental design

REVIEW QUESTIONS

To ensure we have a firm understanding of what we covered in this chapter, let's finish it off by answering the following questions. You can find the answers at the end of the book.

1. In order to control threats to validity, the most powerful design is:

    a. One-shot case study.

    b. Posttest-only control group design.

    c. Solomon four-group design.

    d. Pretest–posttest control group design.

2. Reactive arrangements include:

    a. The placebo effect.

    b. The John Henry effect.

    c. The Hawthorne effect.

    d. All of the above.

3. The idea that people who score high on the posttest tend to score lower on the same test if it is taken again, is called:

    a. Maturation.

    b. Mortality.

    c. Regression to the mean.

    d. The effect of testing.

4. We would reject a null hypothesis if:

    a. Our p value is equal to our alpha value.

    b. Our p value is less than our alpha value.

    c. Our p value is greater than our alpha value.

    d. None of the above.

5. In evaluating potential instruments for a study, we should be concerned with:

    a. Sampling validity.

    b. The effect of testing.

    c. Item validity.

    d. Both a and c.

6. When we conduct experimental research, which of the following designs could we use?

    a. Survey.

    b. Correlational.

    c. One-shot case study.

    d. Pearson's r.

7. The threats to validity that can be controlled by a Solomon four-group design include:

    a. History.

    b. Testing.

    c. Mortality.

    d. All of the above.

8. The count of the number of males and females in a room would be considered:

    a. Interval data.

    b. Ordinal data.

    c. Nominal data.

    d. Ratio data.

9. Which threat to internal validity is most severe?

    a. History.

    b. Testing.

    c. Mortality.

    d. They are all equally severe.

10. Of the following, the best way to establish cause and effect is by using a:

    a. Solomon four-group design.

    b. Correlational design.

    c. One-group pretest–posttest design.

    d. All of these are equally effective.

11. When two data sets are positively correlated it means:

    a. As values in one data set get larger, so do values in the other data set.

    b. As values in one data set get smaller, values in the other data set get larger.

    c. As values in one data set get smaller, values in the other data set stay about the same.

    d. None of the above.

12. A placebo effect can happen in:

    a. Educational research.

    b. Medical research.

    c. Psychological research.

    d. All of the above.

13. Our recognized ability to not be able to control for a threat to the validity of our study is:

    a. An assumption of the study.

    b. The significance of the study.

    c. A limitation of the study.

    d. A delimitation of the study.

14. A teacher being transferred to another school during the middle of a research study might cause an effect of:

    a. Mortality.

    b. History.

    c. Selection.

    d. Maturation.

15. Chapter 1 of your dissertation will include:

    a. The problem statement, research question, and procedures.

    b. The research question, the research purpose, and the review of literature.

    c. The research problem, the research purpose, and the research question.

    d. The research problem, the review of literature, and the research method.

16. The generalizability of the results of your study is affected by:

    a. Threats to the internal validity of your study.

    b. Threats to the external validity of your study.

    c. Neither a nor b.

    d. Both a and b.

17. Hypotheses are an integral part of:

    a. Survey studies.

    b. Correlational studies.

    c. Experimental studies.

    d. All of the above.

18. The best way to ensure randomization of participants in your study is through:

    a. Using preexisting groups.

    b. Using volunteers.

    c. A random number generator.

    d. None of the above.

19. The difference between the pretest–posttest control group design and the quasi-experimental nonequivalent control group design is:

    a. In the pretest–posttest design, participants are randomly assigned to groups and the treatment randomly assigned to a group; in the quasi-experimental study, treatments are randomly assigned to preexisting groups.

    b. In the pretest–posttest design, participants in pretesting groups are used.

    c. There is no randomization in either group.

    d. They both control for all threats to validity.

20. The primary concern of the pretest–posttest control group design is:

    a. The threat of multiple-treatment interference.

    b. The effect of pretest–treatment interaction.

c. The effect of history.

d. The effect of maturation.

✓ *Progress Check for Chapter 3*
of a Quantitative Dissertation Proposal

Earlier in the book, I included Chapters 1 and 2 for a study involving an industrial waste dump. Since then, we've talked about the major component parts of Chapter 3 of your dissertation: the population and sampling, the instruments, the specific research method you will use, and the procedures you would follow. In Appendix C at the end of the book, I've included Chapter 3 of a quantitative proposal for a study using a static-group comparison.

LET'S CONTINUE WRITING OUR OWN DISSERTATION PROPOSAL

Earlier you developed Chapters 1 and 2 for a quantitative dissertation proposal you might write. At this point, let's extend your proposal by including Chapter 3. As I said earlier, once you have finished, take a break from writing. Wait a few days and then reread what you wrote. In many instances, you will find areas that aren't clear, points you should have included, and material that isn't needed. Just keep on writing; you'll get the hang of it soon.

APPENDIX 5.1. Example of a Descriptive Research Study

In order to help you better understand the entire process of a descriptive study, I have included the study's problem and purpose statements and research questions that would be included in Chapter 1. As you will see, each of these sections is brief but does cover the pertinent material.

Items from Chapter 1 of Your Proposal

Problem Statement

Government officials in a quickly growing suburban community in South Florida are concerned that their parks and recreation facilities are not meeting the needs of residents, especially of residents with school-age children. Before developing a plan to expand their facilities, the officials want to determine constituents' feelings about the quality of existing parks and recreation facilities, and to what degree residents perceive there is a need for additional facilities.

Purpose Statement

The purpose of this study is to better understand residents' feelings about the quality and number of existing parks and recreation facilities, as well as the perceived need for additional facilities as the population grows.

Research Questions

1. Are there currently enough parks and recreation facilities in the city?
2. How do residents rate the quality of parks and recreation facilities in the city?
3. Is there a need for additional parks and recreation facilities as the city grows?

Research Hypothesis

Not applicable.

Research Limitations

The results of this study are limited to citizens in this particular community. The ability to generalize these results to other populations or communities is unknown.

Items from Chapter 3 of Your Proposal

The Quantitative Paradigm

In this study, the researcher serves as an objective observer and is independent from the actual study. The research process is deductive and value-free, and the results will be used to explain citizens' feelings about recreation facilities in their city. Based on this, the use of a quantitative survey approach is appropriate.

The Research Design

Due to the desire to collect data only reflecting their citizens' current opinions, this study will use a survey research method.

Participants and Sampling

The town that is the focus of this research is a quickly growing suburb of a major city in South Florida. Traditionally, residents of the town have considered it a "bedroom community" and have commuted to jobs in the larger metropolitan area. In the past 10 years, however, the town's population has doubled in size to approximately 30,000 residents. Ninety percent of the residents represent an equal number of non-Hispanic Whites and African Americans, with about 10% of the population describing themselves as Hispanic. The median household income is $45,000; families average two children per household. The names and addresses of citizens will be identified through utility company records. A sample of 1,500 (i.e., 5%) residents will be randomly selected to participate in the study.

Instruments

A web-based survey consisting of demographic data, as well as the following three questions, will be developed:

1. On a scale of 1 (*very dissatisfied*) to 5 (*very satisfied*), how would you rate the number of parks and recreation facilities in our town?
2. On a scale of 1 (*very dissatisfied*) to 5 (*very satisfied*), how would you rate the quality of our parks and recreation facilities?
3. How many additional parks and recreation facilities do you think should be built?

Research Procedures

After the survey has been developed and the sample selected, a letter will be included in the selected residents' utility bill asking them to participate in the study. In order to decrease costs, and increase the probability of participation, rather than having residents complete a paper form and return it to the researchers, a website will be developed to collect the data. The number of responses will be monitored; it may be necessary to randomly sample and solicit other participants from the population until the sample size of 1,500 (i.e., 5%) is reached.

Plans for Data Analysis

Once an adequate amount of data has been collected (i.e., 1,500 responses), descriptive statistics will be computed and analyzed. Data verification is not an issue, or not controllable, in this study. The results are limited to citizens in this particular study and the degree to which they can be generalized to other populations or communities is unknown.

Ethical Considerations

Data from all participants will be anonymized, and no participants will be identified by name or by any other manner during or after the course of the study. All data will be kept in a locked filing cabinet and destroyed after 1 year.

Plans for Presenting the Results

All results will be included in the final dissertation report and a summary report based on the results will be delivered to interested government officials.

Summary

This study is designed to determine citizens' opinions of the number and quality of parks and recreation facilities in the city. A random sample of participants will be selected for participation in the study. Using data collected from a web-based form, the researcher will descriptively analyze the data and report the results to interested government officials.

APPENDIX 5.2. Example of a Correlational Research Study

Items from Chapter 1 of Your Proposal

In order to help you better understand the entire process of a correlational study, I have included the study's problem and purpose statements and research question that would be included in Chapter 1. As you will see, each of these sections is brief but does cover the pertinent material.

Problem Statement

University officials are concerned with the low grade-point averages (GPAs) of first-year students. Research suggests that a lack of regular contact with a faculty advisor may contribute to this problem.

Research Purpose

The purpose of this study is to examine the relationship between the number of faculty advisor conferences and the GPA of first-year college students.

Research Question

Is there a correlation between the GPA and a student's number of visits with a faculty advisor during the first year of college?

Research Hypothesis

Not applicable.

Research Limitations

1. Intentional misrepresentation by a student of their GPA and/or wrongful estimates of the number of visits with their advisor may limit the generalizability of the results.
2. Mortality (e.g., students failing out or leaving the university for other reasons) may affect the generalizability of the results.

Items from Chapter 3 of Your Proposal

The Quantitative Paradigm

In this study, the researcher serves as an objective observer and is independent from the actual study. The research process is deductive and value-free, and the results will be used to determine whether a relationship exists between a given student's GPA and the number of their advisor visits during a term. Based on this, the use of a quantitative correlational approach is appropriate.

The Research Design

Due to the investigation of the relationship between two quantitative data sets, this study will use a correlational research method.

Participants and Sampling

All first-year students will serve as the population for this study. In order to ensure the highest degree of accuracy, there will be no formal sampling process. Administrators would like to get as representative a sample as possible, so the whole population will be studied. Due to the voluntary nature of participation, however, a minimum sample size, using power analysis or using published standards, will be computed. If an adequate sample size is not reached, additional contacts by email may be necessary. Once an adequate sample size has responded, the data will be analyzed.

Instruments

A self-reported number of students' visits with their advisor and GPA will be collected via an online database. The researcher is responsible for developing the online survey system. To help ensure validity, the online survey system will be designed so that erroneous GPA (e.g., greater than 4.00 or negative values) information or an unlikely number of visits with an advisor (e.g., greater than 20.00) cannot be entered.

The Research Procedures

Knowing that students are more likely to respond to a person with recognized authority, the administration will contact all students with instructions on entering their student number, GPA, and number of visits with their advisor during the prior term. The results will be monitored until an adequate number of responses have been recorded. It is possible that administrators will need to send a follow-up message to students, reminding those who have not participated to enter their information into the system, until the desired sample size is reached.

Plans for Data Analysis

Once an adequate amount of data has been collected, descriptive statistics and the Pearson r correlation coefficient will be computed. With the exception of ensuring that only students registered in the prior term participated in the study, and an adequate number of students enrolled in the university participate in the study, other data verification is not an issue, or not controllable, in this study. The results are limited to students in this particular study. The ability to generalize these results to other populations is unknown.

Ethical Considerations

Once collected and verified to be from a student enrolled in the prior term, data from all participants will be anonymized, and no students will be identified by name or by any other manner during the remainder of the study. All data will be kept in a locked filing cabinet and destroyed after 1 year.

Plans for Presenting the Results

All results will be presented in the dissertation report. A summary report based on the results will also be delivered to interested administrators within the university.

Summary

Administrators are concerned with the low GPAs of first-year students. In order to determine whether a possible relationship exists between a student's GPA and their self-reported number of visits to their academic advisor during a term, these data will be collected and analyzed. A report showing the results will be developed and included in the dissertation report, as well as delivered to interested administrators in the university.

APPENDIX 5.3. Example of a Quasi-Experimental Research Study

In order to help you better understand the entire process of a quasi-experimental study, I have included the study's problem and purpose statements, research question, and hypothesis that would be included in Chapter 1. As you will see, each of these sections is brief but does cover the pertinent material.

Items from Chapter 1 of Your Proposal

Problem Statement

Due to the stress placed on them on a daily basis, many stockbrokers complain of high levels of anxiety. This directly affects their day-to-day quality of life.

Purpose Statement

The purpose of this research is to determine whether there are interventions that could be used to lower the levels of anxiety experienced by stockbrokers.

Research Question

Will daily exercise help stockbrokers lower their levels of anxiety?

Research Hypothesis

Stockbrokers who participate in a daily exercise program will report significantly lower levels of anxiety than coworkers who do not participate in a daily program of exercise.

Research Limitations

Threats to the validity of the results, including regression to the mean, selection interaction, and pretest–treatment interaction, may limit the generalizability of the results.

Employees electing not to participate, or who are deemed physically unable to participate, may affect the results and their generalizability.

Items from Chapter 3 of Your Proposal

The Quantitative Paradigm

In this study, the researcher serves as an objective observer and is independent from the actual study. The research process is deductive and value-free, and the results will be used to determine whether a relationship exists between participation in an exercise program and levels of anxiety. Based on this, the use of a quantitative approach is appropriate.

The Research Design

This study will use a quasi-experimental, nonequivalent control group design to investigate the effect of an exercise program assigned to one of two preexisting groups.

Participants and Sampling

Employees of ABC Trading work in two buildings, with about 15 brokers at each location. One of the locations will be randomly chosen with all workers at the location invited to participate in the program while at work.

Instruments

Levels of anxiety will be measured using the State–Trait Anxiety Inventory (STAI; Spielberger, 1975, 1983). The STAI is a set of two 20-item, self-report scales designed to measure a respondent's overall susceptibility to anxiety (i.e., trait anxiety), as well as anxiety at a given point in time (i.e., state anxiety). Scores on the STAI range from 20 to 80, with lower scores indicating calmness and serenity, and with higher scores indicating increasing levels of tension, apprehension, and fearfulness. The STAI has been shown to be a reliable and valid measure of this construct.

The Research Procedures

Before the start of the study, all brokers at both locations will be required to take the STAI. Upon completion, the scores will be tabulated for each participant and saved in an Excel worksheet; the hard copies of the STAI will also be saved in a separate location. One of the locations will be randomly chosen and the exercise program will be introduced and explained. Employees will be encouraged, but not required, to attend and, after passing a company-administered health screening, will be permitted to begin attending the sessions. Employees will be given an exercise log and asked to track their class attendance. At the end of the first 10 weeks of the program, employees at both locations will again be asked to complete the STAI. The exercise logs from the group participating in the exercise classes will also be examined to ensure that participants were taking part in the program. Scores from both the pretest and posttest will be analyzed descriptively and inferentially to test the hypothesis.

Ethical Considerations

Administrators must ensure that all employees desiring to participate are medically screened and cleared prior to the first class. In order to allow for matching data from both administrations of the STAI, employees will be assigned an anonymous user ID known only to the researcher. Employees will use this ID to identify themselves on each administration of the STAI; following that, employees will not be identified by name or by any other manner during or after the course of the study. All data will be kept in a locked filing cabinet and destroyed after 1 year.

Plans for Presenting the Results

All results will be included in the dissertation report. A summary report based on the results of the data analysis will be delivered to interested administrators within the brokerage house.

Summary

This study will investigate the effects of an in-house exercise program on stockbrokers' levels of anxiety. One group of employees will be randomly selected and asked to participate in an exercise program offered during work hours; a control group will not be offered the program. Levels of anxiety will be compared both prior to and after the study to determine the effects of the program.

APPENDIX 5.4. Example of an Experimental Research Study

In order to help you better understand the entire process of an experimental study, I have included the study's problem and purpose statements, research question, and hypothesis that would be included in Chapter 1. As you will see, each of these sections is brief but does cover the pertinent material.

Items from Chapter 1 of Your Proposal

Problem Statement

Students aspiring to earn a master's degree in business administration (MBA) are, in most instances, required to take the Graduate Management Admission Test (GMAT) as part of their admissions process. Scores on the GMAT range from zero to 800; students with higher scores are generally admitted to higher-level MBA programs. Successful Tutoring, a private, for-profit tutoring company, wants to investigate possible modifications to their programs in an effort to help their clients potentially raise their GMAT score. More specifically, recent literature has suggested that the gender of the instructor may affect student performance.

Purpose Statement

The purpose of this study is to investigate the effect of instructor gender on scores from a practice GMAT test.

Research Question

Will instructor gender affect the practice GMAT scores of students being tutored in a private, for-profit tutoring program, depending on the gender of the instructor?

Research Hypothesis

There will be a significant difference in practice GMAT scores between students who have a male instructor and students who have a female instructor.

Research Limitations

The chosen research method may not control for the pretest–treatment threat to external validity. Because of that threat, generalization to other groups outside of the study may be limited.

Items from Chapter 3 of Your Proposal

The Quantitative Paradigm

In this study, the researcher serves as an objective observer and is independent from the actual study. The research process is deductive and value-free, and the results will be used to determine whether a relationship exists between success on the GMAT and the gender of the instructor in a test preparation service. Based on this objective, the use of a quantitative approach is appropriate.

The Research Design

This study will use a pretest–posttest control group design to test the hypothesis. Clients will be randomly assigned to one of two groups wherein both instructors will cover the same material. Students will be pretested using a practice version of the GMAT and, after 4 weeks of instruction, posttested with a practice version of the GMAT. Scores will be compiled and statistically analyzed in order to test the hypothesis.

Participants and Sampling

Each spring, while preparing for the following fall semester, a large number of students enroll in tutoring programs to prepare for the GMAT. Successful Tutoring, a private, for-profit tutoring company, has an average of 50 students starting their 4-week program each week from March through May. In order to test the firm's hypothesis, management will randomly assign registering students into one of two sections: one with a male instructor and one with a female instructor.

Instrument Used

The GMAT, published by the Graduate Management Admission Council, is a standardized assessment that measures test takers' levels of analytical writing skills, integrated reasoning, quantitative ability, and verbal fluency. It is used as part of admissions applications by business schools throughout the United States and has been shown to be highly predictive of achievement in those schools. For this study, achievement will be measured using practice GMAT examinations available at the publisher's official website (*www.mba.com*).

The Research Procedures

Management at Successful Tutoring will select a random sample of 30 clients from the 50 clients who generally start a class in a given week. These clients will be randomly assigned, in groups of 15, to one of two preexisting instructors: one female and one male. Prior to starting the program, clients will be asked to sign a confidentiality form giving administrators permission to view their examination scores while enrolled in the tutoring program, as well as an assurance of anonymity and any reporting of scores only in the aggregate. Should a client not agree to sign the form, he or she will be placed into another class and another client randomly chosen from the initial population to take his or her place. This process will continue until the two classes of 15 students have been formed.

During the two class sessions each week, the instructors will cover the same material, and both instructors will be encouraged to use traditional face-to-face teaching tools (lectures, PowerPoint presentations, etc.). All students will receive identical homework activities. At the end of the 4-week term, all students will be tested using a separate version of the practice GMAT. Appropriate descriptive and inferential statistical tools will then be used to test the hypothesis.

Plans for Data Analysis

Descriptive statistics will be computed for all participants: both the population and for each group. A repeated-measures analysis of variance (ANOVA) will be used to compare differences in postintervention scores on the practice GMAT. Preintervention scores from the practice GMAT will be used to control for differences in the groups prior to participating in the class.

Ethical Considerations

Students will be assigned an anonymous user ID that will be used for group identification, as well as matching preintervention and postintervention scores on the practice GMAT. Beyond that, students will not be identified by name or by any other manner during the remainder of the study. All data will be kept in a locked filing cabinet and destroyed after 1 year.

Plans for Presenting the Results

All results will be included in the dissertation report and a report will be written and delivered to the administration at Successful Tutoring. Given their permission, the work would be anonymized and submitted to appropriate journals and conferences.

Summary

This study will investigate the concerns of owners of a private tutoring company regarding the interaction between achievement and instructor gender. Students will be randomly assigned to one of two groups: one taught by a male and the other by a female. Pre- and posttest scores will be compared in order to answer the research question and hypothesis.

APPENDIX 5.5. Threats to the Validity of an Experimental Study

Design	Threats to Internal Validity							Threats to External Validity		
	History	Maturation	Testing	Instrument	Regression	Selection	Mortality	Selection–treatment interaction	Pretest–treatment interaction	Multiple treatment interference
One-shot case study	N	N	N/A	N/A	N/A	N/A	N	N/A	N/A	N/A
One-group pretest–posttest	N	N	N	N	N	N/A	Y	N/A	N	N/A
Static group comparison	Y	N	N/A	N/A	N/A	N	N	N	N/A	N/A
Pretest–posttest control group	Y	Y	Y	Y	Y	Y	Y	Y	N	Y
Posttest-only control group	Y	Y	N/A	N/A	N/A	Y	N	Y	N/A	N/A
Solomon four-group	Y	Y	Y	Y	Y	Y	Y	Y	Y	N/A
Nonequivalent control group	Y	Y	Y	Y	N	Y	Y	N	N	N/A
Time series	N	Y	Y	N	Y	N/A	Y	N/A	N	N/A
Counterbalanced	Y	Y	Y	Y	Y	Y	Y	N	N	N

Keep in mind that there are other effects created by the researcher that the design cannot control for. These include specificity of variables, treatment diffusion, experimenter effects, and reactive arrangements.

CHAPTER SIX

Qualitative Research Methods

Introduction

Imagine a scenario in which a friend is telling you about a surprise birthday party she recently attended. "It was great," she said, "there must have been 100 people there." After the previous chapter, we know she's using quantitative data to tell us the number of partygoers, but, in this case, do we really know what was so great about the party or would we like to know more? If we're really interested, we could ask questions such as:

* Who was there?
* Where was the party?
* Were there a lot of gifts?
* When did it start? When was it over?
* How did the celebrant react?

By asking questions such as these, and a multitude of others, we will have a much better picture of the party; not only do we know how many people were there but we know a lot of details that will give us a far better picture of what happened. In short, we've collected qualitative data (i.e., the answers to the questions we asked) to better understand the quantitative data (i.e., the number of people at the party). In the next chapter, we talk about using the two types of data together for a mixed methods approach; for now, let's focus on just the qualitative data. Just as we did in the prior chapter, I will supply references to the major authors in the field. Remember, in this book we're focusing on writing proposals; when we need to get into even more detail about the methods we'll use, or the statistical tests we'll employ, you'll find other books indispensable.

An Overview of Qualitative Methodologies

In discussing quantitative research, we spent our time talking about data types, the different methodologies, and hypothesis testing. In short, we talked about data that define an event and agreed that quantitative research tells us "if" something happened. For example, we can use numeric data to tell us whether test scores went up, weight goes down, or gas prices stay the same. Again, while this is interesting information, it really doesn't tell us much more than the numeric measurement of whatever we are looking at.

In qualitative research, we collect text-based data to answer the "Who?", "What?", "When?", "Where?", and "Why" questions that our grade school teachers insisted we learn. We do this in three ways (Hesse-Biber & Leavy, 2011):

1. Exploratory research is used to investigate social life.
2. Descriptive research allows us to describe social life.
3. Explanatory research allows us to explain an aspect of social life.

Conducting research of this type usually involves one of the six most common qualitative approaches:

1. Narrative studies: one person's account or story about a series of connected events (Clandinin, 2013; Kohler-Riessman, 2008).

2. Phenomenological studies: the description of what an experience means to a person, or to a small group of people, who lived the experience, and can retell the story of that experience (Moustakas, 1994; Sokolowski, 1999).

3. Ethnographic studies: the description of a specific culture or group (Fetterman, 2010; Murchison, 2010).

4. Case studies: a manner by which the researcher can answer questions arising from events that actually happened to a specific person or a group of people at a specific point in time (Stake, 1995, 2005; Yin, 2013).

5. Grounded theory studies: the development of a theory constructed from the results of qualitative data collected and analyzed from a group of respondents (Charmaz, 2014; Glaser & Strauss, 1967).

6. Content analysis: a method of objectively analyzing recorded communication, such as books, transcripts, websites, and other forms of the written word, in order to make objective inferences (Holsti, 1969). Because we are not working directly with participants in this type of study, **content analysis** is often referred to as *unobtrusive research* (Babbie, 2012).

We'll discuss each of these methods in much more detail later in the chapter. Before we do, however, we need to do two things: first, we discuss the role of the researcher in qualitative studies, and second, we look at the format of a qualitative dissertation proposal.

The Role of the Researcher

If you think back to our discussions on quantitative (i.e., positivist) research, you'll remember that we wanted to keep the researcher out of the picture. Ideally, this means that only the causes (i.e., the independent variables) we are investigating would influence the effects (i.e., the dependent variables) that we're measuring. Because of this, we often say that quantitative research is approached from an etic perspective (outsider perspective). In qualitative research, however, we generally find that the research is conducted from an **emic perspective** (insider perspective) by direct involvement, collaboration, and interaction with the research participants. Because of this, qualitative researchers can be viewed as their own data collection tools. While a given research method may call for resources such as interview guidelines, recordings, and other text-based resources, it's ultimately the role of the qualitative researcher to immerse him- or herself directly into the study and collect the data he or she needs. As you'll see in our examples, while each design may call for a different approach by the researcher, the idea of active participation remains the same.

The Format of a Qualitative Dissertation Proposal

As I noted very early in this book, most dissertations include five chapters. The first three chapters, the Introduction, Review of Literature, and Research Methods, are included in the dissertation proposal. The final two chapters, the Results and Conclusions, are added after your study has been completed. The completed five chapters represent the dissertation report.

As we learned at that point, the different types of studies, and the requirements of a specific university, may call for a slightly different model. For example, Table 6.1 shows a commonly called-for three-chapter outline for a qualitative proposal. You can see that the items called for are the same as for the quantitative proposal in the previous chapter. As we discuss them, however, you'll see that the content may vary somewhat. For example, as you can already see, although Chapter 2 is still named the Review of Literature, there is far less content; again, we'll discuss the reasoning for this change, and give examples, as we move forward.

Chapter 1 of a Qualitative Dissertation Proposal:
The Introduction

Even though there is a large degree of similarity between Chapter 1 in both approaches, there are minor exceptions. We discuss those as we get to them, but

TABLE 6.1. A Three-Chapter Qualitative Dissertation Proposal

Chapter 1: Introduction

- Background
- Statement of the Problem
- Significance of the Study
- Purpose of the Study (i.e., the Central Purpose)
- Research Questions
- Definitions of Terms
- Assumptions
- Limitations
- Delimitations
- Conclusion

Chapter 2: Review of the Literature

Unlike quantitative studies where the review of literature serves as a theoretical basis for the study, the literature review for a qualitative study often starts small and is added to while or after the data are collected. This allows for a better understanding of topics introduced during data collection, as well as for the development of additional research questions as needed.

Chapter 3: Research Methods

- The Qualitative Paradigm
- Research Design
- Participants and Sampling
- Instruments
- Research Procedures
- Plans for Data Analysis
- Ethical Considerations
- Plans for Presenting the Results
- Summary

for now we start by discussing the background of the problem, the statement of the problem, and the importance of the study.

The Background, Statement of the Problem, and Significance of the Study

As it was for quantitative research, the background in a qualitative study tells the genesis of the problem or the area of opportunity you wish to address. To really understand what I'm talking about, let's use an example that many of us in South Florida are far too familiar with.

If you live where I do, there's a good chance that you'll eventually experience one of the hurricanes that visit us from time to time. Fortunately, between Hurricane Donna in 1960 and Hurricane Andrew in 1992, there were no major storms in our area. When Andrew did hit, it was catastrophic. In the days following the storm, it was obvious that most residents didn't have the knowledge, skills, or tools needed to make their lives safe and as comfortable as possible after the storm passed. The same thing happened in 2004 and 2005, when we were hit with hurricanes Jeanne, Frances, and Wilma; our population had grown tremendously since 1992 and again, many residents weren't ready for these storms and their aftermath. There was no electricity, many people did not have appropriate supplies of food and water, and if a person did have a generator, gasoline was difficult to find; in short, a 12-hour storm radically changed a lot of lives. Taken together, we now have a good understanding of the problem faced by the hurricane victims, we know the background of the problem, and we understand why it's significant. But let's just state this very clearly to make sure:

- The background of the problem includes the information about the history of hurricanes in South Florida, the fact that many people were unprepared for past hurricanes, population growth since then, and so on.
- The actual problem is that most people are not prepared for a major storm. This is compounded over time with the arrival of new residents, many of whom have never experienced a major tropical storm.
- The significance of the study is easy to ascertain; people who are better prepared for a storm in terms of supplies and knowledge of what to do before, during, and after the storm will be better able to cope with the storm.

At this point, it seems it would be fairly easy to conduct a study to collect the data we need. For example, we might conduct phenomenological research by focusing on a group of people who had previously experienced a storm by asking, "What was your experience with the hurricane?" In answering this question, the respondents could tell us how they prepared, what they did during the storm itself, and how they coped with the storm's aftermath. Analyzing these data could lead to findings that would better educate newcomers about what to expect about and how to prepare for a hurricane. In another case, if we wanted to learn about one person's lived experience during the storm, we might ask, "What was it like to live through a hurricane?" By conducting a narrative study, we might be able to share this person's story and, especially if he or she had had a bad experience, use it to motivate other residents to take action before another storm hit. Having said all of that, let's look at another example.

A couple of years ago, a friend, who works in the sales department of an insurance company, told me about a problem they were having at her office. The issue began when her supervisor, whom everyone liked and worked well with, decided to retire. The manager in charge of my friend's department, and three other departments, interviewed several people and ultimately found someone to fill the supervisor's position.

Once hired, management was very impressed with their new employee: he seemed friendly, had a good management style, and brought some new ideas for reorganization that might ultimately lead to greater efficiencies. Unfortunately, my friend and the other employees in the sales department were not so impressed; they found out very quickly that, while he had good management and interpersonal skills, he knew very little about the insurance business itself. Unfortunately, this lack of knowledge seemed to be negatively affecting sales; the employees in my friend's department just weren't as motivated as they had been with their former supervisor.

Again, the background of the problem, the problem itself, and the significance are clear:

- Background: The company hired a new manager for the sales department. The manager had good administrative and interpersonal skills but knew very little about the insurance business.
- Problem: The new manager's lack of knowledge about the insurance business led to a lack of truly effective leadership; because of this situation, employee morale and productivity went down.
- Significance: Lower sales mean less profit.

As you can see, the problem statement, along with its background and significance, are the same in a qualitative study as they are in a quantitative study. Keeping that in mind, let's move forward with writing the rest of the introduction to our study.

Purpose Statement

Here again you'll find the purpose statement for a qualitative study is pretty much the same as for a quantitative study. It will include the participants and the location of the study but, unlike quantitative studies, where we focused on a specific set of variables, the focus in qualitative studies will be the major issue or research opportunity that we want to investigate. We call this the **central phenomenon**. Let's set the stage for writing a qualitative purpose statement using this problem statement:

Despite the availability of public transportation, many people who live outside of the city drive their cars to work daily. Government officials are concerned with traffic congestion, the potential lack of parking facilities, and air pollution within the city.

Here the background is clear. Despite ample opportunities to use public transportation, many people living in the suburbs choose to drive their own vehicles to work. This leads to problems with air pollution, a lack of parking facilities, and congested streets throughout the city. The significance of addressing these problems is obvious—we all want cleaner, less crowded cities, and places to work—and the purpose of this study (i.e., its central phenomenon) is to understand why workers choose to drive in from the suburbs rather than take readily available public transportation.

The purpose of this study is to understand why commuters choose to drive to work in the city rather than use public transportation.

Let's look at other problem and purpose statements focusing on issues faced by many undocumented immigrants in our country:

Undocumented immigrants from foreign countries are entering the United States in record numbers. It is unknown why so few of these immigrants risk deportation rather than attempt to become a permanent resident or citizen.

The purpose of this study is to understand reasons why undocumented immigrants do not attempt to become a U.S. citizen or permanent resident rather than face the risk of deportation.

In both of these examples, what we're interested in investigating is becoming clear; now we need to focus on exactly what we want to know.

Research Questions

As we saw with quantitative studies, we've created an inverted pyramid: we have a wide problem area that we narrowed down to a purpose for our research. Before we move forward, keep in mind what we said about the constructivist nature of qualitative research. Herein we will "construct" knowledge from a postpositivist perspective. We believe there is no absolute truth—rather, what we learn is based on our interaction with the environment. Given that belief, we have to ensure that what we already know doesn't negatively affect our data collection and analysis. For example, if I heard from our neighbor that trains into and out of the city were constantly late, it could easily affect my ability to objectively listen to other reasons given for driving to work rather than using mass transit. Although we'll talk more about it later, this leads us sometimes to practice *epoché*, or **bracketing**: this is the idea that we must suspend our judgment—that is, "empty our minds" of any preconceived notions or ideas when we collect and analyze our data. At the same time, if we worry too much about the future or what others are calling for, we are not conducting research in the moment; it's important to focus on what we want to know by emphasizing the idea of "What is happening, or what do I want to know, right now?"

Following that, we can evaluate the research questions we write, much as we did with our problem statements and research questions in a quantitative study:

1. Your research questions must be derived from the purpose statement.
2. Your research questions must be clear and focused.
3. You must be interested in conducting the research necessary to answer the question.
4. You must be able to handle the scope of the research question.

5. You have the necessary time, knowledge, and research skills you need to conduct the study.

6. You must be able to collect and analyze data to answer the question.

7. Answering the question has theoretical or practical significance.

8. You must ensure that it is ethical to conduct the research.

By ensuring that we follow these guidelines, within the context of our problem statement and research purpose, we soon get a feel for exactly what we want to learn from our proposed study. Let's wrap this section up with an example that shows a problem statement with background and its significance, the central purpose, and a research question related to a young child's memories of growing up in London during World War II:

> **Problem Statement:** World War II raged in the European and Pacific theaters from 1939 to 1945. While there were many horrific events that defined the war, the German bombing of innocent civilians in London stands out as one of the most tragic. Researchers have noted that most of what is known and written about is how the war affected the soldiers and adults in England; little has been written from purely a child's perspective. Research conducted in this area can add to our overall understanding of the impact of the war and give us a better picture of how the individual lives of youngsters in the middle of the conflict were affected.

> **Purpose Statement:** The purpose of this study is to interview adults who were young children who lived in London during the Nazi bombings of the city. It is felt that what can be learned from their perspective can give a better overall picture of how London's citizens were affected by the blitzkriegs.

> **Research Question:** What was the lived experience of young children living in London during the German bombings of the city during World War II?

As you can see, the problem and purpose statements, as well as the research question, meet the criteria outlined above. Together they could clearly focus a study in this area, the results of which could enlighten historians to another facet of the war's impact. As an interesting side note, sometimes I'm asked where I get all of the ideas for case studies for my texts. The answer is simple; some are contrived, others are lived experiences, and still others are based on experiences of my friends. In this case, an elderly neighbor of mine was a youngster living in London at that time; his stories are engaging, informative, and horrific. A word to the wise: Never miss the opportunity to listen to the lived history of our elders; unfortunately, so much of it passes away with the years.

Other Parts of Chapter 1

Obviously, there are other things in Chapter 1 that we've not discussed (e.g., limitations, assumptions, definitions of terms), but they're the same for qualitative studies as they were for quantitative studies. We include them in the examples in the appendices at the end of this chapter, but, for now, let's move on to our next step. For now, to summarize what we've talked about up to this point in the chapter, I've modified the quantitative proposal developed in Appendix C into a qualitative proposal in Appendix D at the end of this book.

Chapter 2 of a Qualitative Dissertation Proposal: The Review of Literature

We talked at great length about the ROL back in Chapter Three of this book by discussing the creation of outlines, how to locate and identify valid literature, concept mapping, and so on. While those are common elements to any good ROL, I also pointed out that literature reviews for quantitative (i.e., deductive) studies tend to be extensive—to the point where the review informs the statement of a hypothesis for testing. As we discussed then, writing those types of reviews is at the very heart of positivist research.

As we've said, because of the inductive, constructivist nature of qualitative studies, the ROLs tend to be much shorter but, much like a quantitative study, they can be used in three separate manners (Creswell & Creswell, 2020):

1. In Chapter 1 of the proposal to aid in understanding the background of the problem, as well as to present an orienting framework for problem investigation.

2. As a stand-alone review in Chapter 2 of the proposal. This is especially true of studies such as ethnographies, where researchers need a good understanding of the research area at the outset.

3. At the completion of a study to aid in comparing and contrasting your results to those of previously published studies. This is especially important in grounded theory studies where researchers want to review the results of their own research in light of prior research.

We may also need to review and include literature if additional research questions arise during the course of your study. For example, in my study investigating the experiences of children living in London during World War II, it's quite possible that other research questions, such as "What happened to your friends and family after the war?" or "What was your perspective on the adult's experience during the war?" might arise. Not only would this cause the scope of our interviews with these children to expand but it's also quite possible that we would need to read additional literature to better understand these questions.

At the same time, as we've said, you have to be careful not to read too extensively into your problem area for fear of finding concepts, ideas, or models that are so compelling that they keep you from looking at your data in more than one manner (Bogdan & Biklen, 2007). This is especially true with qualitative research: we want to "construct" our results based on the data we collect; we don't need a strong theoretical base to work from. Because we've already discussed writing ROLs, we won't include a new one here; instead, we focus specifically on the components of Chapter 3.

Chapter 3 of a Qualitative Dissertation Proposal: Research Methods

As we saw in Table 6.1, the first part of Chapter 3 calls for a discussion of the qualitative paradigm or, as it is sometimes called, our research "lens" (Charmaz, 2014). At that point, we agreed that the paradigm we chose would be driven by:

1. Our belief about what is ethical and valuable; we called this our **axiology**.
2. Our beliefs about reality; we called this our **ontology**.
3. Our beliefs about our role in the research process; we called this our **epistemology**.

We then learned that the research method we choose is determined by the combination of our axiology, our ontology, and our epistemology.

The Qualitative Paradigm

In the proposed study of children living in London during World War II, it is imperative that we establish fair, respectful, and trusting rapport between all parties (i.e., our axiology). This relationship must exist knowing that the knowledge uncovered is contextual, with researchers being respectful of varying viewpoints and the subjective truths that might arise from interactions with multiple participants (i.e., our ontology). Research in this subject area calls for close interaction between the researcher and the adults who experienced the Nazi bombings during their childhood, with knowledge constructed from the relationships developed during the research process (i.e., our epistemology). The relationship among our axiology, ontology, and epistemology calls for a qualitative approach in answering the research questions.

Before we begin talking about selecting the right qualitative design, it's important to note that we've already defined a lot of what we need for Chapter 3 of a qualitative proposal when we discussed Chapter 3 for a quantitative study. We need to write an introduction and can use some of the same approaches to sampling, particularly purposive, convenience, and snowball sampling. We primarily use interview protocols as our data collection tools for qualitative studies, and we need to discuss any ethical issues that might arise in our study. Given that, in this chapter, we focus on the five common qualitative designs and the procedures we can use to conduct a qualitative study. An example of Chapter 3 for each design is shown in Appendices 6.1–6.6 at the end of this chapter.

The Research Design

In order to understand how each design works, we start our case studies with examples of problem statements, purpose statements, and research questions that would normally be presented in Chapter 1. Based on that, we discuss the component parts of Chapter 3 for each of the qualitative designs. Keep in mind that we're writing a dissertation proposal, so our plan needs to be laid out in exact detail; we don't want the results of any of our studies to be negatively affected by something that wasn't well thought through or implemented.

Narrative Research

While we may have never referred to them as such, we're all familiar with **narrative research** in the form of books, television, and movies. For example, Ralph David Abernathy's (1991) *And the Walls Came Tumbling Down* tells us of the life story of Dr. Martin Luther King Jr., and we learn about the life of Mozart in the movie *Amadeus*. While we may just refer to these as a book or movie, researchers consider these as representative of just one of the commonly accepted narrative approaches (Creswell & Creswell, 2020):

- **Biographical narrative:** An account of experiences in a person's life written by someone other than the subject of the study. The book about Dr. King and the movie about Mozart would fall into this category.

- **Autobiographical narrative:** An account of a person's life written by the subject of the story; these are sometimes called "life stories" or "life histories." For example, *The Autobiography of Benjamin Franklin* (Franklin, 2019) was a personal account of the author's life from birth until his death in 1790.

- **Personal history stories:** These are accounts of personal experiences based on specific episodes or events within the subject's life. This can be as simple as a daily personal diary, or as compelling as the late Dan Wheeless's recounting of his daily struggles with epilepsy (LaPlante, 2016).

- **Oral history:** The recording and reporting of other people's reaction to, or "reflections on" an event that has occurred. In many instances, I refer to these as "Where were you when?" stories; these could include their reactions to events, such as the first men landing on the moon in 1969, or the terrorist attacks of 9/11.

Despite the approach we take, when we conduct a narrative study, we're interested in the meaning of a lived experience. We can do this by completing the sentence below:

If I could discover the meaning of one person's lived experience,
I would ask the person _____.

For example, using this statement, if I wanted to learn about one person's lived experience with extreme mountain climbing, I could end the sentence with "What is it like to climb a mountain with an elevation of over 20,000 feet?", thereby allowing the climber to tell us his or her story. Of course, a narrative doesn't have to be as dramatic as a climb up one of the world's highest peaks; it could be something as simple as a typical day at work, or as extensive as a person's life story. For example, my late grandfather co-invented an apparatus for weaving wool, cotton, and man-made fiber yarns with stretchable nylon (Harris & Hester, 1958), thereby allowing fabric of this type to be made more effectively and efficiently. Had I the opportunity to speak with him, I might end the sentence with something as broad as:

What role did you play in the development of the new apparatus?

We could then use information from our interviews, along with ancillary material such as the actual patent form, to write our narrative. Obviously, a study of this type is not as simple and straightforward as it might seem; we'll expand this reflection further when we talk later about identifying data sources and making plans for data collection and analysis. For now, Appendix 6.1 presents a narrative of children migrating from Cuba in the early 1960s in "The Case of the Unfortunate Departure."

Phenomenological Research

The goal of a **phenomenological research** study is to better understand the subjective, lived experience of a particular phenomenon as it was experienced by a person or a group of people (Billups, 2021). This approach can be focused with the statement below:

If I could discover the shared lived experiences of one quality or phenomenon in others, I would want to know _____.

While this may sound similar to narrative research, in this case, you're generally increasing the number of participants and narrowing the focus of your study. For example, if you wanted to better understand one aspect of a military recruiting sergeant's career, you might ask the following question:

What made you want to become a recruiting sergeant?

This study will require you to interview more than one recruiting sergeant; your goal is to understand, from a broader perspective, the reasons for taking on a pretty tough job.

In another case, you might interview college students in a French class about their experiences after studying in Paris for one semester; you could fill in the blank with something as narrow as:

What was it like going to school in a country where the native language isn't English?

As you can imagine, in both of these cases, because you will be interviewing more than one person, your data collection and analysis will be more complicated than that of a narrative study. Because of that complexity, it's imperative that we put a lot of detail in our plans for data collection and analysis to help ensure the accuracy of our results. At the same time, we must practice *epoché* (i.e., "bracketing"), a technique that allows us to work within a phenomenological study with an open mind. By doing this, we don't let our personal preconceptions or prejudices affect the way we conduct our study. In order to get a better feel for how this works, I've slightly modified the narrative study in Appendix 6.1 and included it in Appendix 6.2, "The Case of Parting from One's Children for Their Safety."

Ethnographic Research

Ethnographic research calls for extended immersion into, or observation of, a group of individuals in order to understand and report on their shared culture (Fetterman, 2010). Many researchers feel that only by spending a great deal of time with the participants of your study can you best report what day-to-day life is like. For example, my wife left Cuba just before the 1959 revolution during which Fidel Castro's loyalists overthrew the government of Fulgencio Batista. I won't get into the politics of the matter but let's just leave it to say that many perished, some were jailed for extended periods of time, many families were torn apart and, luckily, some escaped.

I've always been interested in the stories of those who survived the revolution and their experiences. The large majority of this group live in Miami and, simply because of age, the group is getting smaller in number every year. I think it's critical that we capture their stories, or else their insight into their history may be lost forever. In order to do so, I would need to immerse myself in the Cuban culture, through family reunions, social events, and at other times and places where these older Cuban refugees meet.

One such place is General Máximo Gómez Park, known to the locals as Domino Park (see Figure 6.1). Located on Calle Ocho (i.e., Southwest 8th Street), in the heart of Miami, it is a social spot popular with the locals. On most days, you can find many older Cuban gentlemen, many of whom are over 70, who came to the United States during or just after the revolution. They make up a large part of the crowd playing serious games of dominos, drinking very strong Cuban coffee, and chatting with friends. There's quite often a lot of stories and remembrances of times gone by, both about their lives growing up in Cuba, as well as life in the United States since their immigration. Again, it's important that we capture their history, or else run the risk of losing it forever. I could start my investigation using the same approach we've used for the other methodologies:

If I could experience a different culture by living in or observing it,
I would ask _____.

In this case, I could complete the sentence by writing "What was it like leaving your homeland because of the revolution and then living in the United States?" In order to answer this question, I could try to immerse myself into the culture of Domino Park. I speak Spanish fluently so I would speak with the players individually, as well as watch and listen to what they said or discussed. By doing this, I would be able to closely observe their lives: the circumstances surrounding why they left, their immersion into the new country and culture, and their lives since they migrated to the United States.

It would be critical that I visit the park and get to know the participants for as long as I felt necessary to learn their stories. I would need to ensure that I spent enough time talking with and observing the players and spectators and ensure that my insights and observations reflect their normal day-to-day lives, as well as any meaningful special occasions. For example, if I visited with them over a period of only 2 weeks, I might not experience the excitement of an event or holiday that might draw parkgoers to another location or venue. For example,

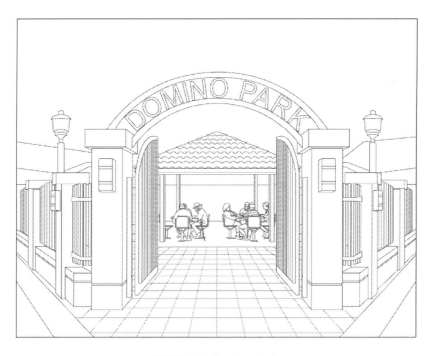

FIGURE 6.1. Domino Park.

the Three-Kings Day parade is celebrated in Spain and in many Latin American countries in early January each year. This event celebrates the Christian traditions of the three Wise Men arriving to Bethlehem with gifts for the baby Jesus. This is a very important day to many in the Cuban community, and thousands attend the parade. While they won't be in Domino Park that day, it would be very important for me to listen to their reflections when I saw them again. This is a key part of their culture.

While this is an example we might not experience, it serves to show the reasoning for an extended immersion into the culture you're studying. The amount of data you might collect could be voluminous; we'll talk more about this as we discuss plans for data analysis. For now, we can move from one adventure to another in Appendix 6.3, "The Case of Climbing the Mountain."

Case Study Research

We've all used or heard the word "case" on a daily basis. Attorneys are willing to take your case, police officers are always investigating cases, and physicians diagnose us with cases of various ailments. When we conduct **case study research,** we're doing much the same thing. We're reporting on events that actually happened to a person or a group of people in a single unit, or as it is called by many researchers, a **bounded system** (Yin, 2013). This simply means that we're trying to understand an event that occurred to a particular person or group at a particular point in time. With that in mind, before we move forward, let me warn you that there are many different definitions, ideas, and approaches to conducting research in a bounded system; there are even researchers who question whether or not case study research should even be labeled as a traditional qualitative approach.

We can begin investigating and writing a case study by completing the following sentence:

If I could discover what actually occurred and was experienced
during one single lived event in a specific location,
I would want to know _____.

I mentioned earlier when we were discussing instruments for a study, that I have a degree in counseling psychology and, having worked in an inner-city mental health crisis center for several years, I've seen quite a few interesting cases. Knowing that, if I had worked with a client with issues that I thought my colleagues could benefit from knowing, I could write a case study focusing on that one individual. In it, I would identify the issue, the approach I took to working with the client, and the results of my intervention. In short, I would end the sentence above with "What is different about this case that might be interesting or educational to my colleagues?" Answering this question would allow my colleagues to learn from my client, the intervention, and the results, and may help them be better prepared to deal with a similar case in the future.

In other instances, I could broaden the scope of my bounded system. For example, our mental health center had a very effective system for working with local physicians, hospitals, and interns from local universities. Other agencies, wishing to emulate our success, might decide to investigate the entire agency's procedures and processes from a case study perspective. By doing this, you can see the bounded system has moved from focusing on one person to focusing on one larger institution. Their findings could then serve as a model for use in their own organization.

However broad your boundary, Merriam (2009) tells us to keep in mind the characteristics of a case study:

1. Particular
   a. It can suggest what and what not to do in a specific case.
   b. It can focus on a specific issue but reflect a general problem.
   c. The author's bias may or may not influence the writing of the case.
2. Descriptive
   a. Demonstrate that many factors may contribute to the complexity of the case and may include information coming from a wide variety of sources.
   b. The study shows the past and current perspectives, and can show the passage of time.
   c. Shows the influence of personalities and opinions on the issue.
   d. Obtains information from a wide variety of sources and presents it in different ways.
3. Background, Evaluation, and Summary
   a. Explains the background and reasons for the particular problem.
   b. Shows why a given intervention worked or failed.
   c. Shows why alternatives to a given intervention were not chosen.
   d. Provides a summarization and conclusion allowing for others to learn from the results.

Knowing this outline will allow us to write a case study that provides an observer's concrete observations, set in the actual context of the case, that are open to a reader's interpretation and, if called for, its implementation. We can see all of this demonstrated in Appendix 6.4 in a study of our old nemesis, "The Case of the Standardized Test."

Grounded Theory Research

The goal of a **grounded theory research** study is to develop a theory for a single phenomenon of living that is shared by others (Charmaz, 2014). In short, we want to develop a theory that describes and explains a phenomenon we are investigating. Based on this definition, the first question that many people have is "What's the difference between a grounded theory study and a phenomenological study? They sound the same." I agree, they do sound similar, but the differences are easy to understand.

As we saw in a phenomenological study, we primarily focused on the lived experience of a group of individuals and didn't rely heavily on material from other sources. For example, with the students studying French, we didn't look into the literature to learn of the experiences of other students—we simply focused on the stories of the students in our French classes. In grounded theory studies, we want to take this process to the next step by collecting data from the participants and using information from other sources to explain (i.e., develop a theory) a given event. We can start with the following statement:

> *If I could discover a theory for a single phenomenon of living as shared by others, I would ask* _____.

For example, there are a lot of people who worked in the corporate world for years but decided to give that up and move into academia; the question then becomes "Why did you leave the corporate world and move into academia?" Using a grounded theory approach, we would move past the idea of basing our results solely on interviews that describe the experience (i.e., the phenomenon) and include information from journal articles, conference presentations, or interviews with former coworkers and managers who might be able to share some insight.

In other cases, we can use grounded theory research to develop a set of "best practices" to guide us in a given endeavor. For example, let's go back to the career of an Army recruiting sergeant. I can only imagine this is a very tough job; any guidelines we could develop might prove to be very helpful. In order to begin, we would identify and interview a group of recruiters and have them tell us their opinions and experiences concerning the best way to recruit young soldiers using questions such as:

1. What are the characteristics of a good recruit?
2. Do you actively advertise (e.g., local newspapers, school bulletins)?
3. Do you visit local schools, job fairs, and the like?
4. Which locations do you find where you're more likely to identify recruits?
5. Once a potential recruit visits your office, what do you do to try to persuade him or her that the military is a good choice?

Of course, there are other questions and it's natural for respondents to expand upon their answers and include material you may not have specifically asked for. It's also acceptable for you to ask follow-up or probing questions. In addition, we could delve into any literature related to the topic (e.g., the magazine *Army Times*), as well as books or journals that focus on human motivation. By collecting and analyzing these data, it's quite possible that we could develop a theory, or a set of best practices, that will help recruiters do their jobs better.

As you can imagine, creating a theory, or a set of best practices, based on data from interviews and other sources, is very time-consuming and requires a focused and well-developed plan for data collection and analysis. Like the other approaches, including a solid research method in your proposal is like creating a road map to success. You can see what I mean in Appendix 6.5, "The Case of Homelessness."

Content Analysis

Using content analysis, researchers are able to make inferences based on the objective and systematic analysis of recorded communication, such as newspapers, books, letters, email messages, and the like. In doing so, researchers look for both the manifest (i.e., apparent) and the latent (i.e., underlying) meaning. Unlike other purely qualitative approaches, content analysis often uses a quantitative component as part of the analysis. This allows researchers to make inferences based on the frequency of certain words or concepts, to test hypotheses, and to conduct evaluations (Neuendorf, 2002).

Suppose, for example, we had the following research question:

Are there differences in presidential approval expressed by participants in the different Sunday morning news discussion programs?

We could answer this question using a content analysis of transcripts of these programs by first defining our evaluation criteria (e.g., Are there specific words, terms, examples, and the like in the transcripts that we would consider positive or negative?). We would then identify the specific networks and programs to be viewed, as well as the scope of our project (e.g., the time of year the study will be conducted, the number of transcripts to be used, the duration of the study).

Using these criteria, we would collect the transcripts needed for our study and carefully read through them, while marking the segments of the transcripts we've identified as being necessary to answer our research question. We would then be able to quantify our results and use them to write a report answering our research question; this entire process is shown in Appendix 6.6, "The Case of the Eyewitnesses."

Participants and Sampling

From the outset, keep in mind that qualitative sampling is generally purposive; we know the group we want to work with, and we'll simply select members of that group to interview. While there are no specific numbers, Creswell and Creswell (2020) provide general guidelines for us to follow (see Table 6.2). As you can see, there are no hard-and-fast rules; words such as "group," "many," or "several" are open to interpretation. Obviously, our research method points us in the right direction, but you as the data collector ultimately determines exactly how many participants or data objects you will need.

TABLE 6.2. Qualitative Sample Sizes

Narrative research	One or more individuals who want to share their life history.
Phenomenology	Several individuals who have shared the same experience.
Grounded theory	A process, an action, or an interaction that involves many individuals.
Ethnography	A group that shares the same culture.
Case study	An event, program, or activity, or more than one individual.
Content analysis	There is no set number of documents one should review for content analysis. The number of resources needed will correspond directly to what is called for by the problem and purpose statements and research questions.

Instrumentation

Keep in mind what I said earlier in the chapter. Due to the nature of qualitative research, in the vast majority of cases the researcher is the data collection tool, and he or she collects data from a variety of sources. In many instances, the way we collect data is obvious: If we want a person's feelings about a phenomenon they experienced, we will most likely conduct a one-to-one interview; in other studies—an ethnography, for example—we become a participant in the group or culture we're observing. While these do seem obvious, don't let that limit your ability to collect the data you need; each of these common approaches can be combined with the others as needed:

1. Interviews: This is the most common way to collect qualitative data. We can use predefined questions and conduct either a structured, semistructured, or unstructured interview (Kvale, 2007).

2. Direct observation: In this case, data are collected from an outsider's perspective by close observation; in many instances, you will take field notes to use for data analysis (Spradley, 1980).

3. Participant observant: As we saw in ethnographic studies, sometimes it's necessary for the researcher to become part of the group that is being studied. While doing so, the researcher can be an active agent of data collection simply by being part of the lived experience (Spradley, 1980).

4. Focus groups: Data are collected from members of a small group who are asked, using a series of guided questions, about their perceptions, beliefs, or attitudes toward an event, products, concepts, and so on (Barbour, 2007).

5. Surveys: This is exactly what it sounds like, asking open-ended questions where you're expecting the participant to provide written answers (Fowler, 2013).

Given the advances in today's technology, also keep in mind that, in some instances, you don't have to be burdened with the "time and place" constraints of years past. Online interviews, video-based remote observations, weblogs, and inter-active chat sessions are all viable tools—as long as you carefully plan your approach to help ensure the validity of the data you collect. As an example, I conducted text-based online focus groups to discuss changes in departmental policy for an agency I was working with (Terrell, 2011). I feel like the data I collected using that approach were exactly what I would have gotten in a face-to-face environment. The key is, if it's valid and the situation calls for it, do what works for you.

As Creswell and Creswell (2020) note, different qualitative approaches may focus on a particular type of data, as shown in Table 6.3.

Sometimes Data Are Easy to Collect

In some cases, our data are easily identified and readily available. If I wanted to conduct a simple survey asking the average adult's opinion of our economy, I could develop the questions I wanted to ask and purposively select, and interview, people as they walked through a shopping center or down the street. There are problems with this approach in that the results represent only those people who were actually at the given location at the time I was there; that would be narrowed further by the actual number of people who would stop and talk to me. While this would be an easy way to collect our data, because of these and other reasons, my results might not be very insightful.

In another case, I received an email from a student asking my opinion of the possibility of offering a specific course; in the email he included a link to a web page where I was to write my feelings. Although I didn't mention it above, asking some-one to take the time to actually compose and write out his or her thoughts is not the most effective means of collecting data—many people simply do not have the time or inclination to give you a complete, well-thought-out answer. This is especially true when you ask someone to handwrite their response.

TABLE 6.3. Qualitative Data Sources

Narrative research	Data are collected primarily through interviews and documents.
Phenomenology	Data are primarily collected from interviews with individuals, although documents and observations may be included.
Grounded theory	Data are primarily collected from interviews and documents.
Ethnography	Data are collected primarily from observations and interviews, but perhaps also from other sources encountered during the extended time in the field.
Case study	Data are collected from multiple sources, such as interviews, observations, documents, and artifacts.
Content analysis	Data are collected from existing published sources, such as journal articles, newspaper articles, reports, organizational documents, and the like.

In yet another example, while conducting a phenomenological study, I might want to ascertain people's feelings about a certain event. To do that, I might watch how people react to the situation and write brief vignettes, called **field notes**, about what I see. For example, several years back I was helping chaperone a group of middle school students to Arlington National Cemetery and we just happened to be there when they buried the last survivor from World War I. I could have easily taken field notes about what I saw, and perhaps spoken with other attendees about the feelings they had during the ceremony. Following that, when I analyzed my data, I'm sure I would have seen themes such as "gratitude," "patriotism," and "honor" emerge, as well as answer my interrogative pronouns:

1. *Who was there?* The actual solider himself; Frank Buckles lived to be 110, he also served in World War II as a civilian merchant seaman and was captured and held as a prisoner of war by Japanese forces. Others in attendance included the president and vice president of the United States, family, friends, other military personnel, other governmental dignitaries, and the like.

2. *What was happening?* They were honoring the last survivor of "the war to end all wars." Some people were crying, others were praying, and still others were standing solemnly.

3. *When did it happen?* Sergeant Buckles died on February 27, 2011, and was buried on March 15, 2011.

4. *Where did it happen?* Frank Buckles was buried in Arlington, Virginia, at Arlington National Cemetery. The cemetery is located just across the Potomac River from Washington, DC.

5. *Why did it happen?* The funeral took place in Arlington to commemorate and honor the last of the soldiers from World War I.

You can see, based on the data I collected and analyzed, it would be relatively easy to write a sound phenomenological paper about what was witnessed.

Sometimes Data Are Not Easy to Collect

In some cases, researchers have been left scurrying when not only do they have to identify the data they need for a certain project but they also have to identify any potential roadblocks to accessing it. For example, as I've mentioned, a lot of my research focuses on determining reasons why students leave college prior to graduation. While working with one of my graduates (Moore, 2014), we focused on a specific demographic: African American students who failed to graduate from an online bachelor's degree program. While we truly believed that developing a grounded theory identifying reasons for attrition might help us develop new procedures and policies, we had to take many steps.

To begin, before we actually ever began contacting possible participants for our study, we had to show both our university, as well as the university that the students left, that our research plan was ethical and didn't negatively affect the prior students in any way. We also had to explain why our study was meaningful to both the university and the students who left the program. Because the study involved working with human participants, we also needed approval from the IRBs of both schools.

Once we got through these steps and keeping in mind that our data would come from a specific source, we had to identify and contact our potential participants: in this case, students who left the program prior to graduation. This meant we had to work with the other university to identify these students, use the information they provided us to contact the former students, and hope that an adequate number would agree to be interviewed. Once a former student volunteered to participate, we had to agree on a mutually acceptable time and place (e.g., in person, by phone) for the actual interview.

Unfortunately, at this point, we ran into a problem. The university supplied us with the names of 44 former students, and we had planned to conduct 12–15 interviews; our feeling was that we would reach **data saturation** at that point and any additional interviews would not tell us anything more than what we had already learned (Creswell & Creswell, 2020).

Our response rate was low and, even after repeated mailings, only seven former students agreed to participate in the study. This, of course, meant we couldn't analyze the data and present them as a grounded theory study; we simply didn't know enough about the experiences that these students faced. Given that problem, what did we do? As we've talked about, qualitative research is far more flexible than quantitative studies. In this case, we were able to focus solely on our central phenomenon: Why did the students leave the online program? We then analyzed their interviews from a phenomenological perspective and discovered the usual reasons: academic failure, a loss of interest in the program, financial concerns, family problems, and so on. In short, we weren't able to develop a theory or set of best practices that could help the school, but we were able to show that these students faced many of the same problems as students from other types of institutions and from other racial and ethnic groups. Our study wasn't a failure; we added that tiny bit of knowledge that told us "The reasons these students left school are no different from the others you've studied. Continue your research."

The Research Procedures

We can't say this often enough. Your procedures lay out, step-by-step, how you will conduct your research. It's imperative that this is well thought out, presented, and followed to ensure the credibility and transferability of your research. We see examples of this procedure in the appendices of this chapter, as well as in Appendix D at the end of the book, where we continue our investigation of the waste treatment plant.

Plans for Data Analysis

There is one thing that most researchers can agree on when it comes to analyzing qualitative data, and that is that there is no one standard way to analyze the data. Unlike quantitative research where we relied on a positivist approach using specific statistical tests, p values, alpha values, and so on, there is no one right way to analyze qualitative data. Keeping in mind the nature of the data, as well as the fact that the researcher is the data collection tool, analysis becomes a synthesis and evaluation of the data that were collected. Doing so requires the identification of patterns, concepts, and relationships in their data, ultimately allowing for research questions to be answered. Before we can do that, however, there are several things to keep in mind.

First, we need to discuss the idea of reliability as it pertains to qualitative data analysis. When we discussed quantitative reliability, we were concerned with the consistency and generalizability of the data we collected; qualitative reliability focuses on the dependability (i.e., the results are consistent and could be repeated) of the data collection process (Lincoln & Guba, 1985). For example, did a group of researchers use the same interview guidelines and did they work together to ensure that they followed the same procedures while collecting their data? In reviewing the transcripts of interviews, are there any obvious errors? In short, you need to tell the reader of your proposal how you plan on ensuring the dependability of your research process.

Following that, you should discuss your plans for familiarizing yourself with the data you've collected. Doing so may require you to transcribe interviews, and then ensure their accuracy by listening to the recordings of the interviews while reading the transcripts again. In another case, if you were involved in an ethnographic study, you might want to reread your field notes before you begin your analysis. The key is that you want to be as familiar with your data as possible by ensuring that the text you are working with is an accurate representation of what you observed, or what the person who was interviewed really said.

Another concept completely foreign to many researchers used to working with numeric data is the idea that qualitative data analysis can begin as the data are being collected; the reasoning for this is simple. As we discussed earlier, starting analysis early allows the researcher to identify other topics to be covered or questions to be asked when interviewing others in your sample. It may also call for the researcher to add to the literature review. This iterative process allows you to develop a much deeper understanding or, as it's often called, a thicker view of your material.

As I said, however, most will agree there is no one best way to analyze qualitative data. At the same time, despite the issues we've discussed, there are common elements within each of the approaches. Remember, these are general guidelines; they may be modified or combined when the researcher thinks it's necessary.

Narrative Analysis

In order to effectively analyze narrative data, Gibbs (2007) suggests beginning by reading the transcripts to look for events, experiences, accounts of things that happened, and the details of the actual narrative you're analyzing (e.g., sequencing, other characters in the story, interactions). This would be followed by creating a written summary showing the beginning and end of the story, as well as the sequence of events within the story. The researcher is then able to identify themes within the story, as well as see how these themes flow together; this would also include identifying "mini-stories or sub-plots" and "emotive language, imagery, use of metaphors, and passages about the narrator's feelings" (p. 64). At this point, it's possible to logically organize these themes and include any ancillary information needed to complete the story (e.g., a published history about the time frame of the story, anecdotes from others). Once finished, a narrative answering the central focus of the study can be written.

Phenomenological Analysis

As discussed by Patton (2001), data analysis in a phenomenological study starts during data collection with the research practicing *epoché* (i.e., bracketing), the idea that data must be collected with an open mind so as not to contaminate the data with personal opinions or preconceptions. At that point, the analysis continues with the researcher reviewing the transcripts for common themes, while attempting to understand the meaning of key phrases both personally and by working with the interviewees. This ultimately allows the researcher to tie these themes and phrases together to better present the story being told by the participants of the study.

Ethnographic Analysis

As I said, there is no one agreed-upon way to analyze qualitative data; this is especially true with ethnographic studies. Keeping in mind that data for these studies can come from interviews, field notes, and other sources, Angrosino (2007) points out that analysis of this type calls for narrowing the data by searching for patterns within the data (i.e., a descriptive approach), as well as searching for meaning within the patterns (i.e., a theoretical approach). This requires looking at data from an insider's (i.e., emic) perspective by trying to understand how the participants in the study report or understand things; it then becomes the job of the researcher (i.e., the etic or outsider perspective) to link the findings of the analysis to data from outsider sources. This process, called **triangulation**, adds to the overall validity of the study. Based on the themes uncovered, it is then the researcher's task to write the report describing the essence of the culture studied. In most instances, this will call for several drafts, often shared with the observed participants for **validation**, until you are satisfied with what you've written.

Case Study Analysis

Data for a case study can come from a multitude of sources, such as interviews, observations, documentation, and other information or data particular to the location and focus of your study. As Baxter and Jack (2008) point out, this "facilitates reaching a holistic understanding of the phenomenon being studied" (p. 554). While an in-depth discussion of specific data-analytic approaches is beyond the scope of this book, Yin (2013) and Stake (1995) point out several distinct approaches, including pattern matching, linking data to propositions, explanation building, synthesis across cases, time–series analysis, **intercase analysis**, **intracase analysis**, categorical aggregation, and direct interpretation. When writing your proposal, it is important that you understand these different types of data analysis and propose the one best suited to the type of case you are proposing.

Grounded Theory Analysis

Obviously, what we've discussed up to this point is just an overview of qualitative data analysis; in writing an actual dissertation proposal and report, we would need far more detail from texts focusing on these topics. At the same time, instead of just talking about how we would analyze grounded theory data, we look at one good example of the entire process. We continue "The Case of Homelessness" we began in Appendix 6.5 by restating the research question:

What are the reasons that females give for living in homeless shelters in New York City?

Figure 6.2 illustrates what the first person we talk to might tell us. If you look closely at the figure, you can see quite a few similar ideas. For example, she mentions only having a high school diploma and alludes to a lack of job skills; obviously, she attributes part of her inability to get a job, and subsequently winding up living in the shelter, to that. In two other places, she mentions a lack of support by friends and family: "My husband decided he didn't want to be married" and "My friends told me I had stayed there too long."

Moving into a homeless shelter was a decision that was just about made for me; I didn't have a whole lot of choices. Before I came here, I graduated from high school and was making a pretty good living working in a shoe store for about 10 years; you know, helping customers, running the cash register, doing most anything the store manager wanted me to do. I was married and between my husband and me, we lived a fairly comfortable life until two things happened. First, my husband decided he didn't want to be married and moved back to be close to his family in California; shortly after that, our store went out of business. We were just a small place, and we couldn't keep up with the competition from the bigger stores. After that, I tried to find other work but, like I said, I only went to high school and there were younger kids willing to work for less than I was making; I just couldn't seem to find anything permanent, or that paid enough. It wasn't long before I had to move out of our apartment, so I moved in with friends and started collecting unemployment assistance while I was looking for work. It seems like trouble comes in twos in my life – I ran out of time to collect unemployment benefits at about the same time my friends told me I had stayed there too long. After all of that, I didn't have much choice. I've been here about four months and I'm still trying to find a good job. Thankfully, I've got my health; if I keep trying, I'll get out of here someday.

FIGURE 6.2. First transcript.

We can label each of the themes we recognize as an **open code** (see Figure 6.3). In addition to the two we just mentioned, we can see the person being interviewed feels she had no choice other than to go into the shelter, and that, despite everything, she is willing to keep trying to move forward with her life.

Our second interview is shown in Figure 6.4, with the open codes for it shown in Figure 6.5. Here again, the idea of not having a choice and problems with friends and family are also issues that led this person to move into a homeless shelter. In this case, you can see that drugs and alcohol are the largest contributing factors.

As you might expect, based on our final transcript (see Figure 6.6), we see many of the same open codes, shown in Figure 6.7, that we saw in the first and second transcripts.

Because there were so many similar open codes in the three transcripts, I've grouped them into categories showing their similarities (see Table 6.4). For example, in the first column, we see that the people interviewed mentioned having no control over moving to the shelter on five separate occasions; this was attributed to several things: moving there with their parents, losing their job, having to move out of their home or apartment, and so on. When I group all of these similar open codes together, and assign names, I've created an **axial code**. By doing this, I have lessened the amount of data I need to deal with; we call this **data reduction**.

I've named the second axial code "Lack of Education or Skills." In two of the cases, one person had dropped out of high school and felt she had no skills; the other graduated from high school but didn't feel like the skills she had learned over the years would allow her to compete with younger applicants who would work for less money. Finally, the third axial code, labeled "Family Problems," is straightforward: divorce, families and friends unwilling to support them on a long-term basis, and alcoholic parents all contributed, to some degree, to the person living in the shelter.

Moving into a homeless shelter was a decision that was just about made for me; I didn't - - - - No choice
have a whole lot of choices. Before I came here, I graduated from high school and was - - - - - Only high school
making a pretty good living working in a shoe store for about 10 years; you know, helping
customers, running the cash register, doing most anything the store manager wanted me - - - - Low skills job
to do. I was married and between my husband and me, we lived a fairly comfortable life _ _ _ _ Married then break-up
until two things happened. First, my husband decided he didn't want to be married and
moved back to be close to his family in California; shortly after that, our store went out ←—— Lost job
of business. We were just a small place, and we couldn't keep up with the competition _ _ _ _ _ Tried to find work
from the bigger stores. After that, I tried to find other work but, like I said, I only went to - - - Only high school
high school and there were younger kids willing to work for less than I was making; I just
couldn't seem to find anything permanent, or that paid enough. It wasn't long before I had
to move out of our apartment, so I moved in with friends and started collecting unemployment - Tried to find work
assistance while I was looking for work. It seems like trouble comes in twos in my life – I
ran out of time to collect unemployment benefits at about the same time my friends told
me I had stayed there too long. After all of that, I didn't have much choice—I've been here - - - No choice
about four months and I'm still trying to find a good job. Thankfully, I've got my health; if I - - Still trying
keep trying, I'll get out of here someday.

FIGURE 6.3. Open codes for first transcript.

I didn't have a choice, I had nowhere else to go. I was in college, and got messed up with the drug scene. At first, it wasn't too bad, typical college stuff – smoking a little dope and drinking a lot. I was able to go to class, and did fairly well; I even finished my degree. When I got my first job, there were several people who were also into the social drug thing. Unfortunately, some of them and their friends were into stronger drugs. I've always tended to be a follower; I went to the parties and did what my friends did - cocaine, a little bit of this, and a little bit of that. I was still doing fairly well at work, but I met my downfall with meth. We were in a fairly bad part of town looking to score some weed, and I started talking to some people who lived there. They seemed like good people and, since I was used to smoking weed, they asked if I wanted something a little stronger. Believe me, that first hit was all it took; I was addicted. From there it was slowly downhill; my work life, my social life and my personal life went to hell. I lost everything I owned, and spent every penny I had, on drugs. I finally hit rock bottom and started looking for help. I tried to go back to my family, but they wouldn't put up with me and kicked me out. After that, I've gone to support groups and they help me make a few bucks; not enough to live alone, but enough to get by. The leaders of those groups pointed me here. I know it would be very easy to get caught up in the drug scene again, but I'm going to try my best to stay clean and work my way out of here.

FIGURE 6.4. Second transcript.

I didn't have a choice, ~~I had nowhere else to go. I was in college, and got messed~~ - - - - - No choice
up with the drug scene. At first, it wasn't too bad, typical college stuff – smoking - - - - Good education
a little dope and drinking a lot. I was able to go to class, and did fairly well; I even
finished my degree. When I got my first job, there were several people who were - - - - Drugs
also into the social drug thing. Unfortunately, some of them and their friends were
into stronger drugs. I've always tended to be a follower; I went to the parties and
did what my friends did - cocaine, a little bit of this, and a little bit of that. I was
still doing fairly well at work, but I met my downfall with meth. We were in a fairly
bad part of town looking to score some weed, and I started talking to some people
who lived there. They seemed like good people and, since I was used to smoking
weed, they asked if I wanted something a little stronger. Believe me, that first hit
was all it took; I was addicted. From there it was slowly downhill; my work life, my - - Lost everything
social life and my personal life went to hell. I lost everything I owned, and spent
every penny I had, on drugs. I finally hit rock bottom and started looking for help. - - - - Looked for help
I tried to go back to my family, but they wouldn't put up with me and kicked me out. - - - Kicked out by family
After that, I've gone to support groups and they help me make a few bucks; not
enough to live alone, but enough to get by. The leaders of those groups pointed me - - - - Willing to try
here. I know it would be very easy to get caught up in the drug scene again, but I'm
going to try my best to stay clean and work my way out of here.

FIGURE 6.5. Open codes for second transcript.

It's pretty simple. Growing up my family was dysfunctional; my parents were alcoholics and my brother and I basically raised ourselves. We all finally wound up in a shelter. I tried to keep going to school, but dropped out when I was 16. I got pregnant and got married to a guy I met in the shelter but, of course, that didn't last. He filed for divorce when I was 17, took our baby and I've never seen either one of them again. I'm trying, believe me, I'm trying. I don't have any real skills to speak of and, without an education and with my background, a lot of folks are scared to hire me. The people in the shelter are nice – I get food and a place to sleep; the churches and other agencies give us clothes. It makes me feel bad that all I do is take from these people; I'm willing to work, but just can't find anything. Like I said, I'm trying, believe me, I'm trying.

FIGURE 6.6. Third transcript.

It's pretty simple. Growing up my family was dysfunctional; my parents were
alcoholics and my brother and I basically raised ourselves. We all finally wound ----- No choice
up in a shelter. I tried to keep going to school, but dropped out when I was 16. ----- Poor education
I got pregnant and got married to a guy I met in the shelter but, of course, ---------- Had child/divorced
that didn't last. He filed for divorce when I was 17, took our baby and I've
never seen either one of them again. I'm trying, believe me, I'm trying. I don't ---- Keeps trying
have any real skills to speak of and, without an education and with my background, --- Poor education
a lot of folks are scared to hire me. The people in the shelter are nice – I get food ---- No skills
and a place to sleep; the churches and other agencies give us clothes. It makes me
feel bad that all I do is take from these people; I'm willing to work, but just can't ----- Willing to work
find anything. Like I said, I'm trying, believe me, I'm trying. ------------------ Keeps trying

FIGURE 6.7. Open codes for third transcript.

TABLE 6.4. Axial and Open Codes

No other option	Lack of education or skills	Family problems
1. The decision was just about made for me.	1. I graduated from high school.	1. My husband decided he didn't want to be married to me anymore.
2. We all finally wound up in a shelter.	2. I only went to high school.	2. Friends told me I had stayed in their homes too long.
3. I didn't have a choice.	3. I dropped out.	3. My family . . . kicked me out.
4. I didn't have much of a choice.	4. I don't have any real skills.	4. My parents were alcoholics.
5. My work life . . . went to hell.	5. I have no real education.	

AN IMPORTANT NOTE

In the second interview, the person said that the biggest contributor to her homelessness was drug addiction. While this is common in many shelters, in our example, it appeared only in this one transcript. It's not uncommon to find open codes that are found only in one or a small number of your transcripts. Because of that, you need not try to develop an axial code based on it.

The final stage in analyzing our data in a grounded theory study is to identify a *selective code* from the axial codes; the remaining axial codes will then be related to it and the entire structure will be used to develop the grounded theory. In this case, the most important code seems to be that the residents who were interviewed felt that they had no option; their personal circumstances caused them to move there, and they didn't have the education, skills, or support network necessary to help them move forward.

Given that information, let's develop a theory based on the selective code "No Other Option," with all other axial codes contributing to it (see Figure 6.8): You can clearly see that the grounded theory we have developed directly represents the data we collected. Our selective code (i.e., the belief that there is no other option) is a function of a given person's lack of a support network, and the need for higher education or an employable skill set. In order to test the theory (or evaluate it over the long term), we would put mechanisms into place to address these issues. One thing that is definitely on the researcher's side is the motivation of each female to leave the shelter; each of them clearly stated a willingness to keep on trying.

Content Analysis

This type of analysis is focused on answering a research question by identifying themes in selected material related to your area of interest. For example, I recently

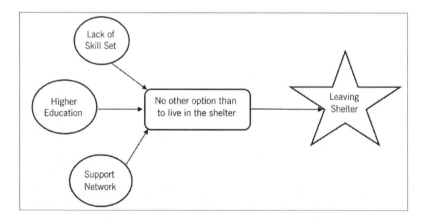

FIGURE 6.8. Grounded theory.

listened to the president's annual State of the Union speech. If I asked the research question, "What did the president specifically focus on?" it would be easy to think back to the major points he made. At the same time, did he reinforce his major themes with minor themes that tied into his overall remarks, or were there subtle comments that reinforced the primary focus of his speech? In order to ascertain that, I could get a transcript of his speech and code it, much as I would for grounded theory research. Upon completion, I would be able to compile these codes and readily identify both the major themes and the other parts of the speech that more discretely supported his statements or beliefs.

In another case, I recently noticed that the classified advertisements in our local newspaper had far fewer job listings than I remember from the job-hunting days of my youth. I also noticed that the job listings that did appear seemed more focused on entry-level or low-skilled jobs. I began to wonder: Does this just happen in my local paper or are the job advertisements similar in other newspapers throughout the United States? Do the job advertisements in the newspaper's online advertisements mirror those in the print version? Obviously, I would need to analyze more than one resource: newspapers from different parts of the country, different websites, and so on. The purpose of my research might be to allow us to better help our students, recent graduates, or anyone else looking for work or to change jobs to find the resources that best suit their needs.

The Validity and Reliability of a Qualitative Study

Before moving forward, we need to discuss reliability and validity in the qualitative context. As you'll remember, in the quantitative designs, reliability was primarily a function of the instruments used to collect data, with the various research designs used to control for the validity of our results. Due to the nature of the data being collected, as well as the fact that the researcher is most often the data collector, these ideas change somewhat in the qualitative designs. Instead of reliability and validity, we focus on the overall **trustworthiness** of our study; this is a function of four factors (Cohen & Crabtree, 2006; Lincoln & Guba, 1985): credibility, transferability, dependability, and confirmability.

Credibility

We can consider **credibility** to be the equivalent of internal validity in a quantitative study. When we establish credibility, we are stating that our study results are believable or credible from the perspective of a participant in the study. This can be done with:

1. Prolonged engagement: Ensure that you spend enough time in your research environment in order to understand the broad setting, the central phenomenon, and the culture of the setting. Prolonged engagement allows you to develop relationships and rapport, and thereby trust and understanding.

2. Persistent observation: While prolonged engagement allows the researcher to understand the breadth of the area under investigation, persistent observation allows for a better understanding of the depth of the organization. This helps the researcher to become open to the multiple factors that may affect the phenomenon being studied, the participants, elements of the organization, and so on.

3. Triangulation: When more than one source of data is being used, this is known as triangulation. For example, if you are using more than one interviewer, check to ensure that the results from each are similar. Triangulation can also be used theoretically by comparing interview results to the valid results of published resources or theories.

4. Peer debriefers: Impartial colleagues can be asked to examine your study's methodology, transcripts, data analysis, and report. These are **peer debriefers**. Their feedback can help you ensure the validity and credibility of your work.

5. Negative case analysis: Referring to data that may contradict the themes you uncovered may be referred to as **negative case analysis**. Talk about and explain the effect of these data to what you might have expected or to those themes common in the majority of the analysis.

6. Referential adequacy: A portion of the data collected may be set aside, archived, and followed by an analysis of the remaining data. Once initial findings are developed, the archived data should be analyzed with the results of both analyses compared for consistency. This is a way of determining that the study has **referential adequacy**.

7. Member checking: As tempting as it sounds, **member checking** doesn't mean for you to go back and have the person you interviewed check the transcript. Rather, you show them the final report or product and ask whether they believe it represents their input accurately.

Transferability

Transferability is often compared to the idea of external validity in quantitative research and is nothing more than attempting to demonstrate that your research findings are applicable in other contexts. This is done by providing a **thick description** of your results. Don't skimp on your words. When you're describing an event, scenario, or situation, go into great detail. This demonstrates the extent to which the results of your study can be transferable to other participants or situations.

Dependability

Much like the function of reliability in quantitative research, **dependability** refers to the consistency and the replicability of the results. This is often demonstrated by an **external auditor** examining and evaluating the research process and the accuracy of the results.

Confirmability

To achieve **confirmability**, the researcher must discuss how neutrality is maintained in the study, and how the results reflect those of the participants with no outside influence. This can be done by using triangulation, as well as:

1. Confirmability audits: This type of audit involves having a researcher not involved in the research project examine both the process and product of the study. This allows for an evaluation of the accuracy of the findings, interpretations, and conclusions based on the data collected.
2. Audit trail: This is a document created by researchers that provides a step-by-step account of the research study. The document helps researchers trace their activities in order to better understand the results of a study.
3. Reflexivity: This entails the researchers' continued awareness that any actions taken on their part may affect the outcomes of the study (i.e., they are conducting the study, as well as collecting and analyzing the data).

As you can surmise, it isn't possible, nor necessary, to use all of these approaches to ensure the trustworthiness of your work. You must choose the tools that work best for the type of study you are conducting. For example, when conducting ethnographies, you have to ensure you're in the research environment for an ample period of time in order to guarantee that you observe the total experience. This approach may not hold true for another type of study. Whatever your approach, when writing your proposal, try your best to convince your reader that you will do everything you can to collect, and report, your results in a valid manner.

Ethical Considerations

As we discussed in Chapter One, it's very important that we ensure we do no psychological or physical harm to anyone involved in our study. As we talked about then, you don't have to read very far into the literature in order to find the work of unscrupulous researchers: the Tuskegee studies, the Milgram studies, and others involving children and animals that are almost too much to believe. As noted, if your proposal involves work with animal or human subjects, you must have it approved by an IRB; its job is to ensure that your research is completely ethical. For example, in the project where we're interviewing young men and women who dropped out of college, one of the things that we have to recognize is that the very act of talking about their experience might traumatize some of the people we're working with. Because of that possibility, our review board insisted we acknowledge that, and inform potential participants prior to the start of our interviews. By doing that, we give the people we want to work with the opportunity to opt out of the study before it even begins. The bottom line is this: As trite as it sounds, let caution be your watchword. If you even suspect something might be unethical, you need to discuss it with your dissertation supervisor and IRB. The bottom line is that if you have any concerns about ethical issues, ensure you include them in your proposal.

Plans for Presenting the Results

This is straightforward. Simply tell your reader what the final product will look like. While yours will be a dissertation report that follows the guidelines of your school and dissertation supervisor, there are other general formats for qualitative studies. Among these you might find evaluative reports, journal articles, or conference presentations. Regardless of the type of presentation you're planning, there are usually explicit guidelines provided by the agency or organization where you will be presenting it.

Summary of Chapter 3 of Your Proposal

The summary of Chapter 3 of your proposal is what the name suggests—a recap of everything you've talked about in the chapter. The reader should be able to read the summary alone and get a good feeling for what the chapter is about.

SUMMARY OF CHAPTER SIX

As we saw in the prior chapter, quantitative data analysis is fairly straightforward: you state your hypothesis and ultimately use a specific test to test it. Qualitative research, on the other hand, is more open-ended. While you are basing your study on the research problem, and the research questions that drive its investigation, keep in mind that things might change. As we saw in the study where we worked with students who left school, sometimes our studies don't work out as planned. The key was that the researcher had to be open to change and willing to make changes, as necessary. I've always found that keeping your mind open, letting the data drive the process, and not getting frustrated when things seemingly go awry are the hallmarks of a good qualitative researcher.

Do You Understand These Key Words and Phrases?	
Autobiographical narrative	Content analysis
Axial codes	Credibility
Axiology	Data reduction
Biographical narrative	Data saturation
Bounded system	Dependability
Bracketing	Emic perspective
Case study research	Epistemology
Central phenomenon	*Epoché*
Confirmability	Ethnographic research

External auditors	Persistent observation
Field notes	Personal history stories
Grounded theory research	Phenomenological research
Intercase analysis	Prolonged engagement
Intracase analysis	Referential adequacy
Member checking	Thick description
Narrative research	Transferability
Negative case analysis	Triangulation
Open codes	Trustworthiness
Peer debriefers	Validation

REVIEW QUESTIONS

Just as we have in prior chapters, let's check our understanding of what we've covered in this chapter by answering the following questions as either true or false. In instances where the answer is false, explain why. You can find the answers at the end of the book.

1. ____ Validation in a qualitative study is primarily concerned with whether or not your interview guidelines cover the entire topic you want to discuss with the person being interviewed.

2. ____ Developing open and axial codes are part of the data reduction process.

3. ____ Having data saturation is the same principle as having an adequate sample size in quantitative research.

4. ____ Member checking includes returning transcripts of recorded sessions to those people interviewed in order to ensure what is written is what they said.

5. ____ Peer debriefers should be familiar with your work in order to provide you with the best insight and evaluation.

6. ____ Field notes are ideas or suggestions given to you by participants in an ethnographic study.

7. ____ A thick description is primarily concerned with the amount of detail provided in your report.

8. ____ A biography of George Washington would be considered a case study.

9. ____ Triangulation can include analysis of data from two sources, or comparison of the results from two different studies.

10. ____ If I were conducting a study by living with the Maoris, a tribe indigenous to New Zealand, it would require using an etic perspective.

11. ____ The central phenomenon can be considered the purpose of a study we want to conduct.

12. ____ The primary data collection tools in a qualitative study are the questions we use as part of an interview.

13. ____ Asking a group of adults to describe their feelings when they first learned that Neil Armstrong had walked on the moon would be an ethnographic study.

14. ____ External auditors should be used sparingly because they have a vested interest in the outcomes of your study.

✓ Progress Check for Chapter 3 of a Qualitative Dissertation Proposal

Earlier in the book, I presented Chapter 1 (the Introduction) and Chapter 2 (the Review of Literature) for a study involving an industrial waste dump. Since then, I've included an example of Chapter 3 for a quantitative study in Appendix C at the end of the book. At this point, I've rewritten the problem, purpose, and research questions and included an example of Chapter 3 for a qualitative study in Appendix D.

LET'S CONTINUE WRITING OUR OWN DISSERTATION PROPOSAL

Earlier in this book, I asked you to develop Chapters 1 and 2 for a quantitative proposal; you then wrote Chapter 3 based on that. In this case, change Chapter 1 to include a qualitative research question and then write Chapter 3 from a qualitative perspective. As I've said all along, after writing, put it aside and pick it up within a week or so; chances are you'll find places where you need to clear things up, expand the material, or simply clarify what you're trying to say. Getting used to addressing a problem from more than one perspective will add to your researcher skills set. Remember, the problem drives the process; we want to have all the tools we need for our investigation.

APPENDIX 6.1. Narrative Study Procedures: The Case of the Unfortunate Departure

Items from Chapter 1 of Your Proposal

Background, Problem, and Significance

Fulgencio Batista reigned as dictator in Cuba from 1952 until 1959. During that time he suspended most social and political rights of Cuba's citizens and further widened the socio-economic gap between rich and poor in the island nation. As the result of a guerilla war against the regime, culminating in the defeat of Batista's troops on January 1, 1959, Fidel Castro assumed power and ruled the communist island until illness forced him to delegate power to his younger brother in 2011.

Soon after Castro became president, rumors circulated that he would begin sending young Cuban children to work camps and military camps in the Soviet Union. Terrified Cuban parents, through a covert Central Intelligence Agency project, began sending their young children to live in foster homes or with friends and relatives in the United States. This effort, code-named *Operación Pedro Pan* (i.e., Operation Peter Pan), helped relocate over 14,000 Cuban youngsters to safety. While the stories of many of these youngsters live on by word of mouth within families, very few have been recorded to share with future generations.

Purpose Statement

The purpose of this study is to help us better understand the lived experience of an adult Cuban immigrant in the United States who entered the country via Operation Peter Pan as a child.

Research Question

What was your lived experience as a Cuban immigrant child before, during, and after your arrival in the United States?

Items from Chapter 3 of Your Proposal

The Qualitative Paradigm

In the proposed study, it is imperative that we establish fair, respectful, and trusting rapport between the researcher and the participants who immigrated to the United States as part of Operation Peter Pan. This relationship must exist knowing that the knowledge uncovered is contextual, with the researcher being respectful of varying viewpoints and the subjective truths that might arise from interactions with multiple participants. Research in this subject area calls for close interaction between the researcher and adults who immigrated to the United States as children via this program. The relationship between these factors calls for a qualitative approach in answering the research question.

The Research Design

Because the researcher wants to understand the lived experience of a person over a period of time, a narrative approach will be used.

Participants and Sampling

The researcher will apply for and receive approval from all institutions involved in the study. Children who participated in the program would now be in their 50s and 60s—however, the exact number of surviving adults who participated in Operation Peter Pan living in the United States is unknown. A recently established Miami-based group, Operation Pedro Pan, focuses on identifying and reuniting as many of these former immigrants as possible. This group would be used to help identify potential participants for the study by posting a notice on their website. Only respondents currently old enough to remember the events of the time would be included in the sample frame, with only one individual purposively selected to participate. Issues that pertain to the study will be discussed with the potential participant (e.g., privacy, emotions related to reliving the event, the right to terminate the session at any time). In the event that the person first identified decides not to participate, another individual will be purposively selected.

Instruments

No specific instrument will be used. Data will be collected via interviews focusing on the study's research question.

The Research Procedures

After sampling is concluded and a suitable subject is recruited, the researcher will establish a mutually agreeable time and place to conduct the first interview (e.g., in person, by phone call, via online chat). The participant will be reminded that the interview is being recorded and will begin with the overarching research question:

> *What was your lived experience as a Cuban immigrant child before, during, and after your arrival in the United States?*

Respondents will reply extemporaneously, with the researcher posing follow-up or probing questions as needed. These interviews will continue until the interviewee and the researcher mutually agree that the story of the departure from Cuba and a new life in the United States has been completely covered. The researcher will then transcribe and analyze the data, upon which the final narrative will be written.

Plans for Data Analysis

After transcription, the researcher will read the data while listening to the recordings in order to ensure accuracy. Notes will be taken in an effort to identify the beginning, middle, and end of the story; further evaluation will attempt to identify transitions, minor stories, emotional statements, and so on, thereby allowing for connection between one stage and the next. Thematic coding will allow for further development of the overall analysis, thereby allowing for a logical "restorying" of the entire event. Additional reference material may be added in order to develop a full explanation and understanding of the adult's experience during his or her immigration to the United States as a child.

Upon completion of the story, the draft will be returned to the interviewee. That person will be asked to verify that all facts, dates, and so on are accurately portrayed. In the event that there are discrepancies, the draft will be modified.

Ethical Considerations

Participants must agree to, and sign a form indicating, informed consent. As noted, participants must be advised of their rights to privacy, as well as the potential for emotional issues arising from their retelling of their story.

Plan for Presenting the Results

The narrative will be included in the dissertation report and provided to the participant and members of Operation Peter Pan, and will be published or presented in suitable venues.

Summary

This study is designed to help us better understand the lived experience of an adult who as a child emigrated from Cuba to the United States during Operation Peter Pan. After recruitment of a suitable participant, the researcher will conduct and transcribe interviews. At completion, a narrative based on the experience will be written.

APPENDIX 6.2. Phenomenological Study Procedures: The Case of Parting from One's Children for Their Safety

The narrative study shown in Appendix 6.1 focused on one individual who left Cuba at an early age, and covered his or her life's story to date. In a phenomenological approach, we use the same story but broaden the research group to the parents involved, and narrow the (time) focus to the event in which the parents sent their child to safety.

Items from Chapter 1 of Your Proposal

Background, Problem, and Significance

Fulgencio Batista reigned as a dictator in Cuba from 1952 until 1959. During that time he suspended most social and political rights of Cuban citizens and further widened the socio-economic gap between rich and poor in the island nation. As the result of a guerilla war fought against the regime, culminating in the defeat of Batista's troops on January 1, 1959, Fidel Castro assumed power and ruled the communist island until poor health led him to take a background role in the government.

Soon after Castro became president, rumors circulated that he would begin sending young Cuban children to work camps and military camps in the Soviet Union. Terrified Cuban parents, through a covert Central Intelligence Agency project, began sending their young children to live in foster homes or with friends and relatives in the United States. This effort, code-named *Operación Pedro Pan* (i.e., Operation Peter Pan), helped relocate over 14,000 Cuban youngsters to safety. While there are many oral stories surrounding this event, little is known about the parents and how they dealt with sending their children to a foreign country, with a real chance of never seeing them again.

Central Purpose

The purpose of this study is to better understand the lived experience of parents at the time they sent their children to the United States during Operation Peter Pan.

Research Question

What was your experience as a parent, sending your child out of Cuba?

Items from Chapter 3 of Your Proposal

The Qualitative Paradigm

In the proposed study, it is imperative that we establish fair, respectful, and trusting rapport between the researcher and the parents whose children immigrated to the United States as part of Operation Peter Pan. This relationship must exist knowing that the knowledge uncovered is contextual, with the researcher being respectful of varying viewpoints and the subjective truths that might arise from interactions with multiple participants. Research in this subject area calls for close interaction between the researcher and adults who sent their child from Cuba during this program. The relationship between these factors calls for a qualitative approach in answering the research question.

The Research Design

Because we want to understand the lived experiences of a group of people at a specific period of time, we will use a phenomenological approach.

Participants and Sampling

The researcher must first apply for and receive approval from all IRBs necessary. Only then will work with an agency to identify potential participants in the study begin. Parents who sent their children from Cuba soon after Castro's ascendance will now be in their late 70s and 80s—however, the exact number of surviving adults living in the United States is unknown. Operation Peter Pan is a Miami-based group focused on identifying and reuniting as many of these former immigrants as possible. Their group will be used to help identify potential participants for the study by posting a notice on their website and by using word of mouth. Respondents will be identified from one of two groups: first, the children of the parents needed for the study may be able to identify and notify their parents, or the parents themselves may volunteer after hearing about or seeing the notice. After the parents electing to participate in the study are screened for any physical or mental issues that might preclude their participation, a random group of 12–15 will be selected for the study. Issues that pertain to the study will be discussed (e.g., privacy, emotions related to reliving the event, the right to terminate the session at any time); in the event that any person identified decides not to participate, another individual will be randomly selected.

Instruments

No specific instrument will be used. Data will be collected via interviews focusing on the study's research question.

The Research Procedures

After a suitable sample is recruited, the researcher will establish a mutually agreeable time and place with each participant to conduct the first interviews (e.g., in person, by phone call, via online chat). The participant will be reminded that the interview is being recorded and will begin with the overarching research question:

> What was your experience, as a parent, sending your child out of Cuba?

Respondents will be allowed to respond extemporaneously, with the researcher adding follow-up or probing questions as needed. The interview will be recorded.

Plans for Data Analysis

After transcription, the researcher will read the data while listening to the recordings in order to ensure accuracy. Following that step, the researcher will analyze the data for common themes that relate directly to the overarching question. The goal of the researcher is to identify common themes within the data and write the story from them. Notes will be taken in an effort to identify the beginning, middle, and end of the story; further evaluation will attempt to identify transitions, substories, emotional statements, and so on, thereby allowing for connection between one stage and the next. Thematic coding will allow for further development of the overall analysis, thereby allowing for a logical "restorying" of the entire event. Additional reference material may be added in order to develop a full explanation and understanding of the child's past experience during his or her immigration to the United States. The initial draft will be returned to the interviewees; they will be asked to verify that all facts, dates, and the like are accurately portrayed. In the event there are discrepancies, the draft will be modified.

Ethical Considerations

Participants must agree to, and sign a document, indicating informed consent. As noted, participants must be advised of their rights to privacy, as well as the potential for emotional issues arising from their retelling of their stories.

Plan for Presenting the Results

The results of the investigation will be included in the dissertation report and a resultant paper will be provided to members of the study and interested parties at Operation Peter Pan. It may be submitted to appropriate conferences and journals focusing on issues related to the subject.

Summary

This study is designed to better understand the lived experience of adults who sent their child from Cuba to the United States during Operation Peter Pan. After recruitment of a suitable sample, the researcher will conduct and transcribe interviews with the selected individuals. Once the data have been analyzed, a phenomenological report, based on the participants' experiences, will be written.

APPENDIX 6.3. Ethnographic Study Procedures: The Case of Climbing the Mountain

Items from Chapter 1 of Your Proposal

Background, Problem, and Significance

Mt. Rainier, in Washington State, is the highest mountain in the continental United States. Over 1.5 million people annually visit the national park surrounding it, with about 10,000 people attempting to reach the 14,411-foot summit. Unfortunately, for many reasons, only about 60% of the climbers actually reach the peak. For those who don't make it, problems such as altitude sickness, the incredible strength and endurance the climb takes, and dangerous changes in weather conditions have all contributed to climbers having to turn back. Even though many experienced climbers attempt to reach the summit with their own unaccompanied group, history shows that groups that hire professional climbing guides have a much higher rate of success. While much is written about climbers, both successful and unsuccessful, little has been written about the rather small community of climbing guide professionals. An understanding of their experiences and lifestyle may provide insight that helps prepare future climbers in their efforts to reach the summit of Mt. Rainier.

Purpose Statement

The purpose of this study is to understand the lifestyle and experiences of professional climbing guides at Mt. Rainier.

The Research Question

What is the lifestyle and lived experiences of climbing guides on Mt. Rainier?

Items from Chapter 3 of Your Proposal

The Qualitative Paradigm

In the proposed study, it is imperative that we establish fair, respectful, and trusting rapport between the researcher and the climbing guides on Mt. Rainier. This relationship must exist because what will be uncovered is contextual. The researcher needs to be respectful of varying viewpoints and the subjective truths that might arise from interactions with multiple participants. Research in this subject area calls for close interaction between the researcher and the guides who will be interviewed. The relationship between these factors calls for a qualitative approach in answering the research question.

The Research Design

Because we want to immerse ourselves in and understand the lived experiences of a group of professional climbing guides, we will use an ethnographic approach.

Participants and Sampling

Due to interaction with human participants, the researcher will apply for and receive permission from the IRB prior to commencing the study. A population of professional climbing guides working on Mt. Rainier will be identified by contacting businesses that advertise and provide guide services to park visitors. The researcher will then purposively contact and ask individual guides for their cooperation in the project. Guides agreeing to participate will be made aware of their role and responsibilities in the study, and the option to leave the study at their discretion.

Instruments

No specific instrument will be used. Data will be collected via informal discussions and observations while working and living with the climbing guides. It is possible that additional information may be included from appropriate published sources, as well as from other persons participating in a particular climb.

The Research Procedures

Data will be collected during a series of guided climbs. The researcher has a climbing background, so climbing and living with the guides should not prove to be problematic. The study will cover five planned climbs over a period of approximately 1 month (i.e., five 4-day climbs with 3 days of rest between each climb). The researcher will participate in all five climbs, live with two of the guides during the rest period, and attend any social gatherings of the guides during the rest period. During the course of the study, information from conversations, as well as actual events occurring during the climb, may be audio or video recorded.

Plans for Data Analysis

At the outset of data analysis, field notes will be reviewed, and transcribed interview transcripts will be compared to the actual recordings. Analysis will continue by searching for patterns or themes within the transcribed interviews, as well as within video and audio recordings, to investigate ways in which the themes or patterns are interconnected; this will allow for an understanding of the climbing lifestyle from the insider's perspective.

From this, an initial draft of the ethnography will be developed and triangulated with other related resources (e.g., books written by climbers, press and magazine reports detailing events occurring on the mountain, interviews with other climbers). These initial drafts will be given to the climbing guides, and they will be asked whether the draft accurately reflects their lifestyle, and whether deletions or additions should be made. In the event there are discrepancies, the draft will be modified. Following all modifications, the final ethnography will be written.

Ethical Considerations

Participants must agree to and sign a document indicating informed consent. As noted, participants must be advised of their right to privacy, as well as the potential for emotional issues arising from recounting stories based on previous climbs.

Plan for Presenting the Results

The ethnography will be included in the dissertation report and submitted for publication in the public press, as well as shared at conferences or with interested outside parties.

Summary

This study is designed to help better understand the lived experiences of professional mountain climbing guides on Mt. Rainier. The researcher will participate in five guided climbs, as well as live with climbing professionals during rest periods between climbs. The researcher will keep field notes, as well as audio and video recordings of experiences during and between climbs. Following transcription and data analysis, an ethnographic report will be written and submitted to interested parties.

APPENDIX 6.4. Case Study Procedures:
The Case of the Standardized Test

Items from Chapter 1 of Your Proposal

Background, Problem, and Significance

Government-mandated standardized testing for children in grades 6–12 is a contentious topic for residents in many states. Many parents and teachers believe that focusing on "teaching to the test" takes away from the true educational experience. Proponents of testing feel that the results allow for measuring students against prescribed standards, thereby addressing student achievement problems as quickly as possible. In reviewing statewide scores, a state superintendent of education noted that one school district had standardized test scores that were consistently higher than those of other districts of its size and demographic makeup. Because of that finding, the superintendent felt that there are lessons to be learned from that district. This could be of value to administrators and teachers in other districts.

Purpose Statement

The purpose of this study is to determine reasons why test scores for one district are consistently higher than those in other districts with similar demographic characteristics.

Research Question

What are the factors in the school district that lead to consistently higher standardized test scores?

Items from Chapter 3 of Your Proposal

The Qualitative Paradigm

In the proposed study, it is imperative that we establish fair, respectful, and trusting rapport between the researcher and the administrators and teachers within the school district. This relationship must exist, with the researcher knowing that the knowledge uncovered is contextual, and with the researcher being respectful of varying viewpoints and the subjective truths that might arise from interactions with multiple participants. Research in this subject area calls for close interaction between the researcher and administration, employees, parents, and students within the school district. The relationship between these factors calls for a qualitative case study approach to answering the research question.

The Research Design

Because we want to investigate one problem in a bounded environment, we will use a case study approach.

Instruments

Semistructured interviews focusing on the overarching research question will be used to collect data from all participants.

Participants and Sampling

Data may come from administrators and teachers, as well as from parents and students as needed, within the school district. Data may also be collected from policies, procedures, or other ancillary published material. Because we are working with human participants, approval from an IRB must be applied for and received prior to any interaction with participants in the study. As noted, initial data collection will begin with published historical documents from both the state and local levels.

The Research Procedures

In this case study, the researcher will investigate perceived causes of success by schools within the district. Keeping in mind that many factors contribute to success, the researcher will review all available historical information prior to the start of the study. Following that, the researcher will use published approaches (e.g., Stake's countenance model) to collect data from administrators, teachers, and students, as needed. Observations and interviews at both the district and the school level will be recorded for transcription, and visits into an actual learning environment may be documented with field notes. Using the data from all sources, the researcher will evaluate and report on the district's practices.

Plans for Data Analysis

Field notes will be reviewed, and data verified, by listening to recordings while reading transcribed interviews. The data analysis is descriptive in nature and based directly on published sources and input from the participants in the study. Concise descriptive, factual data from interviews, observations, and district documentation will be used to present the background of the school system and its success. Standard evaluation procedures (e.g., Stake's countenance model) will be used to describe reasons for consistently high scores on the standardized tests. The completed case study will be reviewed by administrators and teachers to ensure the accuracy of events, material gathered, and any personal quotes. The results may be triangulated with reports from other high-achieving districts with similar ethnographic characteristics.

Ethical Considerations

Participants must agree to and sign a document indicating informed consent. As noted, participants must be advised of their rights to privacy, as well as their right to withdraw from the study at their own request.

Plan for Presenting the Results

The results of the case study will be included in the dissertation report and presented to administrators at the state and local level. The results will include perceived indicators of success, or best practices, in the school district, as well as suggestions by the participants to raise future achievement. The report will conclude with a summarization of the study, as well as conclusions that were drawn from it.

Summary

This case study is designed to help ascertain reasons that students in the school district being investigated consistently score higher on standardized tests than students from surrounding school districts. Interviews with students, parents, teachers, and administrators, as well as direct observations and information from published and external resources, will be used to better understand the district's educational practices. Information from all sources will be analyzed and presented as a set of best practices for consideration by administrators in other districts.

APPENDIX 6.5. Grounded Theory Procedures: The Case of Homelessness

Items from Chapter 1 of Your Proposal

Background, Problem, and Significance

Since the early 1980s, the population of New York City has grown from approximately 7.1 million to slightly over 8.8 million (i.e., approximately 13%). At the same time, the average number of persons staying in homeless shelters each night in the city has increased by well over 500% (i.e., from approximately 15,000 to over 80,000). Historically, persons staying in shelters were single males but, unfortunately, in the last 30 years the number of females living in homeless shelters has grown at a faster rate than that of the overall population. Many experts are interested in gaining a better understanding of the circumstances leading to the precipitous growth rate in this female population.

Purpose Statement

The purpose of this study is to ascertain the reasons for the dramatic increase in the number of females staying in homeless shelters in New York City.

Research Question

What are the reasons that females give for living in homeless shelters in New York City?

Items from Chapter 3 of Your Proposal

The Qualitative Paradigm

In the proposed study, it is imperative that we establish fair, respectful, and trusting rapport between the researcher and females living in the homeless shelters. This relationship must exist knowing that the knowledge uncovered is contextual, with the researcher being respectful of varying viewpoints and the subjective truths that might arise from interactions with multiple participants. Research in this subject area calls for close interaction between the researcher and the females in these shelters. The relationship between these factors calls for a qualitative approach to answering the research question.

The Research Design

Because we want to develop a theory or approach to understand circumstances leading to females choosing or being forced to live in homeless shelters, a grounded theory method will be used.

Participants and Sampling

Data will be collected from females living in a homeless shelter in New York City. In this type of study, at least 12–15 participants will be required. Prior to any interaction with human participants, the researcher must apply for and receive IRB approval. Following that approval, a purposive sample of females from the shelter will be identified and interviewed.

Instruments

Data will be collected from females living in a homeless shelter using semistructured interviews focusing on the question "What are the circumstances that led you to live in this shelter?" These data may be supplemented with information from other published resources.

The Research Procedures

Prior to the start of the study, the researcher will familiarize themself with the history and current status of homelessness in the United States, and particularly New York City, by reading available literature related to the subject. Following selection into the sample, participants will be asked to sign an informed consent agreement noting that their participation is voluntary, that their interviews will be recorded, and that they will not be identified by name in reports written from the interviews. The interviewee will be further assured that participation in the interviews will not, in any manner, interfere with, or interrupt, the government services they are receiving. The interviewee will then be asked to agree to a convenient time and place for the interview; all sessions will be recorded for future transcription and analysis.

Plans for Data Analysis

Verification will begin by spending ample time interviewing; this allows for the development of a thick description upon which the theory can be developed. These interviews will be verified by comparing transcripts to the recorded sessions for accuracy. The data will be analyzed using a constant comparative approach. Interview transcripts will be coded for like ideas, thoughts, or statements (i.e., open codes); these will then be further analyzed by combining like themes, represented by open codes, into axial codes. One axial code will be chosen as the selective code upon which the resultant theory will be developed. The final report will be shown to the participants (i.e., member checking) to ensure it represents their input. Finally, a peer debriefer will review the report to determine the clarity, accuracy, and consistency of the work.

Ethical Considerations

Participants must agree to and sign a document indicating their informed consent. As noted, participants must be advised of their rights to privacy and that participation in the interviews will, in no way, negatively affect their housing situation.

Plan for Presenting the Results

The results of the grounded theory will be included in the dissertation report and published in journals focusing on societal issues.

Summary

This study is designed to better understand the characteristics of females living in homeless shelters in New York City, as well as to gain a better understanding of the circumstances that led them to living in the shelter. Interviews with females in the shelters will focus on their backgrounds and their personal circumstances that led them to live in the shelters. The data will be analyzed, and a grounded theory developed, focusing on gaining a better understanding of this growing population.

APPENDIX 6.6. Content Analysis Procedures:
The Case of the Eyewitnesses

Items from Chapter 1 of Your Proposal

Background, Problem, and Significance

In the last decade, students have witnessed over 400 instances of gun violence in schools. These have ranged from the major tragedy at Robb Elementary School to cases in which a firearm was used during an at-school altercation resulting in only minor injuries. When these events occur, there is an outpouring of citizens' concerns—in many instances focused on the ready availability of firearms for purchase in the United States. Many argue that increasing gun control in the United States, especially as it relates to children at school, is called for; others express their constitutional rights to legally obtain and carry firearms. Many voters have asked members of Congress to pass legislation to address this problem, but to no avail.

Purpose Statement

The purpose of this study is to analyze newspaper accounts of these violent incidents while focusing on members of Congress's recommendations for addressing the problem.

Research Question

Are there common recommendations made by members of Congress to address instances of gun violence in U.S. schools?

Items from Chapter 3 of Your Proposal

The Qualitative Paradigm

This research calls for the unobtrusive collection and analysis of newspaper articles reporting incidences of gun violence and members of Congress's suggestion on how these problems may be addressed. The researcher must realize that facts reported in a given reporter's statement are contextual, and must be respectful of varying viewpoints and the subjective truths. This research is unobtrusive in that it does not call for interaction between the researcher and the members of Congress. The relationship between these factors calls for content analysis in order to answer the research question.

The Research Design

Because we are investigating published reports of politicians' comments with no direct interaction between the researcher and a member of Congress, we use content analysis to answer the research question.

Instruments

No formal instruments are required for this study. The research will be focused on the analysis of published newspaper reports.

Participants and Sampling

Newspapers from four major metropolitan areas within the United States will be randomly chosen, with data purposively collected on articles covering the past five instances of gun violence in the schools.

The Research Procedures and Plans for Data Analysis

In this content analysis, the researcher will contextually analyze the newspaper articles by thoroughly reading each, while marking words or phrases that a member of Congress used to address actions that could possibly be taken to redress problems of this type. It is anticipated that specific terms and actions to be taken will be easily identifiable but may not be consistent between articles, even when they are reporting on a specific member of Congress. Upon completion of the analysis, the results will be quantified by counting the number of references in a transcript to a particular action or description. This will continue until all transcripts have been read and coded. An overall summation of the occurrence of specific words, phrases, and observations should result in identifiable recommendations common to the members of Congress identified in the study.

Ethical Considerations

Due to the use of printed historical newspaper articles, there are no ethical considerations other than the truthful analysis and reporting of the actual text of the articles used.

Plan for Presenting the Results

The results of the content analysis will be presented to interested parties, including members of Congress, media outlets, and individual citizens. The results will include a presentation of areas of consistency between the articles, as well as statements mentioned less frequently but that might be considered of interest to readers. The report will conclude with a summarization of the study, as well as conclusions drawn from it.

Summary

This content analysis is designed to help better understand the reaction of politicians to acts of school violence involving firearms. Articles from purposively selected newspapers from across the country will be read, and words, phrases, or statements used by each member of Congress will be marked. The results will be quantified by totaling the number of consistent statements or observations within each of the transcripts; an overall summation should result in the development of themes with a report written for interested politicians, media outlets, and individual citizens.

CHAPTER SEVEN

Mixed Methods Research Designs

Introduction

As I mentioned earlier, it is not too long ago that most researchers fell into one of two camps: quantitative or qualitative. Researchers on both sides were adamant that the differences between the two approaches were so significant that there would never be a need for them to merge. In a very real way, it reminds me of Rudyard Kipling (1940, p. 233) when he wrote, "Oh, East is East, and West is West, and never the twain shall meet."

Fortunately, in the late 1980s and early 1990s, researchers began to call for a truce and an end to the "paradigm" wars, with the idea that no major problem area can be studied exclusively with one research method alone (e.g., Bazely, 2004; Creswell, 2014; Creswell & Plano Clark, 2017; Johnson & Onwuegbuzie, 2004; Morse & Niehaur, 2009). Of the many authors writing about mixed methods research, Tashakkori and Teddlie (2003) perhaps described it best in calling for the use of whatever philosophical or methodological approach that works in a particular research study. In short, researchers began embracing the idea of "the right tool for the job."

As for me, I took 10 or 12 classes focusing specifically on quantitative methods; a qualitative class was an option, but one that I, and most of my peers, chose not to take. Unfortunately, that decision came back to haunt me as I finished my dissertation. As I discussed earlier in the book, I was interested in elementary school student motivation and measured it using a commonly available quantitative scale. To my surprise, after working with young students for over a year, I found my interventions had not worked; there was no significant difference in their level of motivation between the start and end of the school year. This meant I had to go back to the children and teachers I worked with during the year to interview them and attempt to understand why my intervention didn't go as planned. Because of that, two things happened.

First, I had to learn to do fundamental qualitative analysis to use the interview data to explain what went wrong. Second, although I didn't realize it at the time, I was conducting a mixed methods study; I just didn't know that's what it was called. That the project was ultimately successful led me to appreciate both qualitative and quantitative research and the idea of using them together in a single research study. Now, after 20 years and a lot of postdoctoral work in qualitative research, I think I'm finally getting the hang of it.

An Overview of Mixed Methods Research

Given the different characteristics of the quantitative and qualitative methodologies, it stands to reason that the combination of the two will result in another unique set of features. Because of that reality, as we move forward, we'll discuss new ways of writing problem statements, research questions, and hypotheses. As usual, we will then be at our "methodological point of departure" and will be able to select the appropriate mixed method approach for our study. Before we move forward, however, there are a few basic concepts we need to cover.

First, many people think that any study in which quantitative and qualitative data are collected is a mixed methods study; this isn't necessarily true. In some cases, it just means we're conducting two studies simultaneously. For example, I could conduct an opinion poll of local school parents by asking them to comment on the characteristics they looked for as they started a search for a new superintendent (i.e., qualitative data). Within the same opinion poll, I could provide them with a list of possible school starting times and ask them to rank them according to their preference (i.e., quantitative data). Although my poll would be asking for responses requiring both types of data, it's not a mixed methods study. Simply put, one set of data is not being used to complement or explain the other by merging or connecting the two (Johnson & Onwuegbuzie, 2004).

Second, mixed methods studies can be considered simultaneous when both quantitative and qualitative data are collected simultaneously, or can be regarded as sequential, where one type of data is collected after the other (Creswell, 2014). These are not part of a larger quantitative study, where multiple variables are observed, manipulated, and measured (e.g., experimental research), nor are they a standard qualitative model (e.g., a case study or grounded theory). Mixed methods studies are just that, an approach to answering research questions that require data collection and analysis of the type called for in a given study.

Even though, as a research method, mixed methods approaches are different from qualitative and quantitative approaches, many of the same tools still apply. For example, if you're collecting quantitative data, your sampling procedures must adhere to the rules and guidelines for studies of that type. Although we talk about it in much greater detail later in the chapter, ideas such as using a small purposive sample for qualitative research and needing a large sample for quantitative research still hold true (Teddlie & Yu, 2007).

Finally, while they are separate methodologies, in order to conduct a good mixed methods study, you should be very familiar with the components of both qualitative and quantitative research methods. In addition to the commonality of tools, the same philosophical underpinnings still apply; the paradigm you choose will be based on your axiology, ontology, and epistemology.

To summarize all of this, before you consider conducting a mixed methods study, ensure that (Bazely, 2004; Terrell, 2012):

1. You have a good overarching knowledge of quantitative and qualitative research.
2. You understand the assumptions underlying each research method.
3. You have a good working knowledge of the analytic procedures and tools related to quantitative and qualitative research.
4. You have the ability to understand and interpret results from the quantitative and qualitative methods.
5. You are willing to accept and forgo methodological prejudices from training in a prior discipline.
6. You understand the different disciplines, audiences, and appropriate studies where mixed methods are acceptable.

Keeping those things in mind, let's start by looking at the format of a mixed methods proposal. Although it will include components of both quantitative and qualitative proposals, we have to expand and modify things just a bit.

The Format of a Mixed Methods Proposal

As we've seen with the qualitative and quantitative approaches, a good dissertation proposal has a format we must follow. Although we saw slight differences in those two approaches, for the most part they are very similar. The same holds true for a mixed methods study, but because it represents both a quantitative and qualitative approach, there are sections that have to be expanded or modified due to the collection of two types of data. To get a good idea of where we're going, let's use the same three-chapter model we used in the previous chapter, add material from the quantitative approaches we discussed earlier in the book, and include Creswell's (2014) suggestions for material specific to mixed methods studies (see Table 7.1). Much of the proposal outline below is the same as those for quantitative and qualitative studies (e.g., Definitions of Terms, Assumptions, Limitations), so let's focus on what is different.

Chapter 1 of a Mixed Methods Dissertation Proposal: The Introduction

In Chapter One of this book, we talked in great detail about the six characteristics of a good problem statement. We agreed that you must have the knowledge, time, and resources to investigate the problem and that it's only a valid problem if you are

TABLE 7.1. Outline for a Mixed Methods Proposal

Chapter 1: Introduction

- Background
- Statement of the Problem
- Significance of the Study
- Purpose of the Study (i.e., the Central Purpose)
- Research Questions
  - Qualitative Questions
  - Quantitative Questions
  - Mixed Methods Questions
- Hypotheses
- Definitions of Terms
- Assumptions
- Limitations
- Delimitations
- Conclusion

Chapter 2: Review of the Literature

At this point, both of the previously discussed approaches to writing the ROL must be considered. The quantitative aspect of the study may be theory driven, while the qualitative aspect may call for the addition of literature during or after data collection.

Chapter 3: Research Methods

- The Mixed Methods Paradigm
- Research Design
- Participants and Sampling
- Instruments
- Research Procedures
- Plans for Data Analysis
  - Qualitative
  - Quantitative
  - Merging (i.e., Mixing)
- Ethical Considerations
- Plans for Presenting the Results
- Summary

interested, and the scope of the problem is manageable. You must be able to collect and analyze data, your study must have theoretical or practical significance, and conducting it must be carried out ethically. If your problem statement doesn't meet all of these criteria, you probably shouldn't spend time trying to investigate it.

As you saw, in each of the problem statements we talked about for quantitative and qualitative studies, we ensured that these characteristics were met. We'll need to do the same thing for mixed methods studies, but for that kind of study, we add a seventh characteristic:

7. Your problem statement must call for collecting, analyzing, and synthesizing both qualitative and quantitative data to answer your research questions and test your hypotheses.

This goal might seem obvious, but it goes back to the earlier statement: just because you collect both quantitative and qualitative data doesn't necessarily make your study a mixed methods study unless one set of data is being used to complement or explain the other by merging or connecting the two.

Background, Statement of the Problem, and Significance of the Study

In a mixed methods study, you need to show that you're writing your problem statement within the framework of a gap in the literature. For example, let's look at the key parts of a problem statement that we defined earlier, the background of the problem, the actual problem, and the significance of the problem. Writing a problem statement in that manner is relatively straightforward. To add the material needed, we need to modify the actual problem and its significance just a bit. We can understand this better by using ideas from the dissertation of one of my students (Bronstein, 2007). In her study, although it was conducted as a qualitative study, she wanted to develop an evaluation checklist and then determine whether it worked as a teaching tool. Despite that, we can modify it slightly for our use. Following is a brief overview of her problem statement:

1. Background: There are many different ways to evaluate Internet websites and many tools that have been used to evaluate them.
2. Problem: There is no tool or checklist explicitly designed for high school students that will teach them to evaluate the Internet as part of the overall instructional process. An instructional tool of this type should be developed and validated to determine its efficacy in the classroom.
3. Significance: The development of such a tool will assist students in learning an overall evaluative approach and in developing a checklist that can be used outside of the classroom.

By looking at this proposal, you can immediately see the existing gap in the literature; while tools do exist to evaluate websites, none have been specifically aimed at teaching secondary students to evaluate websites using a checklist. To develop the checklist, we would need to collect data from existing literature and evaluation experts (i.e., qualitative data). We could then develop and validate a checklist for our students to evaluate websites (i.e., quantitative data). As we did earlier, we'll use fictitious references to the literature to develop a problem statement for our use:

> Studies (Bridgewater, 2010; Jones, 2011; Smith, 2012) have demonstrated a multitude of ways in which the content and presentation of material on an Internet website can be evaluated. To date, no evaluative tool has been developed specifically for secondary students to be used as part of the instructional process. Research of this type is called for (Johnson, 2013; Miller, 2013), with the intention of developing an instrument that can be used as a teaching tool, as well as for evaluation outside of the classroom environment.

As you can see, all of the criteria for a mixed methods problem statement have been met; there is a valid background to the problem, and the problem and investigating its significance is well stated. Most important for this discussion is that both types of data are called for to address the overall purpose of the study.

Another of my students (Howles, 2007), a computer science professor, was interested in looking at the effect of learning communities on attrition from beginning computer programming courses. Prior to her investigation, there were a multitude of studies investigating the relationship between student connectivity and achievement, but none had focused specifically on its effect on computer science students. Again, let's modify her problem statement just a bit to meet the criteria for a mixed methods study:

> *Student-to-student interaction in online communities of practice (COPs)*
> *can lead to higher achievement and lower attrition in college-level science-*
> *oriented coursework (Caulfield, 2012; Knox, 2011). Despite its success,*
> *there is a lack of literature examining the effect of COPs in computer science*
> *and technology curriculums. These same researchers, and others (e.g., Ellis,*
> *2013; Lieber, 2013), have called for expanding the investigation of COPs*
> *into fields not yet investigated; it is their belief that research of this type can*
> *lead to higher levels of success in those fields.*

You can see that our criteria have been met; there is sufficient background and there is an apparent problem calling for new research in this area. My student investigated the problem by looking at the interaction of connectivity, based on interaction in the COPs (i.e., qualitative data) and achievement (i.e., quantitative data). The significance of her research is obvious.

Purpose Statement

At this point, we've told the reader the problem we're investigating, its background, and why our research is significant. Now it's time to explain the purpose of our study. We need to define what we want to do, and we want to make it clear to the reader why both types of data are required to investigate our problem area. Creswell (2014) points out that due to the broader nature of mixed methods research, purpose statements are likely to be lengthier than the purpose statements we've written up to this point. He further contends that a good purpose statement for a mixed methods study comprises four parts: the intent of the study, the design of the study, the data we need to answer our research questions or test our hypotheses, and the rationale behind what we propose to do. Let's start with an example from an investigation in which I am currently involved.

As you might know, quite a few South Florida residents are retirees who have moved here from northern states to get away from the snow, sleet, and otherwise miserable weather they experienced for most of their lives. After relocating, many of these former "snowbirds" live in retirement communities with others of their same age, who have similar interests and similar lifestyles. Many of these new residents will tell you it's the best time of their life; in fact, many of them may be celebrating too much! Here's what I mean (keep in mind, the facts are true but, to keep from cluttering up our reference list, the references are fictitious):

> Despite efforts by governmental agencies and medical professionals, the rate of sexually transmitted diseases (STDs) has increased throughout recent years. Nowhere is this growth more prevalent than in persons over 55 (Rigolo, 2018). Between 2015 and 2020, the overall rate of STDs grew 25%, with some communities experiencing an increase of nearly 90%. This has led to an increased demand for medical services, issues of public health, and the overall well-being of citizens affected by the STDs. To date, there have been countless studies on the causes and growth rate of these diseases (e.g., McEwen, 2009; Nunnelly, 2021; Pinkerton, 2022), but there has been no research uncovered focusing specifically on adults older than 55.

From this problem, I can easily develop a focused purpose statement. Let's see whether Creswell's (2014) criteria have been met:

1. The intent of the study is to better understand the reasons for the rise in STD cases among senior citizens.
2. The study will use a mixed method for answering research questions and testing hypotheses.
3. Data will include information from interviews (i.e., qualitative data), the health department, and surveys (i.e., quantitative data).
4. The rationale is the development of prevention programs designed to help seniors maintain a healthy lifestyle.

In this case, we have met the criteria indicating that we have a sound central purpose statement. In the next example, while we'll discuss particular mixed methods designs later in the chapter, we use one of them simply to show how it will fit into the purpose statement. This time we're interested in investigating the efficacy of a weight loss program. In our study, we monitor the results of one specific weight loss program. At the end of the study, we'll interview our participants to try to find out what worked and what did not work, in their effort to lose weight. Let's start with this problem statement. Again, rather than fill the reference list with material other than what you need, I've included fictitious references:

> *Problems related to weight gain (e.g., diabetes, coronary disease) have risen sharply in the past two decades (e.g., Dunn, 2012; Frank, 2005; Hester, 2011; Pfahl, 2018). While battling weight gain is important to many people, research has shown that participation in organized weight loss programs is not as effective as was once thought (Carise, 2014; Putnam, 2012). An investigation of factors contributing to success in these programs could lead participants to healthier lifestyles and fewer medical programs.*

The background and significance of the problem is clear, and to investigate it, we need to collect quantitative weight data, as well as qualitative data from interviews with people participating in the program. This allows us to state a valid purpose statement:

The intent of this study is to determine if and how participants were
successful in a weight loss program. A sequential–explanatory design will
be used to collect the amount of weight lost or gained by each participant,
as well as interview data describing each person's individual experience. It
is hoped that the results of the study will help in the creation of a set of best
practices designed to help a person in his or her effort to lose weight.

The intent of this purpose statement is clear: The researchers want to investigate a given weight loss program to determine a participant's level of success, as well as their personal experiences. A sequential–explanatory design will collect weight and interview data from the individual participants. The rationale of the study is obvious: The researchers want to better understand the specific ways by which participants were successful or unsuccessful in their efforts.

Research Questions

Based on our purpose statements, it should be fairly easy to state research questions for each scenario. At the same time, because we're collecting both types of data, we need to expand our effort by also developing a mixed methods research question. To understand the big picture, we need to state a research question focused on the quantitative data, another one specifically for the qualitative data, and finally, a research question investigating the interaction of both types of data (Johnson & Onwuegbuzie, 2004). For instance, with the first example, our quantitative research question might read:

What is the rate of STDs in the population being investigated?

In this case, per our purpose statement, we would collect numeric data from the health department and directly from the participants. Given that our ultimate goal would be to better understand the reasons for the increase in diseases of this type, our qualitative research question for our participants could be:

What are the causes of the increased rate of STDs in persons over the
age of 55?

Asking this question would leave plenty of room in an interview to ask follow-up questions regarding participants' knowledge of STDs, their level of sexual activity, the number of partners of the person being interviewed, any precautions they use to prevent infection, and so on. We could then combine the quantitative and qualitative research questions and write an overarching mixed methods research question to ask:

> *Does a lack of knowledge of the causes of an STD help explain the*
> *increase of STDs in the population of adults over the age of 55?*

In this case, we're combining the knowledge gained from each research question to better understand the bigger picture. For example, if adults in our study had little or no knowledge of what STDs are, or how they are transmitted, the development and administration of an educational program focusing on these issues could be called for. By participating in the class, adults would at least have the knowledge required to help decrease the rate by which these diseases are spreading. If it were found that the adults were knowledgeable about STDs and how they are spread, then a program aimed at encouraging prevention could be developed.

In the case of the weight loss investigation, we would collect numeric data directly from the participant about the number of pounds they lost or gained based on a quantitative research question:

> *How much weight did you gain or lose during the weight loss program?*

We could then ask a qualitative research question that explains his or her success (or maybe a lack thereof) by asking:

> *What did you do to affect your weight change*
> *during the weight loss program?*

As we know from earlier chapters, this is the type of question we would ask as part of a phenomenological study. Just as we did in those cases, this question would allow for follow-up or probing questions, such as the types of food eaten, dining schedules, the amount of exercise the participant was involved in, or situational factors that may have contributed to their results in the program. Based on that information, we could develop a mixed methods research question, such as:

> *Does using multiple methods contribute to success*
> *in a weight loss program?*

By stating our question in this manner, we're able to consider answers from all respondents to better understand how to lose weight.

Hypotheses for Mixed Methods Studies

When researchers first began accepting the idea of mixed methods studies, because quantitative data are collected, they felt a hypothesis should always be stated. As we saw above, that idea has changed throughout the years, with more and more studies simply having a research question that focuses on the quantitative data. In this case,

I could compare clients' weights before the program and after the program to see whether there was a significant change:

Will there be a significant difference in participants' weights before the weight loss program and after the weight loss program?

If I wanted to expand my investigation and compare weight loss between two different programs, I could start with the following quantitative research question:

Are there significant differences in weight loss between Program A and Program B?

If we wanted to reframe this statement as a hypothesis, it would be relatively easy. Just as was the case when we discussed hypotheses earlier in the book, hypotheses in mixed methods studies can be directional or nondirectional, and they are tested using the null hypothesis. In this case, our independent variable is "program" and has two levels: Program A and Program B; our dependent variable is weight lost or gained. Given that information, our research hypothesis would read:

There will be a significant difference in weight loss between Program A and Program B.

Just as in the case above, we could combine this hypothesis with our qualitative research question to create the overarching mixed methods question.

For the next example, let's look at a paper I published a few years back (Terrell, 2014)—in it I focused on whether a student's learning style (Kolb, 1984) is predictive of success in an online graduate program. The study was called for by the higher-than-average attrition rates from these types of programs, and is significant due to the loss of, among other things, the amount of money spent, and the time invested in, a program from which a student ultimately doesn't graduate. When I originally conducted the study, it was purely quantitative. I used the Kolb Interest Inventory (Kolb, 1984) to determine learning style (i.e., the independent variable), where each student was identified as having one of four learning preferences (i.e., the levels of the independent variable). I then compared the attrition rate (i.e., the dependent variable) between the different styles by investigating the following hypothesis:

There will be a significant difference in attrition from an online graduate program between students with different preferred learning styles.

I collected these data over 7 years and, once I analyzed them, I found to my surprise that there was no significant difference in attrition among the four groups. While I didn't think of it when I initially analyzed the data, this would have been the perfect opportunity to extend this quantitative study into a mixed methods study. Using the following research question, I could interview former students to find out whether they felt their preferred learning style contributed to their lack of success in the program:

> *Did your learning style (i.e., the way you prefer to learn) affect your success in the program?*

I could then tie these two ideas together to ask a mixed methods research question:

> *Is there an interaction between learning style and attrition in a limited residency doctoral program?*

The Remaining Sections of Chapter 1

As you can see in Table 7.1, there is nothing else that is new or different that needs to be discussed in Chapter 1 of our mixed methods study. We'll see that the same holds true in Chapter 3: There are parts where we won't need to go into great detail (e.g., instruments). At the same time, as you can imagine, the simple act of including a mixed methods research question greatly affects some of the other things we will discuss.

Chapter 2 of a Mixed Methods Dissertation Proposal: The Review of Literature

We've seen in the earlier chapters how to write a good ROL for quantitative and qualitative studies. We use the same guidelines for each of those approaches now for our mixed methods study, but we have to take more of a hybrid approach. You must include literature from the theoretical perspective upon which you can base your quantitative hypotheses, but you must also include literature supporting the qualitative design. Beyond that, we must also include literature from other mixed methods studies in your problem area. We need to consider and incorporate the content of those publications. Still, we also need to pay strict attention to the particular mixed methods design chosen by the author and the procedures they used to implement it. Only by including literature from these three separate approaches can we build an effective research method in Chapter 3.

Chapter 3 of a Mixed Methods Dissertation Proposal: The Research Methods

When we discussed Chapter 3 for both the quantitative and qualitative studies, we spent most of our time talking about how to support our work with an appropriate paradigm, choose the appropriate research design, and detail the procedures needed to carry out a successful study. Here we need to concentrate on those three issues again but, as you might expect, they will be modified and expanded due to collecting and analyzing both types of data for the same study.

The Mixed Methods Paradigm

In a mixed methods study, we refer to the quantitative and qualitative methods singularly as **strands** of the study; each strand represents the component parts of that given approach (i.e., the research question, how data are collected, how data are analyzed). In our mixed methods paradigm, we must consider both the qualitative and quantitative strands. The quantitative strand must be deductive and value-free, with the researcher serving as an independent objective observer. The qualitative strand calls for the researcher to contact the participants, with a fair, respectful, and trusting rapport established between all parties. The researcher must also remember that the qualitative data collected is within the context of the study and must be respectful of input from multiple participants. Situations wherein both qualitative and quantitative strands are needed to answer a research question call for a mixed methods approach.

The Research Design

One of the basic beliefs I have about teaching research and statistics is that students need to focus on and understand what they are going to need, most of the time. In other situations, when a student needs to work with a statistical tool or research method that is out of the ordinary or more advanced, they can deal with them on a case-by-case basis. Given that, instead of spending a lot of time on the multitude of mixed methods designs, we will focus on the three designs a doctoral student is most likely to encounter or use as the basis of his or her dissertation research. The question then becomes "My paradigm calls for a mixed methods design; what are they and how do I pick the right one for my study?" I faced a similar problem in my earlier text (Terrell, 2012) where I needed a "guide" to help my students select the appropriate statistical test for a quantitative design. Much as was the case there, I've slightly modified the work of Creswell and Plano Clark (2017) to help us choose the appropriate mixed methods research design by answering four overarching questions:

* *Question 1: Do our qualitative and quantitative strands interact?* Simply put, this question asks whether the two strands are independent of each other, or does one influence the other? As we just saw, sequential designs are interactive; as a study progresses, we can use the results of one strand to influence our actions while implementing the other strand. If our strands interact only at the end of the study, we say they are independent of each other.

* *Question 2: What is the priority of our strategy?* We can design our study using three priorities: Each reflects the relative importance of one strand over the other when answering the research questions. When our quantitative and qualitative

strands contribute, to the same degree, this is an **equal priority** design. In other cases, it makes sense that more emphasis is on the quantitative aspect of the study (i.e., a **quantitative priority**); at different times, the qualitative strand is more important (i.e., a **qualitative priority**).

  * *Question 3: What is the timing (i.e., the sequence) of our strands?* This may seem a lot like the priority of our strategy, but the sequence of the strands is different from the importance of each strand. We can run the qualitative assessment before or after (sequential) the quantitative, or run the two concurrently. For example, in the case of attrition in limited-residency programs, our timing was sequential; we addressed our overarching research question by collecting the quantitative data first (i.e., a student's learning style), followed by qualitative data (i.e., opinions as to why students leave particular types of programs). Online counseling for depression may also lend itself to a concurrent approach. We could collect quantitative data each week by having each client complete the Beck Depression Inventory. At the same time, qualitative data could be collected from weekly counseling sessions. They could be integrated to answer research questions regarding the efficacy of online counseling for depression.

  * *Question 4: When are the strands mixed?* To eventually answer our mixed methods research questions, at some point, we will have to integrate, or mix, our strands. In this case, we have two choices: We either mix them during data collection or mix them during interpretation. For example, in the counseling example above, we said that our strands are concurrent (i.e., they are both conducted independently). This means the two strands are mixed only at the end of the study when both types of data are used together to answer the research questions. In the investigation of attrition, we collected and analyzed quantitative data that identified the students' learning styles. The analysis results influenced the questions we asked during the interviews (i.e., the qualitative data collection); this means we are mixing the strands during data collection.

The Three Major Mixed Methods Designs

The answers to the questions about the qualitative and quantitative strands, along with the research problem, will suggest which of the three most common mixed methods designs to choose: sequential–explanatory, sequential–exploratory, or convergent (Creswell & Plano Clark, 2017; Johnson & Onwuegbuzie, 2004). An overview of these relationships is shown in Table 7.2. Keep in mind that while there are other, more advanced mixed methods designs, these are the three most commonly used. The following explanations all grow from my earlier work (Terrell, 2012).

The Sequential–Explanatory Design

I have alluded to this type of study several times before; it is used in situations where we need to use qualitative data to explain, or better understand, a set of quantitative data (see Figure 7.1). Its use is determined by:

TABLE 7.2. Design Selection Criteria

Design	Interaction	Priority	Timing	Mixing
Convergent	Independent	Equal emphasis	Concurrent	During interpretation
Sequential–explanatory	Interactive	Quantitative emphasis	Sequential–quantitative first	During data collection
Sequential–exploratory	Interactive	Qualitative emphasis	Sequential–qualitative first	During data collection

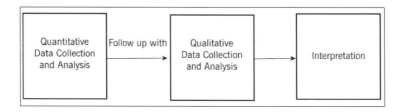

FIGURE 7.1. Sequential–explanatory design.

1. Interaction: The quantitative and qualitative strands interact.
2. Priority: The quantitative strand takes precedence.
3. Timing: The quantitative strand precedes the qualitative strand.
4. Integration: The strands are mixed during data collection.

Thinking back to my own dissertation, as you will remember, I worked with a group of fifth graders for a whole school year. I measured the students' levels of intrinsic motivation (i.e., quantitative data) at the beginning and end of the school year using a previously developed and validated motivation inventory. When I found that the intervention I performed didn't result in higher motivation for the students in my experimental group, I interviewed them (i.e., I collected qualitative data), analyzed the data, and then interpreted the two sets of data together. As I've said before, my results simply showed that the students didn't understand the feedback tool we had used; based on that, we made changes and successfully conducted the study again. You can see an outline of another example of this type of study in Appendix 7.1 at the end of this chapter.

The Sequential–Exploratory Design

We use this design in cases where we collect qualitative data first, and then use quantitative data to help us better understand our problem area (see Figure 7.2). It's most often used in situations where we need to quantify the results of a qualitative investigation:

1. Interaction: The qualitative and quantitative strands interact.
2. Priority: The qualitative strand takes precedence.
3. Timing: The qualitative strand precedes the quantitative strand.
4. Integration: The strands are mixed during data collection.

It should be noted that the order of the words in each design's name might be reversed. For example, some authors write "sequential–exploratory," while others may write "exploratory–sequential" (e.g., Walker & Baxter, 2019). Don't let this confuse you; either way is acceptable. A sequential–exploratory approach is often used as a valid way to create an examination, survey, or questionnaire. For example, right now I have a student working on a dissertation focusing on the role of information systems in future organizations. His plan is to collect the data he needs from interviews with information technology officers at a number of corporations by asking their opinions on the topic. Obviously, he could conduct a purely qualitative study, but there are many factors (e.g., the number of interviews needed and the time to conduct them, transcription costs) that might keep him from collecting the data he needs for his study. Knowing that, I've asked him to approach it from a mixed methods perspective.

First, he will interview a representative sample of persons in these roles to learn their opinions on the topic and, second, he will search the literature for other studies, questionnaires, or surveys that are like or similar to this topic. Following this preliminary work, he will create a survey and have it completed by a pilot group of participants in order to help establish its validity and reliability. In short, my student will have collected qualitative data to develop the instrument, and then will have collected quantitative data to evaluate it. Because this system meets the four criteria established above, we are using a **sequential–exploratory design**. In order to reinforce this, I've included another example of a sequential–exploratory design in Appendix 7.2.

 **A WORD OF CAUTION**

In the last two paragraphs, I gave you a high-level synopsis of developing a survey. As I've said before, creating a valid data collection instrument requires a lot of expertise and experience. For example, once a survey is initially developed, it must

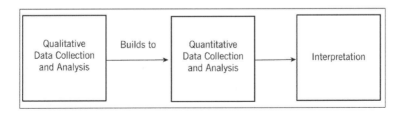

FIGURE 7.2. Sequential–exploratory design.

be pilot tested and then validated using very specific statistical tools. And since this book is about the process of writing a dissertation proposal, we can leave the details of testing and validating a survey for some other book.

The Convergent Design

The **convergent design** is used when we need to have a better understanding of our research area and must do so by collecting quantitative and qualitative data at the same time, analyzing each separately, merging the two sets of results, and then interpreting them together (see Figure 7.3). In this case, our four questions are answered by:

1. Interaction: The quantitative and qualitative strands are independent.
2. Priority: There is equal emphasis on both strands.
3. Timing: The strands are implemented concurrently.
4. Integration: The strands are mixed during interpretation.

Several years back one of my graduate students wrote her dissertation based on the theory that anonymity would increase students' willingness to interact with a teacher during class. In order to investigate the theory, she randomly selected one of the classes of introductory computer programming offered each term at her college. She set up the classroom so that each student had personal access to a computer. Students could then send anonymous messages containing content or lecture-specific questions to the instructor during class. The students' questions would appear on a screen at the front of the classroom; this allowed the instructor to directly answer the question or address it in the context of her lecture.

In order to actually investigate the theory, my student collected the number of messages for the class each week, as well as a measurement of communication apprehension; she also interviewed a small group of students each week to get their input on how they perceived the value of the anonymous messages, their willingness to use the messages, and whether or not the questions asked by

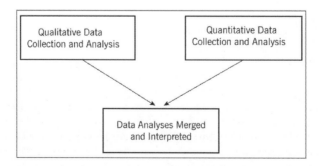

FIGURE 7.3. Convergent design.

other students contributed to their understanding of the material. Notice that she wasn't conducting an experimental study, she was investigating the theory itself; she wanted to know whether the ability to anonymously ask messages affected her students' willingness to participate in class. At the end of the study, she analyzed the quantitative data to look for trends over time and coded the qualitative data to determine whether common themes arose from them. After both sets of data had been analyzed, they were merged and synthesized, allowing her to develop a better understanding of the overall usage of the messages, their effect on students' willingness to participate in class, and a better understanding of the underlying theory. As a side note, although this is a good example of a convergent design, the question remains "What did she find out?" Unfortunately, not much; the number of questions didn't increase over time seemingly because the students did not perceive the value of having their questions posed this way. In order to get an even better understanding of this mixed approach, I've included another example in Appendix 7.3.

Participants and Sampling

In the preceding section, you may have noticed that I didn't mention exactly how we select samples before conducting our studies. That's because, before we look at the basic designs, it would be difficult to determine how large samples need to be for each type of data collected. There are a few things we have to consider and a few rules of thumb (Teddlie & Yu, 2007).

First, because you're dealing with both types of data, you must keep in mind the guidelines we've followed up to this point. It's best to have randomly selected, quantitative samples that are large enough for generalization to the population they were selected from. We tend to have much smaller samples of qualitative data and they are usually purposively selected.

Second, the different designs may call for samples drawn from the same population, or it may be permissible, or desirable, to take our samples from different populations. The question becomes "How do we know what to do in a given situation?" Creswell (2014) acknowledges these issues and has developed rules of thumb when trying to create a sample for your mixed methods study. Obviously, situations will arise where these general guidelines need to be modified, but for now, in this general approach, we'll stick to the basics (Teddlie & Yu, 2007).

Sampling for a Convergent Design

In a convergent design, it's best to have a random sample of quantitative data and a purposive sample of qualitative data drawn from the same population. As I just said, this rule may be affected by things such as the availability of the time and money necessary for analyzing a large amount of qualitative data or how we're going to use the different types of data when they are merged. As we saw with my student studying communication apprehension, she was able to randomly select a given class from a number that were taught, and then purposively select a smaller number of students to be interviewed.

Sampling for a Sequential–Explanatory Design

For sequential–explanatory designs, the ideal situation is to be able to draw your samples from the same population. You select your quantitative data randomly, keeping in mind the basic rules of generalizability for all quantitative studies, and then purposively select a smaller sample of participants from whom you'll collect qualitative data. Because the overarching goal of this type of design is to use the qualitative results to explain the quantitative data, Creswell (2014) suggests simply asking for an appropriate number of volunteers from the randomly selected group to be interviewed. For example, thinking back to the discussion about my dissertation, I randomly selected the students to participate in the study and then purposively selected from them a smaller group whose opinions would help explain the results.

Sampling for a Sequential–Exploratory Design

Finally, sampling for a sequential–exploratory design depends upon the overall goal of your study. If you simply want to use the quantitative data to help explain the qualitative results, you should purposively select your sample members to interview, and then collect quantitative data from a random sample created from that same sample.

For example, in one study we developed an instrument for measuring connectivity in online education (Terrell et al., 2009). Because high levels of interaction have been shown to predict success in virtual classrooms, we wanted to develop a survey that would help us identify potential problems before the problems resulted in low levels of student achievement or attrition. To do that, we selected a small sample of our students and interviewed them concerning how they felt about interaction with their peers and faculty in an online environment; our goal was to be able to measure how connected they felt to one another. We used the results of the interviews to develop the survey and then administered and validated it on a larger, randomly chosen, group of students in the same program. Obviously, there is quite a bit more involved in creating a quality survey; if you ever get to that point, authors like Fink (2016) can point you in the right direction.

Instrumentation

Here again, we have to be careful to ensure that the instrumentation we plan to use to collect our data are valid and reliable (Johnson & Turner, 2003). At the same time, we want to ensure they complement one another. For example, in the convergent design where my student investigated the use of instant messaging in class, she collected information from the communication apprehension survey, while at the same time she interviewed her students about their experiences using the text messages. Clearly, in that case, she had to ensure that the quantitative survey instrument demonstrated validity and reliability, but she also had to develop interview questions that focused specifically on her investigation. In this case, she used a semi-structured interview where she was able to focus specifically on the students' experience with the messaging tool. It's easy to underestimate how difficult it is to find a previously developed survey tool, or especially having to develop one on our own. I can't emphasize enough how important it is to match the tools to the data you need, as well as to how the data will be used in cross-analysis. Again, we're talking about the use of surveys here; go to the experts to tell you how to actually develop them.

The Research Procedures

As we've seen throughout the book, in our procedures sections we need to establish a good plan we can follow as we carry out our research (Creswell & Plano Clark, 2017). However, in conducting a mixed methods study, we have to somewhat change our mindset. With the quantitative and qualitative designs, we thought in a linear fashion: one step in our research plan led logically to the next. In the mixed methods approaches, however, you have to consider the fact that you might collect both types of data sequentially or concurrently and, regardless of the design you need, your plan will have to reflect that type of data collection. We will see examples of this in the appendices of this chapter, as well as in Appendix D at the end of the book, where we continue our investigation of the waste treatment plant started in Appendix A.

Plans for Data Analysis

As we've said from the outset, the key to data analysis for a mixed methods study is to first be able to understand and then be able to analyze the individual data sets you've collected. You need to test the hypotheses or research questions based on the quantitative data, and appropriately analyze the data to answer your qualitative research questions (Onwuegbuzie & Leech, 2006). Only by understanding those analysis tools will you be able to understand how to merge (i.e., mix) the two data sets to answer the mixed methods research questions. As we saw in Figures 7.1 and 7.2, the data are analyzed after each phase in the sequential designs, integrated, and then interpreted. In the convergent design (see Figure 7.3), the data are collected concurrently, merged, and then interpreted. Following these steps, you'll be able to accurately answer your mixed methods research questions.

Ethical Considerations

Just as we've counseled earlier, we need to ensure that our research study does no physical or psychological harm to our participants. Your proposal needs to outline your plans for obtaining IRB approval from your institution, as well as the manner by which you'll inform the participants of their rights to privacy, their choice to leave the study at any time, that the interviews will be recorded, and so on.

Plans for Presenting the Results

As with the earlier approaches, our plan will reflect the audience interested in, or requesting, the investigation. This could be a company, a school board, a government official, or whomever else has a problem or research area that can best be answered using a mixed methods approach. You may also consider presenting it at a conference or submitting it to an appropriate journal. The key to our plan is to develop and present our audience with a quality report that accurately reflects the findings that address their inquiry or concerns.

Summary

The summary of the proposal is just that, a recap of what you want to do. Start by briefly describing your problem, purpose, research questions, and hypotheses. Briefly describe your design and plans for data analysis, and then provide a summary of exactly what you're proposing. Always keep in mind that a reader should be able to go to the summary of your chapter and get a good feel for what you are proposing.

Summary of Chapter Seven

The end of the quantitative and qualitative paradigm wars brought with it great news: Now, instead of understanding "if" with quantitative data and "how" or "why" with qualitative data, we can combine the two and get a much better understanding of our research problem and questions. In this chapter, we only talked about the three most used mixed methods designs: the sequential–explanatory, the sequential–exploratory, and the convergent designs. There are other higher-level designs, but those are best left for a book specifically designed for mixed methods research. Keep in mind, when you first start using these approaches, that they require a different mindset. Let me encourage you to keep at it; the fruit of your labors will be well worth it.

Do You Understand These Key Words and Phrases?	
Convergent design	Quantitative priority
Equal priority	Sequential–explanatory design
Merge or mix	Sequential–exploratory design
Qualitative priority	Strands

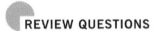

REVIEW QUESTIONS

As usual, let's check our understanding of what we've covered in this chapter by answering the following questions as either true or false. In instances where the answer is false, please explain why. You can find the answers at the end of the book.

1. ____ Using qualitative and quantitative data in a study always calls for a mixed methods design.

2. ____ Merging or mixing your qualitative and quantitative data is necessary only in certain instances.

3. _____ It is imperative to have a qualitative, a quantitative, and a mixed methods research question in your mixed methods study.

4. _____ Sequential–explanatory and sequential–exploratory studies call for data analysis of each data set to occur simultaneously.

5. _____ There are only three types of mixed methods designs.

6. _____ It is acceptable to use different sampling approaches and sample sizes for collecting qualitative and quantitative data in a mixed methods study.

7. _____ Equal priority should always be given to all strands in a mixed methods study.

8. _____ In a sequential–explanatory study, you should collect qualitative data, followed by quantitative data, in order to better answer the mixed methods research question.

9. _____ A researcher should never use a standard inferential tool, such as an ANOVA, to analyze quantitative data in a mixed methods study.

10. _____ The sequence and priority in a mixed methods study are essentially the same thing.

✓ Progress Check for Chapter 3 of a Mixed Methods Dissertation Proposal: The Research Methods

Earlier in this book, I presented Chapter 1 (the Introduction) and Chapter 2 (the Review of Literature) for a study involving an industrial waste dump. Since then, I've included an example of Chapter 3 for a quantitative study in Appendix C, and a qualitative study in Appendix D. In Appendix E, I've revised some of the contents of Chapter 1 (e.g., the problem statement, research questions) and have written the investigation of the industrial waste dump from a mixed methods perspective.

LET'S CONTINUE WRITING OUR OWN DISSERTATION PROPOSAL

In the earlier chapters, you've identified a research problem, stated your research questions and hypotheses, and then developed either a qualitative or a quantitative proposal based on what you wanted to investigate. Just as we did before, I want you to go back to Chapter 1 and rewrite it to include the content needed for a mixed methods study; this means you will need to make a revised problem statement, a change in your purpose statement, and include qualitative, quantitative, and mixed methods research questions. Following that, develop Chapter 3 for your study. Depending on the problem, ensure that your timing, sequencing, mixing, and data analysis dictate the design you choose. Because this type of study calls for us to move from the linear approach we saw in the earlier methodologies, make sure your research procedures are detailed and specific enough to give you the answers you need.

APPENDIX 7.1. Sequential–Explanatory Design: The Case of the Tutors

Items from Chapter 1 of Your Proposal

Background, Problem, and Significance

The owners of star-pupil.com are in business to tutor high school students in their class-work, as well as to prepare them to take standardized college entrance exams. The company hires well-qualified tutors to work with students either face-to-face or in an online video chat room. In order to ensure the quality of their tutors, the owners of star-pupil.com have students evaluate each new tutor after a student's initial session with the new tutor. The owners have had negative experiences with tutors in the past and feel this feedback is neces-sary to address any concerns or problems at the outset. Hiring good tutors not only increases the chances of success by their students, it helps ensure the viability of their company.

Purpose Statement

The purpose of this study is to evaluate new tutors to ensure they are meeting the needs of their students.

Quantitative Research Question

How well do new tutors score on student evaluations?

Qualitative Research Question

What are student expectations from a high-quality tutor?

Mixed Methods Research Question

Can a tutor's scores on a student evaluation be explained by a student's expectations of what should be provided by a high-quality tutor?

Items from Chapter 3 of Your Proposal

The Mixed Methods Paradigm

This study calls for the researcher to be an independent and objective observer while design-ing instruments to collect student evaluations of new tutors at star-pupil.com. At the same time, the researcher must establish fair, respectful, and trusting rapport between him- or herself and the students who are being tutored and then interviewed; this relationship must exist knowing that the knowledge uncovered is contextual, with the researcher being respect-ful of varying viewpoints and the subjective truths that might arise from interactions with multiple participants. Research in this subject area calls for data from interviews, conducted after survey completion, that will be used to explain student evaluations of the tutors. This relationship between the collection and use of quantitative and qualitative data calls for a mixed methods approach.

Research Design

Quantitative survey data will be collected and analyzed to rate the efficacy of new tutors within the organization. Qualitative data will then be collected and analyzed to help better understand or interpret the results of the quantitative analysis. The results from both analyses will be mixed and analyzed in order to explain or better understand the mixed methods research question. The desired priority of the data types, the sequence in which the data will be collected, the point at which they will be integrated, and their interaction calls for a sequential–explanatory mixed methods research method.

Participants and Sampling

Students typically learn about star-pupil.com from other students, advertisements on the Internet, or from guidance counselors. Upon enrollment, they are matched with a tutor whose specialty area is that in which the student needs help, and they generally meet virtually or face-to-face for 2–10 hours. This quantitative phase of the study will use all students (i.e., a convenience sample) assigned to a new tutor over the first 3 months of that tutor's employment; the historical average for this time period will be 12 students. Fifty percent of students enrolled will be randomly selected to be interviewed.

Instruments

The researcher will collect quantitative data using a publicly available, commonly used student satisfaction survey. Qualitative data will be collected from semistructured interviews focusing on explaining the results of the quantitative analysis.

Research Procedures

Participants for the study will be identified as students who work with a new tutor during their first 3 months of employment (i.e., a convenience sample). Prior to completing the satisfaction survey, students must sign an agreement acknowledging their willingness to participate, as well as their rights to privacy, their willingness to have the interviews recorded, and the opportunity to withdraw from the study at any time. Upon completion and the analysis of data from the quantitative surveys, a random sample of 50% of the students will be chosen to be interviewed based on themes emanating from the quantitative data analysis. Upon completion of the data analysis, the researcher creates a report answering the research questions based on the results.

Plans for Data Analysis

The data from the surveys will be inferentially analyzed, with the results used to inform interview questions for qualitative data collection. The results of both analyses will be integrated and used to answer the overarching mixed methods research question.

Ethical Considerations

As noted above, students must sign an agreement acknowledging their willingness to participate, as well as their right to privacy, their permission to have the interviews recorded, and their opportunity to withdraw from the study at any time.

Plan for Presenting the Results

A report based on the findings will be presented in Chapters 4 and 5 of the dissertation report. A copy of the report will be given to the owners of the tutoring service.

Summary

The owners of star-pupil.com want to ensure that their tutors are effective and offer the best services to their clients. This study is designed to collect data on student satisfaction, after a newly hired employee's first 3 months, using a commonly available student satisfaction survey. This step is followed by conducting interviews with a random sample of the students completing the surveys. The quantitative data set will be analyzed and followed by a qualitative analysis aimed at gaining a better understanding of the quantitative results. These results will serve as a basis for a report to be delivered to the company's owners.

APPENDIX 7.2. Sequential–Exploratory Design: The Case of the Academies

Items from Chapter 1 of Your Proposal

Background, Problem, and Significance

Being accepted to a prestigious U.S. military academy is a difficult task; with an acceptance rate hovering around 10%, these schools only take top scholars from their respective high schools, most of whom have exemplary records of service to the community and the school, athletic prowess, and standardized test scores in the upper 5%. It is estimated that it costs taxpayers well over $300,000 for students to attend one of the academies, after which they are required to spend 8 years on active duty in the military. Unfortunately, the attrition rate from these academies averages over 10%. This results in temporal and financial loss on the part of the student and academy, but also the missed opportunity of a nonadmitted student who may have successfully completed the 4-year program.

Purpose Statement

The purpose of this study is to develop a screening tool that may help admissions officers better identify applicants who will successfully complete the program.

Qualitative Research Question

What leads a student to make the decision to leave a military academy?

Quantitative Research Question

Are there identifiable factors that can predict attrition from a military academy?

Mixed Methods Research Question

Do the results of the analysis of the qualitative data of factors leading to attrition align with the factors identified by an instrument developed to predict attrition?

Items from Chapter 3 of Your Proposal

The Mixed Methods Paradigm

While conducting the interviews, the researcher must establish fair, respectful, and trusting rapport between him- or herself and the military academy personnel being interviewed. This relationship must exist knowing that the knowledge uncovered is contextual, with the researcher being respectful of varying viewpoints and the subjective truths that might arise from interactions with multiple participants. The researcher must remain independent and objective while developing, validating, and administering the survey instrument. This relationship between the collection and use of quantitative and qualitative data calls for a mixed methods research method.

Participants and Sampling

Military academies enroll hundreds of students every fall; between 10 and 20% of these students leave prior to graduation. This study uses a purposive sample of students who failed to graduate within the past year.

Research Design

Qualitative data will be collected from faculty and administration at the military academy. From that, a quantitative survey instrument will be developed, validated, and pilot tested with a sample of students who left the academy prior to graduation. The interaction between the strands, desired priority of the strands, timing of the strands, and the point at which the data are mixed, call for a sequential–exploratory mixed methods research approach.

Instruments

An attrition prediction instrument will be developed by first interviewing faculty and administration at the military academy and gaining their insight on the reasons they believe a student in the academy leaves prior to graduation. From the interviews, common themes will be identified upon which questions for the survey will be developed. The instrument will be shown to a selected group of administrators and faculty to ascertain their expert opinions as to the validity of the instrument; changes may be made based on their input. Following the successful development of the survey, it will be administered to a pilot group of students who recently left the academy; the results of the pilot test will be analyzed for construct validity and reliability.

The Research Procedures

At the outset of the study, any requirements of the academy's IRB must be met. Following that, a representative sample of faculty and administrators at the academy will be purposively sampled to be interviewed using a semistructured approach based on the qualitative research question. Once the interviews have been completed, the data will be analyzed, relevant themes identified, and a survey instrument based on those themes developed. Members of the representative sample of faculty and administration will be asked to review the survey, with their input possibly leading to changes in the survey itself.

Once the survey has been deemed valid, a purposive sample of students who recently left the academy prior to graduation will be identified and their participation solicited. These prior students will be assured of their confidentiality, and that all results will be anonymous and will never be used to identify a given person. After an adequate number of surveys have been completed, the results will be analyzed to demonstrate the reliability and validity of the instrument.

Plans for Data Analysis

Data from interviews with faculty and administrators will be qualitatively analyzed to identify themes or patterns that those personnel believe are indicative of a student leaving the academy prior to graduation. An initial instrument will be developed and returned to the faculty and administrators for review. Once the survey has been completed by a purposive sample of students who recently left the academy, the results will be analyzed for validity and reliability.

Ethical Considerations

Former students must be assured that all results of the study remain anonymous, and that taking the survey may result in reliving events that were initially traumatic and may have caused emotional or interpersonal stress or anxiety.

Plan for Presenting the Results

A report detailing the developmental process, as well as the results of the pilot test, will be presented in Chapters 4 and 5 of the dissertation report, and delivered to administration at the academy.

Summary

Highly qualified students are selected each year to attend prestigious military academies. When students leave the academies prior to graduation, the time lost by both the student and the academy is significant, and so too is the loss of the tremendous amount of money required for an education at an institution of this type. In this study, it is proposed to develop an instrument that will help administrators identify, and perhaps remediate or counsel, students in danger of leaving the academy prior to graduation.

APPENDIX 7.3. Convergent Design: The Case of Calling It In

Items from Chapter 1 of Your Proposal

Background, Problem, and Significance

Information systems (IS) professionals often work an inordinate number of hours to ensure that the technology needs of the organization they work for are being supported. In a particular data processing company, members of management have become concerned about a perceived significant increase in the number of sick days taken by employees in their IS department. Members of upper management are concerned that this increase in sick days may indicate employee dissatisfaction with the working environment, and that ultimately this could negatively affect customer service and corporate profits.

Purpose Statement

The purpose of this study is to understand the reasons for an increase in the number of sick days taken by employees in a particular company's IS department.

Quantitative Research Question

Is the number of sick days taken by employees in the organization's IS department different from those in other departments within the organization?

Qualitative Research Question

How do employees perceive working conditions in the IS department?

Mixed Methods Research Question

Is there a relationship between working conditions in the IS department and the number of sick days taken by employees in that department?

Hypothesis

Employees in the IS department take a significantly higher number of sick days than employees in other departments because they are typically overworked on a daily basis.

Items from Chapter 3 of Your Proposal

The Mixed Methods Paradigm

This study calls for the researcher to be an independent, objective observer while collecting quantitative data representing the number of sick days taken by employees in the IS department, as well as other departments within the organization. At the same time, the researcher must establish fair, respectful, and trusting rapport between him- or herself and employees in the IS department; this relationship must exist knowing that the knowledge uncovered is contextual, with the researcher being respectful of varying viewpoints and the subjective truths that might arise from interactions with multiple participants. Research in this subject area calls for data from a series of interviews with these participants that will then be used to attempt to explain the number of sick days taken by employees in the IS department. This relationship calls for a convergent mixed methods approach.

The Research Design

In this case, the quantitative and qualitative strands will be conducted simultaneously in order to answer the respective research questions. This first step will be followed by merging and analyzing the two data sets in order to answer the mixed methods research question. Because of this goal, a convergent mixed methods design is called for.

Participants and Sampling

Data for the number of sick days taken by all employees will be obtained from human resource records, de-identified, and then each record marked as being from an IS employee or from someone in another department outside of IS. Currently, there are 35 employees in the IS department; a random sample of 10–12 employees will be selected to be interviewed.

Instruments

There are no formal instruments for the quantitative data; it will be collected by a simple count of sick days taken for each employee. The qualitative data will be collected via a semi-structured interview focused on the qualitative research question.

Research Procedures

At the outset of the study, the researcher will work with upper management to identify personnel in the human resources department who will be able to access and format the needed data on sick days taken by employees in the organization. Following that step, management in the IS department will be contacted to help identify a random sample of 10–12 employees within the department. After employees sign an agreement indicating their awareness of privacy and participation issues, a mutually convenient time and place will be scheduled for the actual interview sessions. Each employee will participate in one interview estimated to take no longer than 1 hour. Once all data are collected, data analysis will begin.

Plans for Data Analysis

An independent sample t $test$ will be used to test the hypothesis that employees in the IS department use significantly more sick days than employees in other departments. The data from the interviews will be transcribed and validated by reviewing the transcripts while replaying the recorded interviews. Phenomenological analysis of the interview transcripts will allow the researcher to identify themes and phrases representing the experiences of the participants. After both sets of data have been analyzed, they will be merged and synthesized to allow for the identification of themes or patterns that may suggest a relationship between the number of sick days an employee uses and his or her perception of the working conditions in their department. The results from the final analysis will allow researchers to answer the mixed methods research question.

Ethical Considerations

Participants must agree to, and sign, a document indicating informed consent. As noted, participants must be advised of the anonymity of their participation and their rights to privacy.

Plan for Presenting the Results

The results will be presented in Chapters 4 and 5 of the dissertation report and a formal report will be written and presented to management in the organization.

Summary

The purpose of this investigation is to examine the relationship between the number of sick days used by IS employees and their perceptions of their working environment. Data will be collected to determine whether employees in the IS department take significantly more sick days than employees in other departments. Concurrently, employees in the IS department will be interviewed to ask them about their perceptions of their work environment. Both data sets will be individually analyzed to answer the qualitative and quantitative research questions, as well as to test the study's hypothesis. The data will then be merged and analyzed to ascertain whether an interaction does exist between the number of sick days used, and employees in the IS department's opinion of their working conditions.

Epilogue

Have We Accomplished What We Set Out to Do?

As I said at the outset, many doctoral students face a roadblock when starting their dissertation. They're perfectly capable of actually writing the paper—it's just difficult for them to get started. I've had the idea "the problem is the problem" for a long time; so, finally in this book I've been able to put to use my experiences with students to help me try to help you. I've laid out the criteria for a good proposal, but I think the most important part of the process is in that first step of articulating a problem. Find a problem you're interested in—something you're willing to dedicate yourself to for a year or more.

I encourage my students to read as much about their problem area as possible. If your professors are like me, they've given you quite a few reading assignments throughout your time in graduate school. Take advantage of the reading assignments if you can; don't waste your time reading about something that doesn't interest you just to complete an assignment. I also encourage my students to take advantage of professional meetings, to speak with others in the field, and to look into myriad other sources that might spark one's interests. When you get to the point where you're starting your dissertation, you need to be *ready* to start—remember, finding the problem is the problem!

Of course, remember all of our guidelines from Chapter One. Unless you can change those guidelines for a problem statement to focus specifically on your proposed research, then you need to reconsider what you want to do:

1. The problem is interesting to you.
2. The scope of the problem is manageable by you.
3. You have the knowledge, the time, and the resources needed to investigate the problem.

4. You can collect and analyze the data related to the problem.

5. You can demonstrate that investigating the problem has theoretical or practical significance.

6. You can show it is ethical to investigate the problem.

Throughout this book, the largest part of the case studies and examples I used were from dissertations written by my students. My students getting started with their study meant thinking through the criteria several times.

There are a couple of things to keep in mind about this book. First, it's a guideline for writing a proposal, not a specific research methods book. I used brief examples to demonstrate how to conduct quantitative, qualitative, and mixed methods research. In many of those case studies, I used fictitious literature simply to get my point across. That's not to say I didn't include some good resources within the text itself; when you read names like Creswell, Gay, Yin, and others, you're in good company. If you need more specific details for any given approach, I've tried to point you toward the best.

In my statistics textbook from 2021, I tried to provide a good outline for how to select the appropriate statistical technique for a given scenario; I've tried to do the same here. As I mentioned, different universities and professors may require different headings and sections in a dissertation proposal. I've given you a good outline from which to work, but be willing to modify it a bit to please the committee at your university. A student presenting before a committee reminds me of the wise words I heard from a professor in my own dissertation committee: "You know you're about to finish when you start winning the arguments." Try your best to do that and build a good foundation to work from.

Finally, there are other things that seem to be just common sense, but that I think bear mentioning. Demonstrate to your faculty and committee that you believe in what you are doing. Any time you submit a document, make sure there are no spelling, formatting, or grammar errors; nothing says "I'm not ready" quicker than sloppy writing. Listen to what your committee says and take constructive advice; dissertation chairs are there to help you—just show them how much you appreciate it. Connect with your committee and don't go missing for months at a time; they have seen the struggles of writing a dissertation and are a wealth of information and support if you take advantage of it. Connect with other students and professionals in the field—you'll be surprised how open they are to you, and how much you can learn from them. Last, and most important, stay focused and don't stop. Doctoral students represent the cream of the crop in higher education; you wouldn't be where you are unless a lot of people have faith in you: your faculty, your committee, your friends, and your family. The opportunity to get a doctoral degree is like being given a key to a door. Getting through the door is important to you: What you do once you're through the door is important to the world.

APPENDIX A

Progress Check for Chapter 1 of a Dissertation Proposal

The Introduction

As I said early in Chapter One of this book, there are several approaches to writing a dissertation proposal and the final dissertation report, but the most common is the five-chapter model. While the names may vary slightly, these five chapters are the Introduction, the Review of Literature, Research Methods, Results, and the Summary. The first three chapters comprise the dissertation proposal and are used to guide our research. After the research has been conducted, the results and summary are added to complete the final dissertation report.

Up to this point, we have discussed the major components of Chapter 1 of a dissertation proposal: problem statements, the research purpose, research questions, and hypotheses. Now I want to do two things. First, I will show you a complete, albeit brief, Chapter 1 of a dissertation proposal. Second, I will include, and explain, other items in Chapter 1 that may or may not be included.

In this case, Chapter 1 is the introduction to a study focusing on the effect of a toxic waste disposal facility on the quality of life of citizens living near to it. This is the type of dissertation one might see in a sociology or health sciences doctoral program; despite that, the framework we'll use is generalizable to many different schools within a university.

Chapter 1: Introduction

Background

Ongoing concerns exist regarding industrial waste, automobile emissions, and other pollutants being released into the earth's soil, water, and atmosphere (Zarocostas, 2009). Many researchers believe issues such as global warming, the extinction of plant and animal species, and increased rates of diseases, such as cancer in humans, can be traced directly back to the release of toxic waste (Wayman, 2013). Failure to address these issues could ultimately affect the viability of life on Earth.

245

Statement of the Problem, Significance, and Purpose

Literally thousands of industrial plants throughout the United States have closed their doors in recent years due to international competition, a sagging economy, or the decreased need for a specific product. Many of these plants used toxic materials, including petroleum-based products and other potentially harmful chemicals, in their manufacturing process. Upon closing, regulations from state and local governments, as well as the Environmental Protection Agency (EPA; 2013), mandate a company's responsibility to ensure all harmful residues are properly disposed of.

In one small southern town, a large factory specializing in the production of weaved cotton material ultimately closed due to competition in 2006 (Casciaro, 2006). As part of their manufacturing process, the company used chemicals to dye the cloth they manufactured, with residue mechanically cleansed prior to its release into a local river. Upon the factory's closure, the cleansing equipment was bought by an outside waste-processing company and kept operational in its original location on the old mill site. Unlike the chemicals used to dye cloth, the new company provided services to manufacturers producing waste from petroleum-, rubber-, and metal-processing facilities locally, and from surrounding states.

Shortly after the newly purchased plant began operation, the residents of the surrounding area began complaining that noxious fumes coming from the plant were causing respiratory and vision _problems_. Many noted that the original mill emitted odors, but the current situation was far worse than they had previously experienced. Because of the current problems, as well as a concern for future health issues, the citizens asked the local government, over a period of years, to provide better oversight or close the reprocessing plant entirely (Adams, 2012; Carter, 2009a, 2009b). Several remedial efforts were made, but the plant's owners filed for bankruptcy and ultimately closed in 2010, leaving thousands of gallons of untreated waste. Local, state, and federal officials have attempted since that time to remediate the problems but, to date, toxic chemicals remain untreated, leaving the EPA to "initiate emergency measures to contain pollution abandoned REEF facility" (Raines, 2012). The _purpose_ of this study is to investigate the personal health complaints made by the citizens to determine their merit.

Research Questions

1. Is the current number of health problems experienced by citizens living close to the processing plant different from those of residents living in other areas?
2. What are the experiences of residents living in communities surrounding the chemical processing plant?

Hypothesis

There will be a significant difference in the number of current health problems experienced by residents living near the waste treatment plant and residents living away from the waste treatment plant.

Definitions of Terms

There are no terms that require specialized definitions in this paper.

Assumptions

Since many of the residents around the mill became unemployed when the original mill closed down, it is assumed they will be truthful in their disclosure of their current health status.

Since many of the residents around the mill became unemployed when the original mill was closed down, it is assumed they will be truthful in their description of the types and frequency of the odors emanating from the waste treatment facility.

Limitations

Due to the types of chemicals processed and the actual cleansing process used by the current owners, the resultant health issues may not be generalizable to the health issues created by the disposal of other chemicals. Because of that, the experiences of residents surrounding the processing plant may not be generalizable to citizens of other communities facing similar problems.

Delimitations

Only residents 18 years or older and who have lived in the surrounding community for more than 10 years will participate in the study.

Summary

This chapter discussed issues related to environmental contamination and its effect on the health of ourselves and our environment. In particular, the chapter focused on the plight of residents in one small town dealing with possible health issues arising from the mismanagement of industrial waste cleansing. The following chapter presents an ROL related to industrial waste and environmental concerns, as well as the effect of such on our ecology and health.

Progress Check for Chapter 1

In this section, I have listed the headings for each of the sections within the introduction and background. For each of these, I have provided an explanation for what is included.

Background

Elements of this section include the history of factory closures throughout the United States, the closure of a specific cloth manufacturing mill, and the subsequent purchase of the plant's chemical disposal equipment by an outside agency. Notice that I have included references to the literature to support statements where needed.

Problem Statement

Within the section you can see that I have intentionally italicized and underscored the word "problem." Local residents are complaining of problems stemming from noxious odors coming from the chemical-cleaning process.

Significance

Local residents are concerned with current health issues, as well as the possibility of future health concerns.

Research Purpose

Again, I have highlighted and italicized "purpose." The overarching purpose is to investigate citizens' complaints of health issues related to the chemical-processing facility.

Research Questions

The first research question could be answered using a survey wherein residents could indicate the number and severity of different types of medical problems. This type of approach could result in a quantitative study.

The second research question would probably be best answered by interviewing residents of the neighborhood to get a better feeling for how their day-to-day lives have been affected by the plant. This type of question would lend itself to a qualitative approach.

Hypothesis

This hypothesis was developed to answer the first research question. Again, a numeric rating scale or something to that effect could be used to collect data.

Assumptions

It is assumed that residents will be truthful and forthcoming about their experiences relating to the chemical-processing facility, as well as to any health issues they believe have arisen from living in proximity to the plant.

Limitations

The actual chemicals being processed and the method by which they are processed may be unique to this situation. Because of that, any results from this study may or may not be applicable to different situations.

Delimitations

Adults over the age of 18 might be more objective in their reporting. Including only residents who had lived in the area for over 10 years would allow for a better historical perspective.

Definitions of Terms

There are no special terms requiring definition.

Progress Check for Chapter 2 of a Dissertation Proposal

The Review of Literature

As noted in Chapter Two of this book, there are different ways to write an ROL: here I will use the generic model I used in that chapter. We continue by writing an ROL for the toxic waste problem paper we started in Appendix A. As you'll remember, the problem dealt with noxious odors emanating from a toxic waste processing facility; residents are concerned that these odors might lead to personal illnesses. The purpose of the study is to investigate these complaints; this goal will be guided by research questions designed to better understand the lived experiences of residents in surrounding communities, as well as to compare incidents of health problems between residents living around the closed factory to national rates of the same types of problems. We can begin by identifying key words that will guide our search:

Key Words: toxic waste, health problems

Using these key words, I identified hundreds of articles in an online database; the following are representative examples followed by an annotation based on each:

Alabama Department of Environmental Management. (2006, October). Hazardous waste: The basics. Available at *https://adem.alabama.gov/programs/land/landforms/HWBasics.pdf*

Hazardous waste, because of quantity; concentration; and physical, chemical, or infectious characteristics, may cause mortality or an increase in illness or have a negative effect on the environment—it also may be ignitable, corrosive, reactive, or toxic. Waste comes from a variety of large and small businesses and manufacturers.

Wayman, E. (2013). Toxic waste sites may cause health problems for millions. *Science News, 183*(10). Available at *www.sciencenews.org/view/generic/id/350205/description/Toxic_waste_sites_may_cause_health_problems_for_millions*

Living near toxic waste may cause health problems to a degree comparable to the effect of infectious diseases. This was quantified through the study of 373 toxic waste sites in India, Indonesia, and the Philippines, where it was shown that exposure may have contributed to the loss of over 800,000 healthy years of a population of about 8.6 million. About two-thirds of the people negatively affected by the chemicals were women and children. Diseases and disorders included mental retardation, anemia, a weakened immune system, and breathing problems. The authors noted that only one hazardous chemical per site was investigated, so the issues may be even greater.

Zarocostas, J. (2009, September 23). Health effects of toxic waste dumped in Côte d'Ivoire need urgent examination, UN expert says. *British Medical Journal, 339.*

Prima facie evidence points to deaths and adverse health problems for people living near the site where 500 tons of toxic waste were dumped from a Dutch ship. The site is near Abidjan, Côte d'Ivoire. Investigators are concerned with the ongoing and future health and environmental consequences of this event.

In reading these articles, two themes became clear: the fact that toxic waste dumping has long-lasting effects and is prevalent, and the fact that exposure to toxic waste gives rise to specific diseases and conditions. The relationship of these two themes to the central question is shown in the figure below.

Based on these data, I can start my ROL. Obviously, an ROL for your dissertation would be far more extensive, but these entries serve as a good example.

Introduction

Throughout the world, toxic chemicals are used in the manufacture of a wide variety of consumer goods and also serve as key components in agriculture, construction, and various service industries (Wayman, 2013). In the United States, federal law mandates the safe cleaning, storage, or destruction of hazardous waste created by the use of such chemicals (Environmental Protection Agency, 2013a). In the case of this study, residents of a small town in the southeastern United States are concerned with possible health problems related to hazardous waste processing by a local plant. In order to better understand these issues, this ROL focuses on the history and prevalence of hazardous waste processing and potential health-related problems related to exposure to hazardous waste.

Hazardous Waste

Per National Geographic (2013), hazardous wastes are

> poisonous byproducts of manufacturing, farming, city septic systems, construction, automotive garages, laboratories, hospitals, and other industries. The waste may be liquid,

solid, or sludge and contain chemicals, heavy metals, radiation, dangerous pathogens, or other toxins. Even households generate hazardous waste from items such as batteries, used computer equipment, and leftover paints or pesticides.

Until the passage of the Resource Conservation and Recovery Act (RCRA) in 1976, regulations for the disposal of hazardous waste were largely nonexistent. The RCRA was passed in an effort to control the increasing amount of toxic waste products produced in the United States by clearly defining hazardous waste, as well as providing regulations for the control, transport, and disposal of such waste.

The RCRA is effective in regulating current and potential future hazardous waste concerns. In order to deal with historic problems, such as the pollution in Love Canal in New York state, first reported in the mid-1950s, Congress enacted the Comprehensive Environmental Response, Compensation, and Liability Act (CERCLA), commonly called the Superfund, in 1980; this act was amended and supported by the Superfund Amendments and Reauthorization Act of 1986 (SARA). These laws allow the EPA to force responsible parties to clean up hazardous waste sites and, when the parties responsible are not identifiable, the agency cleans the sites using money from a designated trust fund. Since the passage of these acts, the EPA has remediated over 10,000 hazardous waste sites—however, there are currently 1,280 Superfund sites with another 62 considered as needing further investigation by the EPA (Superfund National Accomplishments Summary Fiscal Year, 2012).

Health Risks

As reported in *Science News* (Wayman, 2013), millions of people are at risk of illness as a result of working or living in the proximity of hazardous waste disposal sites. Higher than expected rates of cancers, cardiac and respiratory problems, and intellectual disability in children have been linked directly to higher than expected levels of lead, arsenic, mercury, and other common chemicals. Other less common chemicals, including hexavalent chromium and trichloroethylene, are also directly linked to illness in human beings (Raloff, 2009; Wayman, 2013; Zarocostas, 2009).

Because of the discovery of previously unknown toxic waste sites, issues in remediating the problems, and problems associated with data collection, researchers call for continued research in this area (Wayman, 2013). Vrijheid (2000) states that "It is difficult to conclude whether these symptoms are an effect of direct toxicologic action of chemicals present in waste sites, an effect of stress and fears related to the waste site, or an effect of reporting bias" (p. 101).

Conclusion

Toxic waste has, and continues to have, negative health effects for humankind and negative effects on Earth's environment. Various governmental, educational, and private sector agencies have linked toxins released from toxic waste dumps directly to various medical conditions and diseases. These same agencies continue to remediate problems related to dumps. At the same time, the agencies identify new areas of concern and opportunities for research. Based on the currently available literature, it is safe to hypothesize that residents living in close proximity to the toxic waste site that is the focus of this study will report higher than expected levels of disease and other medical conditions.

Progress Check for Chapter 3
of a Quantitative Dissertation Proposal

In the first two appendices, we saw that the first chapter of our dissertation lays the groundwork for our study (problem, research purpose, research questions, and hypothesis) and the second chapter reviews literature, so as to demonstrate that we have become subject-area experts. Remember, the hypothesis for our study, if called for, is also developed from what we learn in the ROL, even though it is generally placed in Chapter 1 for readability.

As you'll remember, in Appendix A, when we were writing Chapter 1 for this study, we included one hypothesis:

> *There will be a significant difference in the number of current health problems experienced by residents living near the waste treatment plant and residents living away from the waste treatment plant.*

We also included two research questions:

1. Is the current number of health problems experienced by citizens living close to the processing plant different from residents living in other areas?
2. What are the experiences of residents living in communities surrounding the chemical processing plant?

At this point, we're ready to develop Chapter 3 of our proposal, the research method. In it, we will design our study to answer the first research question and test the hypothesis; we'll investigate the second research question in Appendix D, when we see an example of a qualitative proposal. Here, we discuss the population and sample for our study, any instruments we may need to collect data, the research design we plan to use, and the exact procedures we'll follow to conduct our study. Keep in mind: Your university or dissertation chair may call for more material than this. Herein we're looking at the very basics of what we need.

Chapter 3: Research Methods

The Quantitative Paradigm

In this study, the researcher serves as an objective observer and is independent from the actual study. The research process will be deductive and value-free, and the results will be used to determine whether a significant difference in health problems exists between residents living near the waste facility and residents living farther than 1 mile away from the facility. Based on this information, the use of a quantitative approach is appropriate.

The Research Design

The study will use a static group comparison research method. Two groups, identified by data indicating the proximity of their residence to the waste facility, will be formed. For this study, residents living within 1 mile of the plant will be considered as a group separate from those living farther than 1 mile away from the facility. Results from surveys completed will be analyzed and used to test the study's hypothesis.

Participants and Sampling

The population of the area directly surrounding the abandoned mill property, defined as living within 1 mile, is approximately 500 residents; there are approximately 13,000 residents in the greater metropolitan area. The city is located in central Alabama at the intersection of two major national highways, with ready access to a major waterway. The population is approximately 70% non-Hispanic White and 25% African American, with the remaining 5% representing Hispanic, Asian/Pacific Islander, and Native American. The median age of residents is approximately 39 years, with females outnumbering males 55 to 45%, respectively. The median income for the area is $26,000, with a median price for a home or condominium at $123,000 (*www.city-data.com/city/Sylacauga-Alabama.html*).

Power analysis indicates the need for a sample size of 372. Due to the inability to easily identify the entire population, true random sampling is not conceivable; because of that problem, a purposive, snowball sample will be identified. Civic leaders (e.g., government officials; educational administrators; leaders of organizations, such as Kiwanis International) known to the researcher will be contacted and asked to both complete the survey, as well as to encourage their members to complete the survey and recruit other participants. Persons completing the survey will be screened for inclusion in the sample (e.g., ages 18 or older), with qualified participants' data stored for analysis.

Instruments

The hypothesis calls for the collection of the number of health problems experienced by residents of the metropolitan area. Due to the focus of the study, the definition of health problems will be delimited to include neurological disorders (e.g., Alzheimer's, seizure disorders) or breathing-related issues (e.g., cancer, bronchitis, pneumonia, asthma). Other data to be collected will include gender, race or ethnicity, age, and residence proximity to the waste facility. A text box to allow for other commentary, and a checkbox to indicate willingness to participate and permission to use the de-identified data, must also be included. Data will be collected using a firewall-protected web-based survey developed by the author.

The Research Procedures

Researchers will first develop the online survey using one of the many online resources of this type. Following that, participant recruitment will begin. Business, civic, and governmental leaders will be approached and asked to participate and recruit other respondents for the survey. This process will continue until the minimum sample size of 372 is reached or surpassed. Once data collection is complete, participants will be coded as living in close proximity to the waste facility (i.e., 1 mile or less) or away from the facility (i.e., greater than 1 mile).

Plans for Data Analysis

Descriptive statistics will be computed and, based on the results, the appropriate inferential test will be used to analyze the data. The hypothesis will be tested using an alpha value of .05; p values less than alpha will result in rejecting the null hypothesis. Effect size indices will be computed in order to determine the effect of the independent variable on the dependent variable. Descriptive statistics and results of the inferential tests will be presented and discussed.

Ethical Considerations

Permission must be obtained from the appropriate IRB. Residents completing the survey must be made aware that their privacy is protected; no results, individual or aggregate, will be able to be tracked back to a single person. Residents should also be warned that reflecting on current or past medical conditions may cause emotional distress; completion of the survey, at any point, is not required.

Plans for Presenting the Results

After the data are analyzed, and the hypothesis tested, all results will be presented in Chapters 4 and 5 of the dissertation report. Additionally, a summary report detailing the results of the study will be developed and made available to government officials, affected residents, or concerned third parties.

Summary

This chapter discussed the research method for investigating health issues related to an abandoned chemical waste facility. Upon completion of data collection, the results of the analysis will be presented in Chapter 4 of the dissertation report. The results of the hypothesis testing and a discussion of the conclusions that are drawn from this study will be presented in Chapter 5.

Progress Check for Chapter 3
of a Qualitative Dissertation Proposal

In this appendix, we use the same problem statement from Appendix A, but focus only on the qualitative research question we included at that point:

What are the experiences of residents living in communities surrounding the chemical processing plant?

We start by presenting our qualitative paradigm, our design, the population and sample for our study, and any instruments we will need to collect data. Following that, the research procedures and plans for data analysis will be presented in great detail. The appendix will close by discussing any ethical considerations and our plans for presenting the results.

Chapter 3: Research Methods

The Qualitative Paradigm

In the proposed study, it is imperative that a fair, respectful, and trusting rapport be established between the researcher and citizens of the community surrounding the waste treatment plant. This relationship must exist knowing that the knowledge uncovered is contextual, with the researcher being respectful of varying viewpoints and the subjective truths that might arise from interactions with multiple participants. Research in this subject area calls for close interaction between the researcher and adults who live in the community surrounding the plant. The relationship between these factors calls for a qualitative approach in answering the research question.

Research Design

Due to the direct focus of the research question on the lived experience of citizens, a qualitative phenomenological design will be used.

Participants and Sampling

The population of the area directly surrounding the abandoned mill property, defined as living within 1 mile, is approximately 500 residents; there are approximately 13,000 residents in the greater metropolitan area. The city is located in central Alabama at the intersection of two major national highways, with ready access to a major waterway. The population is approximately 70% non-Hispanic White and 25% African American, with the remaining 5% representing Hispanic, Asian/Pacific Islander, and Native American. The median age of residents is approximately 39 years, with females outnumbering males 55 to 45%, respectively. The median income for the area is $26,000, with a median price for a home or condominium at $123,000 (*www.city-data.com/city/Sylacauga-Alabama.html*).

A study of this type requires a sample size of 12–15 participants. In order to recruit participants, a purposive, snowball sampling approach will be used. Citizens living in the community, including business, civic, and governmental leaders known to the researcher, will be contacted and asked to participate in the study, as well as to identify other potential participants. Persons identified will be screened for inclusion in the sample (e.g., ages 18 or older, living in the immediate vicinity of the plant), with qualified participants' data stored for analysis.

Instruments

The research question calls for a resident's description of life living in the vicinity of the waste treatment plant. Demographic data will be collected, followed by semistructured interviews focused on the research question.

Research Procedures

At the outset, IRB approval must be granted before participant recruitment can begin. Business, civic, and governmental leaders will be approached and asked to participate and recruit other respondents for interviews. This process will continue until the minimum sample size of 12–15 participants is reached or surpassed. Participants will be contacted and a convenient time and place for the interviews will be established. Each interview is expected to last approximately 1 hour, with all sessions recorded and transcribed.

Plans for Data Analysis

All recordings will be transcribed; the data will be verified by reading through the transcripts while listening to the recordings. Once verified, the data will be analyzed using a phenomenological approach by looking for common themes that relate directly to the study's research question. Notes will be taken in an effort to identify the beginning, middle, and end of the story; further evaluation will attempt to identify transitions, stories, and emotional statements, thereby allowing for connection between each phenomenon. Thematic coding will then allow for further development of the overall analysis, thereby allowing for a logical "restorying" of the entire event. Additional reference material from published sources (e.g., newspapers, government documents) may be used to develop a complete explanation and understanding of the residents' experiences. The initial draft will be returned to the interviewees: They will be asked to verify that all facts are accurately presented. In the event discrepancies are noted, the draft will be modified as needed.

Ethical Considerations

Permission must be obtained from the appropriate IRB. Residents completing the survey must be made aware that their privacy is protected: No results, individual or aggregate, can be tracked back to a single person. Residents should also be warned that reflection on current or past events and experiences may cause emotional distress and that they can end the interview at any time.

Plans for Presenting the Results

After the data are analyzed, all results will be presented in Chapters 4 and 5 of the dissertation report. Additionally, a summary report detailing the results of the study will be developed and made available to government officials, affected residents, and concerned third parties.

Summary

This chapter discussed the research method for investigating the lived experiences of residents living in the community surrounding the toxic waste facility. Residents will be interviewed and the data analyzed from a phenomenological perspective. The results of the analysis will be presented in Chapter 4 of the dissertation report, with a discussion of the conclusions drawn to be presented in Chapter 5.

Progress Check for Chapter 3
of a Mixed Methods Dissertation Proposal

In Appendices A and B, we laid the framework for a good quantitative study about problems with a chemical recycling plant by using this problem statement:

Shortly after beginning operation, the residents of the surrounding area began complaining that noxious fumes coming from the plant were causing respiratory and vision problems.

Again, we assume that the majority of the material presented in Appendices A and B (i.e., Chapter 1: Introduction and Chapter 2: Review of Literature) meet our purposes for a mixed methods proposal. Keep in mind, however, that we're covering only the basics here; you may be asked for more material. In this case, we need to create research questions that call for the collection of both quantitative and qualitative data. So let's assume that we've developed a survey that asks residents to rank the severity of health problems in their community (quantitative data):

What is the severity of the health-related issues in residents living in the community around the chemical recycling plant?

A survey listing the various health problems will be used to answer this research question by asking respondents to rank severity on a scale of 0 (*not severe*) to 7 (*very severe*). For example, respiratory problems could include asthma, cancer, bronchial infections, and the like. The researcher will then follow up during his or her interviews by asking respondents to reflect on their personal lifestyle choices and how these choices might contribute to these health problems (qualitative data):

Do residents take precautions to guard their overall health (e.g., watch their diet, exercise regularly)? Are there other factors that may contribute to poorer health (e.g., excessive alcohol consumption, smoking)?

When these two questions are combined, it will result in the development of the mixed methods research question:

Is there an interaction between lifestyle choices made by the residents in the community and their perceived rate and severity of health problems caused by the abandoned chemical plant?

Using this problem statement and our research questions, we've set the stage for the third chapter of our proposal.

Chapter 3: Research Methods

Mixed Methods Paradigm

While interviewing the participants, the researcher must establish fair, respectful, and trusting rapport between him- or herself and the residents involved in the study. This relationship must exist knowing that the knowledge uncovered is contextual, with the researcher being respectful of varying viewpoints and the subjective truths that might arise from interactions with multiple participants. The researcher must remain independent and objective while developing, validating, and administering the survey instrument. This relationship between the collection and use of quantitative and qualitative data calls for a mixed methods approach.

The Research Design

In this case, the research questions call for the sequential collection and individual analysis, as well as the mixing, of quantitative and qualitative data. Based on that requirement, a mixed methods, sequential–explanatory design is called for. Research Question 1 will be answered using survey data regarding the perceived severity of symptoms of a given resident; research Question 2 will be answered using data from the interviews addressing personal health habits. Results of the analyses will be mixed in order to answer the third research question.

Participants and Sampling

Due to the inability of easily identifying the entire population of residents living within 1 mile of the abandoned mill property, true random sampling is unachievable. Because of that, a purposive, snowball sample of 100 residents (i.e., 20%) will be identified. Following approval from the university's IRB, citizens known to the researcher will be contacted and asked to both complete the survey, as well as encourage other residents to complete the survey and recruit other participants. Persons completing the survey will be screened for inclusion in the sample (e.g., ages 18 or older, living within 1 mile of the property), with qualified participants' demographic and survey data stored for analysis. From the sample of participants who completed the survey, a random sample of 20 potential interviewees will be selected. Each participant will be contacted, and the study explained to him or her. Respondents who agree to participate will be informed of their right to privacy, and of the possibility of adverse psychological issues that may arise from reliving their experiences via the interview; they will also be notified of their right to withdraw from the study at any point. If a minimum of 10 participants cannot be enlisted from the randomly selected group of 20, an additional random sampling of the participants who completed the survey will be called for.

259

Instruments

In this study, two data collection instruments are required. For the first question, an online survey will be developed that asks residents about the severity of personal illnesses caused by the chemical factory. Respondents will be asked to rate the severity of any personal disease or condition they believe is related to the chemical plant. The scale will range from 0 (*not severe*) to 7 (*severe*)—for example, this might be the first item on the survey:

1. How severe are your problems related to asthma?   0   1   2   3   4   5   6   7   N/A

The respondent also has a choice of N/A (not applicable) in cases in which he or she has not experienced the illness or condition.

The second research question focuses on the personal health habits of participants in the study. Participants will be interviewed and asked to comment on their personal health habits. The interview will begin with an overarching question:

What do you regularly do to ensure you stay healthy?

This question will enable the interviewer to ask follow-up or probing questions, such as:

1. Tell me about your daily eating habits.
2. Describe any health issues you have experienced that you believe stem directly from living near the waste treatment plant.
3. Do you regularly go for medical and dental checkups?
4. Do you use tobacco products or drink alcoholic beverages?

In addition to both surveys, demographic data will be collected on gender, race or ethnicity, age, and residence proximity to the waste facility.

The Research Procedures

Prior to beginning the study, the required survey will be developed and permission to use it obtained from the IRB. After obtaining consent forms from participants, they will be asked to complete the survey; the data from those surveys will then be descriptively and inferentially analyzed in order to answer the first research question.

After identifying a smaller sample to be interviewed, a convenient time and place will be established and the interviews will be conducted and recorded. At the conclusion of each interview, the recording will be transcribed by a professional transcriptionist; upon completion, the researcher will compare the recordings and transcriptions for consistency. Issues raised during the interviews may allow for expansion of those ideas in subsequent interviews. This process continues until a minimum of 20 participants have been interviewed, or until the researcher feels that a degree of data saturation has been reached that would preclude conducting further interviews. Data from the analysis of the transcripts will be used to answer the second research question.

Once the data have been analyzed, and the quantitative and qualitative research questions answered, the two data sets will be merged and analyzed. The resulting data will be analyzed and used to answer the overarching, mixed methods research question.

Plans for Data Analysis

The web-based quantitative data collection site will be designed so as to preclude data entry errors, thereby assuring the researcher of the validity of the data collected. Because of that validity, quantitative data analysis will include the appropriate descriptive and inferential tools. Completion of the quantitative data analysis will allow for answering the first research question.

Qualitative data analysis will begin during data collection by focusing on collecting valid data by practicing *epoché*; upon completion the researcher will analyze the transcripts for common themes, attempting to understand the meaning of key phrases both personally and by working with the interviewees. This method ultimately allows the researcher to tie these themes and phrases together to present the story being told by the participants in the study. These results will be used by the researcher to answer the second research question.

The results of the individual analysis and mixing of the quantitative and qualitative data sets will be used to answer the overarching, mixed methods research question.

Ethical Considerations

The researcher must ensure that participants in the study are included by their own free will and volition, and that they have been advised of their rights and potentially negative issues related to participation in the study. Care has to be taken in developing the survey questionnaire and the interview guidelines to allow for the collection and analysis of valid data, and ultimately the development of a sound dissertation report and other summary presentations.

Plans for Presenting the Results

The results of the study are presented in Chapters 4 and 5 of the dissertation. Summary reports may be derived from that information and delivered to concerned citizens and governmental authorities.

Conclusion

This chapter discusses the research method for investigating health issues related to an abandoned chemical waste facility. Quantitative data concerning specific health concerns are collected via a questionnaire, while information regarding lifestyle choices is the focus of individual interviews. Upon the individual analysis of the two data sets, the sets will be merged and analyzed so that all of the research questions can be answered. The results of the study and a discussion of the conclusions that may be drawn from this study are presented in Chapters 4 and 5, respectively.

Sample Proposal
for a Four-Chapter Dissertation

As we've discussed throughout the text, most dissertations have five chapters. Of these, Chapter 1: Introduction, Chapter 2: Review of Literature, and Chapter 3: Methodology, make up the proposal for your dissertation. As I said in the introduction,

> the proposal will act as your "road map" by identifying and discussing the problem you want to investigate, your plan for conducting your research, how you will collect and analyze data and, finally, how you intend on reporting the results.

Once you have completed your research, you then write and include Chapter 4: Results and Chapter 5: Conclusions. The five chapters, taken together, make up your dissertation report.

While the five-chapter dissertation model is most commonly used, there are universities and colleges that require students to write dissertations ranging from four to nine chapters. Of these, other than the five-chapter model, the four-chapter format is most often used. The content of the four-chapter and the five-chapter formats is essentially the same: the difference lies in the placement of material within each chapter. Let's start by looking at typical chapter headings for a four-chapter quantitative dissertation:

1. Chapter 1: Introduction
2. Chapter 2: Methods and Procedures
3. Chapter 3: Results
4. Chapter 4: Discussion

In this case, Chapters 1 and 2 make up the dissertation proposal; all four taken together are the dissertation report. The key difference between this and a dissertation with five chapters is that there isn't a chapter dedicated solely to reviewing the literature. Since we emphasized the importance of the literature review throughout the text, let's look in detail at Chapters 1 and 2 of a quantitative study to see how this is handled.

Chapter 1 of the Proposal: Introduction

In Chapter 1, we have most of the same sections as in the five-chapter model:

1. Introduction: Here, we want to introduce the reader to the problem area by synthesizing and presenting what is already known.

2. Statement of the Problem: As discussed in Chapter 2 of this text, the problem statement must meet the six characteristics of a good problem:

    a. The topic must be interesting to the researcher.

    b. The scope of the research must be manageable by the researcher.

    c. The researcher must have the time, knowledge, and resources necessary to conduct the research.

    d. The research must be ethical.

    e. The study must have theoretical significance.

    f. The researcher must be able to collect and analyze data.

When you write the problem statement, remember that it must be clear and concise, must include all variables to be considered and should not interject the researcher's bias.

3. Purpose of the Study: This should be written following the same guidelines we discussed earlier for the five-chapter model.

4. Review of Literature: Here, again, you will follow the general guidelines for the five-chapter model. Attention should be paid to the broad knowledge domain you are interested in investigating, followed by a focused ROL more closely aligned with your area of inquiry.

5. Rationale for the Study: This is the significance of your study. Contrary to the way it was described for the five-chapter model, instead of the background, the problem, and the significance of the problem, in the four-chapter model we have separate sections for the introduction (i.e., background), the statement of the problem, and the rationale (i.e., the significance of the study).

Chapter 2 of the Proposal: Methods and Procedures

Chapter 2 includes many of the elements we have typically seen in Chapters 1 and 3 of the five-chapter model:

1. Definitions of terms: Like the five-chapter format, this includes definitions of terms specific to the study, or that may not be understood by the reader.

2. Research questions: Earlier in the text, we included research questions to further narrow down the area of inquiry defined by the problem and purpose statements. Here, we further narrow down the purpose of the study by basing it on findings from the ROL. The research questions should be written using the same guidelines and in the same format as those in the five-chapter model.

3. Independent and dependent variables: The independent variable is the "cause" being investigated. For example, if I wanted to examine the effect of gasoline type on miles per gallon, the independent variable would be gasoline type. The dependent variable is the "effect"; in this case, miles per gallon, in a study.

4. Hypotheses: Taken together, the problem, purpose, and research questions allow us to write a hypothesis about events that have, or will, occur. Testing a hypothesis involves investigating the relationship between the cause and effect.

5. Research method: A plan developed to answer your research questions and, when necessary, test your hypotheses. There are several different designs (e.g., experimental, causal–comparative, posttest-only design).

6. Identifying the population and sample: The population includes all members of a group being investigated; the sample includes a subset of the population.

7. Data collection procedures: A step-by-step, very detailed plan for collecting data from your population or sample necessary to answer your research questions or test your hypotheses.

8. Instrumentation: Data collection tools or surveys needed to collect the data necessary to answer your research questions or test your hypotheses.

9. Statistical analysis: A detailed plan for how you will use the appropriate descriptive and inferential statistical tools to answer your research questions or test your hypotheses.

10. Summary: A brief overview of the methods and procedures that will be used in the study.

Qualitative and Mixed Methods Proposals

The guidelines for Chapters 1 and 2 for qualitative and mixed methods studies generally follow those for the quantitative model. Notable differences are a discussion of the role of the researcher during data collection, how participants will be identified and recruited, ways of determining the validity of the data, and covering any consideration not otherwise covered earlier in the study. These, and other issues covered in Chapters 1–3 of the five-chapter model must be taken into consideration when writing the proposal for a four-chapter dissertation.

Conclusion

As we've discussed, the five-chapter dissertation model is most commonly used but there are universities and colleges that require different formats. In this case, it was easy to see that Chapters 1 and 2 of the four-chapter structure were really nothing more than the rearrangement and consolidation of material from Chapters 1–3 in the five-chapter approach. What we've looked at here is just one example of how a four-chapter model might be written. The key is this: Follow the guidelines of your dissertation chair and university.

Answers to Review Questions

Chapter One Review Questions

1. *Birth weights of babies born to drug-addicted mothers.* This example doesn't meet most of the criteria for a good problem statement. Based on what is alluded to, however, a good problem statement investigating the birth weights of drug-addicted mothers versus mothers who are not drug addicts could be developed. If that were the case, we would have to assume the problem is interesting to the researcher; that the scope is manageable for him or her; and that the researcher has the knowledge, resources, and time needed to answer the research question. We would also need to ensure that the problem can be researched through data analysis, that it is significant, and that there is no bias on the part of the researcher. If we were part of a research group in a specific hospital investigating this problem, we could reframe and refocus the vague problem statement that we have so that it meets our criteria for a good problem statement:

   The birth weight of babies in Maryville Hospital born to drug-addicted mothers is significantly lower than the hospital's average birth weight.

2. *Employees working in the older section of an industrial plant are concerned with the effects of asbestos used in building the plant.* This problem is somewhat clear but there are certainly many issues with it. First, the scope of the problem is probably not manageable and the workers likely do not have the knowledge needed. If we had professionals who were interested in the problem, and had the time and resources necessary, we could identify a practical problem that is significant, could be investigated through the collection of data, and would be ethical. We could then state a clear unbiased problem statement including all variables to be investigated:

   There is a threat to employee health posed by the effects of asbestos in older sections of the industrial plant.

3. *Farmers in the United States are concerned that strict immigration laws will not allow them to hire enough farmhands to reap their annual harvests.* The research problem is certainly implied but is not clear: It seems that the farmers are hiring a lot of immigrants for fieldwork and stricter laws will cut down the labor pool. This could affect their ability to harvest their crops, leading to financial losses. The biggest problems here are the scope and the specificity of the variable "farmhand." Given their recent passage of strict immigration laws in Georgia, we could meet all of our criteria by creating a better focus:

> *Farmers in Georgia are concerned that strict immigration laws will not allow them to hire enough migrant farmhands to reap their annual harvests.*

4. *Publishers are concerned that the ever-increasing costs of printing traditional textbooks will cause decision makers in the elementary school market to opt for electronic textbooks.* This seems to be a valid problem but there are some issues with it. We can assume that the publishers have the interest, are comfortable in terms of the knowledge needed, and so on, and can collect data to investigate their problem. It is certainly practical and there are no ethical issues. However, what about the scope of the problem? Is this aimed at one company or the publishing industry in general? Narrowing the problem statement to one company, thereby increasing its focus, would probably be advisable:

> *Management at Anytime Publishing is concerned that their publishing costs for traditional textbooks will lead decision makers in the elementary school market to opt for electronic textbooks.*

5. *Subscriber feelings toward anonymous text messages used for advertising.* This isn't a good problem statement simply because it lacks most of the criteria needed for one. There doesn't seem to be a theoretical or practical reason to conduct an investigation, the scope of the problem is undefined, we don't know the service or product the subscriber has purchased, and so on. In short, we don't know the problem and too many characteristics of a good problem are missing for us to move forward.

6. *Is there a difference in recovery times among patients who receive medication for back injuries, patients who receive physical therapy for back injuries, and patients who receive a combination of medication and physical therapy for back injuries?* This is not a problem statement, it is a question. A problem is implied, however. Investigators may need better knowledge about which approach is best, allowing them to determine the best way to shorten recovery times for their patients. It is certainly ethical and we can assume the scope is manageable and researchers have the time and other requirements to investigate the problem. It seems that they are not interjecting bias and all variables are included. Given that, it could be worded as a problem:

> *Health care professionals have not evaluated the efficacy of various rehabilitation approaches to back injuries and their effect on patient recovery times.*

7. *Engineering students at Wattsamatta University are concerned that changes in gravitational pull during the 28-day lunar cycle are affecting the structure of the microwave tower on their classroom building.* This problem seems a little far-fetched but let's examine the criteria. First, engineering students are clearly interested and should be able to collect and analyze data reflecting the integrity of the tower's structure. The problem has practical significance and is ethical to investigate. Given that there is no personal bias, all variables are included, and it is stated clearly, it is definitely a good problem statement.

8. *High-altitude climbers are concerned with hypoxia; the inability of the human body to perform due to a generalized lack of oxygen in the body.* This is an interesting problem statement. There is certainly a relationship between the ability to climb at higher altitudes and hypoxia. At the same time, what does "high altitude" mean? Obviously, the problem is different for climbers on relatively small mountains (e.g., Mt. Baker at 10,786 feet) and much higher mountains (e.g., Denali at 20,310 feet). We have to assume that the other criteria, such as investigator interest and comfort in terms of knowledge, time, and resources, are met. Given that, it might be better to state the problem in more exact terms:

    Climbers of peaks higher than 20,000 feet are concerned with hypoxia, the inability of the human body to perform due to a generalized lack of oxygen in the body.

9. *Clients at an inner-city mental health facility who are suffering from depression and are working with therapists using a psychoanalytic approach are not responding to therapy as effectively and efficiently as those working with therapists using a cognitive-behavioral approach.* This is a well-stated problem, all variables are included, and there is no personal bias. We have to assume that the person conducting the study is comfortable in terms of his or her knowledge, time, and resources and that he or she is interested in the problem. Given the specificity of the location, the scope seems manageable, and by using tools, such as the Beck Depression Inventory, therapists can collect and analyze data. Finally, there is a practical reason to investigate what is an ethical study.

10. *This study will investigate morale between soldiers wearing camouflage uniforms versus those wearing khaki uniforms.* There is no apparent problem here, given that evaluating the remaining criteria isn't called for.

Chapter Two Review Questions

The Case of Distance Counseling

Given what we know, suppose we wanted to determine whether it takes therapists the same number of sessions to deal effectively with depression cases in a traditional versus a distance approach. How would we write our purpose statement? What would be a good research question to investigate? How would we state our research and null hypotheses?

Purpose Statement: The purpose of this study is to determine whether there is a difference in the number of sessions needed to effectively treat depression between clients receiving therapy in a distance format and clients receiving therapy in a traditional format.

Research Question: Is there a difference in the number of sessions needed for treating depression between clients receiving therapy in a traditional setting and clients receiving therapy in a distance setting?

Research Hypothesis: *There will be a significant difference in the number of counseling sessions for treating depression between clients in a traditional setting and clients in a distance setting.*

Null Hypothesis: *There will be no significant difference in the number of counseling sessions for treating depression between clients in a traditional setting and clients in a distance setting.*

The Case of the New Teacher

Purpose Statement: The purpose of this study is to determine whether there are differences in the number of parent–teacher conferences between nonaffluent schools and affluent schools.

Research Question: Is there a difference in the number of parent–teacher conferences in nonaffluent schools and affluent schools?

Research Hypothesis: *There will be significantly fewer parent–teacher conferences in nonaffluent schools than in affluent schools.*

Null Hypothesis: *There will be no significant difference in the number of parent–teacher conferences between nonaffluent schools and affluent schools.*

The Case of Being Exactly Right

Purpose Statement: The purpose of this study is to develop software that will control waste-cleansing equipment to maintain a temperature of exactly 155°F.

Research Question: Is it possible to develop software that will maintain a steady temperature of 155°F?

Research Hypothesis: *There will be a significant difference between the temperature of equipment controlled by our new software and 155°F.*

Null Hypothesis: *There will be no significant difference between the temperature of equipment controlled by our new software and 155°F.*

The Case of "Does It Really Work?"

Purpose Statement: The purpose of this study is to compare achievement between students taking an online anatomy and physiology course, and those taking an anatomy and physiology course in a traditional classroom.

Research Question: Can students taking an online anatomy and physiology course have achievement levels equal to students taking an anatomy and physiology course in the classroom?

Research Hypothesis: *There will be a significant difference in achievement between students taking an online anatomy and physiology course and students taking the same course in the classroom.*

Null Hypothesis: *There will be no significant difference in achievement between students taking an online anatomy and physiology course and students taking the same course in the classroom.*

The Case of Advertising

Purpose Statement: The purpose of this study is to investigate the differences in teacher recruitment in Pike County based on advertisements in newspapers, and teacher recruitment from Internet-based advertising.

Research Question: Will the use of Internet-based advertising result in more applicants than advertising in newspapers in Pike County?

Research Hypothesis: *There will be a significantly larger number of job applicants from Internet-based advertising than from newspaper advertising.*

Null Hypothesis: *There will be no significant difference in the number of job applicants from Internet-based advertising versus from newspaper advertising.*

The Case of Learning to Speak

Purpose Statement: The purpose of this study is to investigate language skills acquired between students learning Spanish in an immersive environment and students being taught in a traditional classroom.

Research Question: Is there a difference in the language skills acquired between students learning Spanish in an immersive environment and students learning Spanish in a traditional classroom environment?

Research Hypothesis: *There will be a significant difference in Spanish language skills after 1 year of instruction between students taught in an immersive environment and students taught in the traditional classroom.*

Null Hypothesis: *There will be no significant difference in Spanish language skills after 1 year of instruction between students taught in an immersive environment and students taught in the traditional classroom.*

Chapter Three Review Questions

1. "Generativity" refers to the ability to generalize what is learned from one research study to another scenario. For example, if we learn that first-year students at a community college react well to assigned mentors, are the results generalizable to first-year students at 4-year colleges? In short, does the study of first-year community college students demonstrate generalizability?

2. The three major components of the ROL are the introduction, the body, and the conclusion. The introduction, in most instances, briefly restates the problem area and research questions. These topics are addressed within the body of the ROL by identifying and reading relevant literature, mapping and synthesizing the literature, and presenting it in a synthesized cogent manner. From this the researcher becomes a subject-matter expert, and is able to identify appropriate methodologies, designs, procedures, and so on to help

guide a study. The conclusion summarizes what was learned in the ROL and, in quantitative studies, allows the researcher to state a testable hypothesis.

3. Identifying and using key words related to his or her research area helps the researcher identify material to be used in his or her ROL. Key words are generally used to search electronic databases and can be identified both through existing personal knowledge about a subject field and the subsequent identification of other key words as you read the literature you've identified.

4. Mapping out the ROL allows the writer to identify themes or common elements in the literature he or she is searching. Doing this allows the researcher to synthesize his or her reporting of the literature, allowing for a clearer, more understandable presentation of what was read.

5. Primary sources of literature are attributed to the major author in a field. For example, if you are reading about psychoanalysis, Sigmund Freud would be a primary source. Secondary sources discuss and report on the work of primary authors in a given field. Generally speaking, when conducting research, we would like to rely on primary sources whenever possible.

6. An annotated bibliography allows you to store information from individual sources of literature as you read them. For example, for each journal article you read, you should create a document that includes the bibliographic reference and a synopsis of what you read. Rather than trying to store complete copies of everything you read, you're keeping a much smaller document that you can use by itself or allow you to refer back to the original source as needed.

Chapter Four Review Questions

1. True.
2. False. Probabilistic sampling gives all members of a population the greatest chance of being selected for a sample.
3. True.
4. True.
5. False. The type of interview you use depends upon the research questions and the information you need. A structured interview allows the respondent to give you only the information you specifically ask for. Semistructured and unstructured interviews allow you to ask follow-up questions or give the person being interviewed complete freedom in answering the question.
6. False. Demographic forms need to be used only when information such as name, gender, ethnicity, age, and the like are being collected.
7. False. Although they are used in different circumstances, these values are strong measures of reliability.
8. False. Projective tests are used to better understand and investigate constructs such as personality, depression, and so on.
9. True.
10. False. Researchers need only be concerned with ethical issues where human or animal subjects are involved.

11. False. Dualism refers to a quantitative researcher's belief that he or she must be objective and separate him- or herself from the problem he or she is investigating.

12. Random sampling is the purest form of probabilistic sampling where every member of a population has an equal opportunity to be selected for the sample. Nonprobabilistic sampling, also known as nonrandom sampling, describes situations in which the researcher does not have the opportunity to create a random sample. Examples include convenience sampling, purposive sampling, and snowball sampling.

13. When cluster sampling, the researcher selects preformed groups (e.g., classrooms) to be included in the sample. When creating a stratified sample, the researcher purposefully divides the population into subsets (e.g., political party within a population of voters) and then randomly samples members from each subset.

14. Validity asks the question, "Is my test or survey measuring what it is supposed to be measuring?", while reliability asks, "Does my test or survey consistently measure what it is measuring?"

15. Populations include all members of the larger group from which you would like to draw the sample representative of the population. Sampling bias is anything that occurs that would cause the characteristics of the sample to be unlike those of the population, thereby creating problems with generalizability.

16. Convergent validity investigates whether the construct you are measuring is correlated with a similar construct. Discriminant validity is used to ensure that the construct you are measuring does not correlate with other constructs that could be considered negative. Construct validity is a combination of acceptable levels of convergent and discriminate validity.

17. With systematic sampling, the sample is created by identifying a population and then selecting every nth member to be part of the sample. In a convenience sample, members are selected from a population because they are readily available.

18. Equivalent forms reliability investigates the consistency of measurement between two alternate forms of the same instrument (e.g., Form A, Form B, Form C). Test–retest reliability looks at consistency over time when the results of an instrument taken at one point in time are correlated with the results of the same instrument taken at a later point in time.

19. Population and sampling frame are synonyms. They both represent a given group from which a sample can be taken.

20. Cronbach's alpha should be used when establishing split-half reliability. This allows researchers to account for the variance in correlation coefficients between the multitude of ways that a given instrument could be split.

Chapter Five Review Questions

1. c	2. d	3. c	4. b	5. d
6. c	7. d	8. c	9. d	10. a
11. a	12. d	13. c	14. b	15. c
16. d	17. c	18. c	19. a	20. b

Chapter Six Review Questions

1. False. In qualitative studies, validity is the consistency of the data collection process.

2. True. Developing open and axial codes are part of data reduction. This is continued in grounded theory studies with the identification of a selective code.

3. False. Data saturation is the point at which the results of an interview do not provide you with anything that wasn't already discussed in earlier interviews.

4. False. Member checking is the verification of the accuracy of a final report by people who were interviewed during the study.

5. False. Peer debriefers should not be familiar with your work. By reviewing your methodology, the data you collected, and your analysis and report, they will be able to provide you with objective feedback.

6. False. Field notes are observations you make, and write down, as part of your research study.

7. True. More detail indicates the thoroughness of your data collection, analysis, and synthesis.

8. False. A biography is a type of narrative study.

9. True. The comparison of results from two sets of data or procedures helps ensure the consistency (i.e., the validity) of your study.

10. False. If I was living with the Maoris, I would want to take an insider's (i.e., emic) perspective.

11. True. The central phenomenon is what we want to investigate; it is the purpose of our study.

12. False. The primary data collection tool in a qualitative study is the researcher.

13. False. In this case, you would be asking more than one person to describe a phenomenon he or she experienced; hence, you would be making a phenomenological study.

14. False. External auditors can give you the perspective of a disinterested person outside the scope of the actual study being conducted.

Chapter Seven Review Questions

1. False. A mixed methods study is based on a problem and a research question that calls for a mixed methods design. Other studies may collect both types of data but they are never merged or analyzed together.

2. False. Answering a mixed methods research question requires that the quantitative and qualitative data be merged and analyzed as such.

3. True. A good mixed methods research study includes a quantitative research question, a qualitative research question, and a mixed methods research question.

4. False. The sequential mixed methods design calls for the data sets to be analyzed separately and then merged.

5. False. There are many different types of mixed methods studies. This book only covers the three most basic designs.

6. True. The type of sampling performed in a study depends on the type of data, the size of the data set needed, and the specific circumstances of the study itself.

7. False. The priority of a given strand is different between methodologies.

8. False. A sequential–explanatory study calls for collecting quantitative data prior to qualitative data. A sequential–exploratory study collects qualitative data prior to quantitative data.

9. False. A researcher should use the appropriate statistical tool to test the quantitative hypothesis.

10. False. Sequencing indicates the point at which data are collected; priority is the order in which the types of data are collected.

Glossary

Note: This glossary contains definitions of all terms presented at the end of the chapters, as well as other research and statistical terms you may encounter as you are writing your proposal.

A priori	Before an event occurs. For example, we decide our alpha value a priori. This means we decide our alpha value prior to the start of a study.
Accidental sampling	See *Convenience sampling.*
Achievement tests	Examinations used to measure a specific content area.
Affective tests	Instruments used to measure constructs; values we know exist but aren't tangible.
Alpha value	The degree of risk we are willing to take when computing inferential statistics. Sometimes referred to as the type I error rate.
Alternate hypothesis	See *Research hypothesis.*
Analysis of covariance (ANCOVA)	A version of the analysis of variance where initial differences in the dependent variable are considered prior to final calculations.
Analysis of variance (ANOVA)	A statistical tool based on an *F* distribution. Varieties of the ANOVA include the one-way ANOVA, the factorial ANOVA, and the multivariate ANOVA (MANOVA).

275

Annotated bibliography	A brief synopsis of each resource (e.g., books, journal articles) that you read as part of your study.
Area under the curve	A value ranging from 0 to 100% representing the percentage of values in a given range under one of the data distributions (e.g., the z distribution and the t distribution).
Assumptions	Characteristics of a data set we assume to be true prior to using a given statistical procedure.
Autobiographical narrative	An account of a person's life written by that person.
Axial code	A code that represents the theme of more than one distinct open code.
Axiology	A researcher's beliefs about what is ethical and valuable.
Background of the problem	Information about the genesis of, or what is known about, your problem area.
Behavioral observation scale	A behavior-based measure used to count the frequency of a given behavior or activity.
Beta	Annotation used to designate the probability of making a type II error.
Between-groups variance	The total amount of variance between data sets representing the levels of an independent variable.
Bibliographic database	Online resource used as a repository primarily for journal articles.
Bimodal	A data distribution with two modes.
Biographical narrative	An account of someone's life story written by someone other than the person.
Bivariate	Involving two data sets. For example, a correlation procedure using two data sets is a bivariate correlation.
Bonferroni test	A post hoc test used with the analysis of variance. When significant overall differences are found, this test runs a series of modified t tests to ascertain which levels of the independent variable are significantly different from one another.
Bounded system	The area of focus in case study research.
Bracketing	In qualitative research, the effort by a researcher to refrain from studying or evaluating an experience, without interjecting their personal feelings or experiences.

Case study research	Research in which specific focus is given to a particular situation, group, or person over an extended period of time.
Categorical data	See *Nominal data*.
Causal–comparative research	A quantitative research design where two or more existing groups are compared.
Cell	The space formed at the intersection of a row and a column in a table. The cell is used to record frequencies of values meeting the criteria of the cell.
Central limit theorem	A theorem is nothing more than a statement of an idea that has proven to be true. For example, the central limit theorem tells us "If a sample size is sufficiently large, the sampling distribution of the mean will be approximately normal."
Central phenomenon	The major issue or research opportunity investigated in qualitative research.
Chi-square goodness-of-fit test	A nonparametric test that compares an observed distribution of nominal data to an expected distribution of nominal data.
Chi-square test of independence	A nonparametric test of association that determines whether similar numbers of occurrences appear in groups of nominal-level data. This is sometimes called a factorial chi-square test.
Cluster sampling	The selection of intact groups within the population in order to get the total number of subjects we need.
Coefficient of determination	The result of squaring Pearson's r in a correlational procedure. It represents the strength of a correlation directly attributable to the independent variable.
Computed range	The range of a quantitative data set computed by subtracting the lowest observed value from the highest observed value.
Computed value of F	The result of an analysis of variance. This value can be compared to a critical value of F to determine whether a null hypothesis should be rejected.
Computed value of p	The probability that data sets being compared are significantly different. This is done by comparing it to a pre-determined *alpha* value.
Computed value of t	This value is output from both independent and dependent sample t tests. In days prior to the use of computers, this value was compared to a table (critical) value of t to determine whether a null hypothesis should be rejected.

Computed value of z	The value of a data point on a normal curve representative of the number of standard deviations above or below the mean.
Concurrent validity	Established when scores from one test are highly correlated to scores from another test when administered to the same group of test takers.
Confidence interval	A range of sample statistics in which there's a given probability that a population parameter exists.
Confirmability	The ability of an outside reader to confirm or substantiate data or a biography based on the data.
Confounding variable	An uncontrolled-for variable in a study that could affect the results of any intervention, treatment, or activity, and their effect on a dependent variable.
Construct	Values that we know exist, such as personality type and learning style, but are not tangible.
Construct validity	The ability of an instrument to measure a nonobservable or hypothetical construct.
Consumer of statistics	A person who uses statistics to interpret data, as well as understand data that others are presenting.
Content analysis	The study of documents or other material in the forms of audio or video recordings, pictures, etc. The results of these analyses afford researchers the opportunity to develop patterns for future communication in a systematic or representative or replicable manner.
Content validity	The degree to which a developed instrument accurately represents the content area or construct it was developed to measure.
Contingency table	A multidimensional table used in a chi-square test when the rows and columns of the table are defined by the levels of the independent variables.
Continuous data	A generic name for interval or ratio-level data; also called quantitative data.
Convenience sampling	A technique that uses subjects who just happen to be in a given place at a given time.
Convergent design	A mixed methods design wherein quantitative and qualitative data are collected and analyzed individually at the same point in the study. The results are then mixed in order to answer the mixed methods research question.

Convergent validity	The degree to which two instruments developed to measure a given construct are related.
Correlation coefficient	Output from any of the correlational procedures. It represents the strength of the relationship between two or more sets of data.
Correlational research	A research method where two or more groups of quantitative data are collected and analyzed to determine whether a positive or negative correlation exists between the sets of data.
Counterbalanced design	An experimental or quasi-experimental study where multiple groups receive all interventions in differing orders; participants are tested after each intervention.
Credibility	See *Validity*.
Criterion-related validity	A measure of whether the results of a given test are correlated to the current or future results of another, previously validated test. Depending on the situation, we might be concerned with the concurrent or predictive validity, or perhaps both, of a test we are considering using.
Criterion validity	The degree to which scores on a developed measurement instrument correlate with other measurements of the same construct or content area.
Criterion variable	The value that is predicted in a correlation procedure.
Critical value	A table value to which one of the computed statistics (e.g., t, z, or F) is compared in order to test a null hypothesis. There are specific tables for each of the respective distributions.
Cronbach's alpha	A measurement of the internal consistency of items in a group. It is most often used as a tool for measuring the internal consistency of items in a scale or other type of measurement instrument.
Data consolidation	The point, when interviewing, that you determine that nothing new or interesting is found in subsequent interviews.
Data reduction	Reducing the amount of raw data you have into more meaningful parts.
Data saturation	The point at which enough data has been collected for analysis to ensure it is representative of the construct or content area being investigated.

Deductive research	A quantitative approach that involves developing a testable hypothesis based on existing theory, published research, or experience. This is followed by collecting and analyzing data to support or reject the hypothesis. For example, a researcher might want to test the efficacy of a pneumonia vaccine shown to work in older adults. The same medication could be administered to younger patients, followed by data collection and analysis. The results would allow the researcher to determine whether the use of the medication with a younger population was warranted.
Definitions of terms	A section within a dissertation or research paper that provides definitions of words or phrases that are unique or specific to the given paper.
Degrees of freedom	The number of scores that are free to vary when describing a particular sample. The method by which they are calculated depends upon the statistical test you are using, but for most calculations, the value is defined as one less than the number of data values.
Delimitations	Factors put into place by a researcher that could possibly affect the results of a given study.
Demographic data forms	Surveys used to collect demographic information, such as gender, ethnicity, race, etc.
Dependability	The degree to which the consistency of research findings, and the detail to which research procedures are developed and documented, that would allow other researchers to replicate a given study.
Dependent-sample t test	Statistical tool used when a study involves one independent variable with two levels and one dependent variable that is measured with quantitative data. In this case, the levels of the independent variable must be related to or correlated with each other.
Dependent variable	The "effect" that is being measured in a study.
Descriptive statistics	Numeric and graphical statistical tools that help us "describe" the data so they can be better used for our decision making. Examples include the mean of a data set or a pie chart.
Differential selection of participants	Using samples that may differ on some characteristic at the outset of the study that may have an effect on the dependent variable.
Directional hypothesis	A hypothesis that implies a "greater than" or a "less than" relationship between the variables being studied. Also called a one-tailed hypothesis.

Discriminant validity	An investigation showing that constructs hypothesized as not being related, are, in fact, not related.
Disordinal interaction	An interaction of two independent variables wherein the values of one independent variable have a dramatically opposite effect on a dependent variable than do values of the second independent variable.
Dissertation	A major research project generally completed as the final part of a doctoral degree. The student focuses on a specific area of interest with guidance from the dissertation chair and committee.
Dissertation chair	A faculty member charged with directing the student through the dissertation process. The chair must be an expert in the content area to be investigated, be intimately familiar with the responsibilities mandated by the university or college, and be willing to serve as the student's advisor and guide.
Dissertation committee	Faculty members work with the dissertation chair and the student to help guide the process. In many instances, committee members may serve specific purposes, such as expertise in data analysis, knowledge of the content area being investigated, etc.
Dissertation defense	A formal student presentation of their completed dissertation made to their dissertation chair, committee, and other interested parties. During the presentation the student may be asked to answer questions, expand upon ideas presented, or better explain results. The dissertation generally ends with formal approval by the dissertation chair and committee; in a very few instances, the chair and committee may ask the student to make minor changes, or to rework larger segments of the paper prior to final approval.
Dissertation proposal	The plan for conducting a dissertation study. Major components include a presentation of the problem to be addressed, a review of related literature, and the methodology that will be used to conduct the study. The proposal generally makes up the first three chapters of a dissertation.
Dissertation report	After a research study has been conducted based on the proposal, chapters discussing the results, findings, and suggestions for future research are included. Taken together, the combined chapters constitute the dissertation report.
Dualism	The act of a researcher in removing themself and having an influence on the research scenario. This is an integral part of positivist research.

Effect size	In parametric statistics, a measure of the degree to which an independent variable affects a dependent variable.
Emic perspective	Perspective of one who is within the environment being studied.
Empirical rule	States that, in a normal distribution, approximately 68.0% of values are within +/– 1 standard deviation from the mean, 95.0% of values are within +/– 2 standard deviations of the mean, and nearly all (99.7%) values are within +/– 3 standard deviations of the mean.
Epistemology	A researcher's beliefs about their role during the research process. Should they be actively involved or act as an observer?
Epoché	The practice of phenomenological researchers whereby the methodologist attempts to refrain from judging the literal, or perceived, existence of a construct being investigated. Many researchers refer to this as starting an investigation with an "empty mind" by neither affirming nor denying the existence of the construct under consideration.
Equal priority	A practice in mixed methods research where the quantitative and qualitative strands are processed simultaneously.
Equal variances assumed/not assumed	A test used in parametric statistics to ensure that the variability within sets of data being compared is equitable. Significant differences in variance call for modification of how computed values in parametric statistics are calculated.
Equivalence coefficient	A numeric value computed to indicate the degree of equivalent forms reliability; values range from 0.00 (no reliability) to 1.00 (very high reliability).
Equivalent forms reliability	The degree to which two tests in a given subject area, given to one group of test takers, correlate.
Ethical research	For a research study to be considered ethical, the researcher must ensure that all participants participate voluntarily, and the participants must not be harmed in any way—socially, physically, or mentally.
Ethnographic research	The extended immersion into, or observation of, a group of individuals in order to understand and report on their shared culture.

Etic perspective	Perspective of one who is not within the environment being studied.
Expected value	Used in chi-square tests as a measure of the number of occurrences of each cell value that the researcher believes should appear. These expected values are compared to the actual number of occurrences in each cell.
Experimental design	A research design wherein participants are sampled in such a manner so as to assure equal representation in groups, classes, etc.
Experimental independent variable	See *Manipulated independent variable.*
Experimental research	A research design wherein participants are sampled in such a manner so as to ensure equal representation in groups, classes, etc.
Experimenter effect	A threat to the validity of a study caused by actions of the researcher that might affect the dependent variable.
External auditors	Persons outside the research study, but with expertise in the field, who examine the validity of the study being conducted.
External validity	The ability of a study's results to be generalized to groups other than the sample and population from which the data were collected.
F Distribution	The plot of F values computed from repeated samples of data.
F value	The value computed in an analysis of variance. It is compared to a critical value of F to interpret hypotheses.
Factorial ANOVA	Statistical tool used when a study involves more than one independent variable, as well as one dependent variable that represents quantitative data.
Fail to reject the null hypothesis	When you are unable to reject the null hypothesis based on the results of your statistical test. This means you are unable to support your research hypothesis.
Field notes	Notes taken while observing a person or action; these will be used as part of the data analysis in answering research questions.

Five-chapter dissertation	A dissertation wherein the first three chapters represent the research proposal. These include Chapter 1: Introduction, Chapter 2: Review of Literature, and Chapter 3: Methodology. After the research is conducted, based on the proposal, Chapters 4 and 5 discuss the data analysis, conclusions that can be drawn based on the results of the data analysis, and recommended future research in the field.
Four-chapter dissertation	A research model similar to the five-chapter model wherein Chapters 1–3 are condensed into two chapters. A research study is conducted based on the proposal with the final two chapters discussing results and future directions.
Frequency distribution table	A table showing the number of occurrences of the various values in a data set.
Generalizability	Establishing evidence that the results of a given research study could be applicable to other populations, times, contexts, etc.
Generativity	The ability of a study to contribute back to the literature in a given field.
Goodness of fit	The degree to which an observed distribution of data values fits the distribution that was expected.
Graphical descriptive statistics	The use of tools such as pie charts, bar charts, and relative frequency diagrams to illustrate the characteristics of a data set.
Grounded theory research	Multiparticipant research focusing on discovering a theory for a single phenomenon of living as shared by others.
Histogram	A graph showing the number of occurrences of the various values in a data set.
History	A threat to the internal validity of a study involving events taking place during the study that may affect the dependent variable.
Hypothesis	A statement that reflects the researcher's beliefs about an event that has occurred or will occur.
Independent-sample *t* test	A statistical tool used when a study involves one independent variable with two levels and one dependent variable that is measured with quantitative data. In this case, the levels of the independent variable cannot be related to or correlated with each other.

Independent variable	In a hypothesis, the variable that is manipulated or controlled for by the researcher. It can be thought of as the "cause" being investigated in a study. For example, if I am investigating the difference in salaries between males and females, the independent variable would be gender.
Inductive research	An approach used when there is no previous theory to test. This involves observing a phenomenon, identifying themes or patterns, and developing a theory based on the results. For example, educators might notice a higher-than-average attrition rate from a given college major or program. From observations or interviews with students leaving the program, a theory explaining the attrition could be developed.
Inferential statistics	Statistical tools used to make decisions or draw inferences about the data we have collected.
Instrument	Any test, survey, interview guideline, etc., used to collect data.
Interaction effect	The simultaneous effect on a dependent variable of two or more independent variables.
Intercase analysis	The action of analyzing data, as a whole, from multiple cases.
Intercept	The point at which the line of best fit crosses the x or y axis on a scatter plot.
Internal validity	The degree to which a research study is able to demonstrate an effective cause-and-effect relationship between a treatment and an outcome.
Interquartile range	The range of values between the first and third quartiles in a data distribution.
Interrater reliability	The extent to which two or more raters (e.g., examiners or observers) agree on the rating of a given evaluation or event.
Interval data	One of two types of data that are called quantitative or continuous. Interval data can theoretically fall anywhere within the range of a given data set. The range can be divided into equal intervals, but this does not imply that the intervals can be directly compared. For example, a student scoring in the 80s on an examination is not twice as smart as a student scoring in the 40s. There is no absolute zero point in an interval-level data set.
Intracase analysis	The action of analyzing data from only one case.

Item validity	The assurance that a question on a test represents material the instrument is designed to measure.
John Henry effect	A threat to external validity caused by a member of a control group performing differently because they perceive a challenge from members of an experimental group. See *Novelty effect*.
Key words	Words identified regarding your topic of research that are generally used to guide the search of a bibliographic database.
Kurtosis	The degree to which a data distribution deviates from normal by being too "peaked" or too "flat."
Latent independent variable	An independent variable that is examined "as is" and is not manipulated by the researcher. Examples include gender and ethnic group.
Leptokurtic	A bell-shaped distribution that is too peaked (i.e., too many values around the mean of a distribution) to be perfectly normally distributed.
Levels of the independent variable	Different values of the independent variable that are investigated to determine whether there is a differing effect on the dependent variable.
Levene's test	A statistical tool for testing the equality of variance in data sets being compared.
Likert scale	A numeric scale used for rating or evaluation.
Limitations	Existing factors that may negatively affect the results of a study. For example, a study investigating STEM education in inner-city schools (i.e., the population) may not be generalizable to students from schools in different locales.
Line of best fit	A graphical technique used in correlational procedures to show the trend of correlations being plotted. A line of best fit that emulates a 45-degree angle demonstrates a strong positive correlation. A line of best fit that appears flatter indicates a lesser degree of correlation.
Logistic regression	A linear regression procedure used to predict the values of a nominal dependent variable.
Lower confidence limit	The smallest value in a confidence interval.
Main effect	The effect of a single independent variable on a dependent variable.

Manipulated (experimental) independent variable	An independent variable where the researcher defines membership into factors or levels. An example would show a researcher placing students in different groups to measure the effect of technology on learning. Sometimes called "experimental independent variable."
Mann–Whitney *U* test	Nonparametric alternative to the independent sample *t* test.
Map out the review of literature (ROL)	The use of graphical tools to show the synthesis of literature resources and topics in your ROL.
Maturation	Any change to a subject (e.g., physical, intellectual) during the course of a study that may affect the dependent variable.
Mean	A measure of central tendency reflecting the average value in a data set. Only used with quantitative data (interval and ratio).
Mean square	A constant used in the calculation of an *F* value computed by dividing the sum of squares value for a specific group by the degrees of freedom for the same group.
Measures of central tendency	Descriptive statistics that help us determine the middle of a data set. Examples include the mean, the median, and the mode.
Measures of dispersion	Descriptive statistics that help determine how spread out a data distribution is. Examples include the range, the standard deviation, and the variance.
Measures of relative standing	Used to compare data points in terms of their relationship within a given data set. Examples include *z* scores and percentiles.
Median	A measure of central tendency that describes the midpoint of data that are ordinal, interval, or ratio level and have been sorted into an ascending or descending sequence.
Member checking	The validation of a final report by people who were interviewed during the study.
Merge or mix	The act of combining the results of previously analyzed quantitative and qualitative data for use in answering a mixed methods research question.

Methodology	A plan devised to direct the implementation of a research study. The primary components include the research design; plans for identifying and recruiting participants; a discussion of instrumentation needed and steps for conducting a study; and the specific procedures or techniques used to identify, select, process, and analyze information about a topic.
Mixed methods research	A research method where both quantitative and qualitative data are collected, and blended, to test hypotheses and answer research questions.
Mode	A measure of central tendency reflecting the value that occurs most often in a data set. Can be used with all types of data.
Mortality	A threat to the internal validity of a study due to the loss of subjects during the course of a study.
Multimodal	A data set having more than one mode.
Multiple comparison test	A test used after the analysis of variance to determine exactly which means are significantly different from one another. An example is the Bonferroni test.
Multiple regression	A regression procedure that uses more than one predictor variable.
Multiple treatment interference	A threat to the external validity of a study due to subjects being exposed to two experimental treatments simultaneously.
Multivariate	Referring to a statistical test that has more than one independent or dependent variable.
Multivariate ANOVA (MANOVA)	Statistical tool used when a study involves any number of independent variables and more than one dependent variable that measures quantitative data.
Narrative research	Exploring and presenting a story about the lived experience of a person.
Negative case analysis	A qualitative approach wherein the researcher identifies and discusses findings that are contrary to results emerging from their research.
Negative correlation	The relationship between two variables in a data set that move opposite of each other. A negative correlation shows that when one variable decreases, the other increases.
Negatively skewed	Skewed to the left (i.e., there are more values below the mean of a quantitative data set than there are above the mean).

Nominal data	Data that are categorical in nature. Examples include gender, ethnic group, and grade in school.
Nondirectional hypothesis	A hypothesis that implies a difference will exist between the variables being studied but no direction is implied. Also called a two-tailed hypothesis.
Nonequivalent control group design	A quasi-experimental design where two or more preexisting groups are pretested, the experimental group(s) receives the intervention, and all groups are posttested.
Nonmanipulated (quasi-) independent variable	An independent variable where the levels are preexisting. An example would include a situation where the independent variable was gender; the levels are male and female.
Nonparametric statistical test	Inferential statistical tools used with nominal or ordinal data or with quantitative data where the distribution is abnormally distributed (e.g., skewed or kurtotic).
Nonprobabilistic sampling	See *Nonrandom sampling.*
Nonrandom sampling	A sampling technique where all members of the population do not have a chance of being selected for a sample taken from it.
Normal distribution	A quantitative distribution wherein the distribution is bell shaped.
Novelty effect	A threat to the external validity of a study due to changes in participants' behavior because of the newness or uniqueness of an intervention.
Null hypothesis	A hypothesis that states there will be no relationship between the variables being studied. The null hypothesis is the antithesis of the research hypothesis.
Numeric descriptive statistics	The use of tools, such as measures of central tendency, measures of dispersion, and measures of relative standing, to illustrate the characteristics of a data set.
Observed value	The actual count of occurrences in a cell of nominal values. It is used in chi-square tests to compare to expected values.
One-group pretest–posttest design	A pre-experimental design tht involves a pretest, intervention, and posttest of one group.
One-sample chi-square test	The comparison of cell frequencies in a nominal distribution to those that would be expected according to a previously defined criterion. See *Chi-square goodness-of-fit test.*

289

One-shot case study	A pre-experimental design wherein an intervention is used with one group, followed by a posttest. None of the threats to validity are controlled for.
One-tailed hypothesis	See *Directional hypothesis.*
One-way ANOVA	A statistical tool used when a study involves one independent variable with three or more levels and one dependent variable that is measured with quantitative data.
Ontology	A researcher's beliefs about reality. Is there only one reality that we can identify and verify, or are there multiple realities that we can construct?
Open codes	Devices used to mark unique ideas, thoughts, or situations within a transcript. Open codes are examined for common characteristics and combined into axial codes.
Ordinal interaction	An interaction effect where the influence of one independent variable remains in the same direction but varies in magnitude across levels of another independent variable.
Ordinal (rank) data	Data that are rank ordered. Examples include order of finish in a race and class standing.
p value	The probability that groups being compared came from the same population.
Paired-samples t test	See *Dependent-sample* t *test.*
Paradigm	A theory about how something should be done or conducted. For example, qualitative and quantitative are two paradigms about how research should be conducted.
Parameter	Any value known about a data set representing an entire population.
Parametric	Pertaining to the use of quantitative data that form a mound-shaped distribution.
Parametric statistical tools	Inferential statistical tools used with quantitative data.
Pearson's r	Output from a correlation procedure using quantitative data sets. Pearson's r can range from -1.00 to $+1.00$ with extremely high values indicating a strong positive correlation; extremely low values indicate a strong negative correlation. Values around zero indicate a weak correlation.

Peer debriefer	A disinterested peer who can review your work, ask questions, and determine whether it is understandable to someone other than the writer.
Percentile	A measure of relative standing that describes the percentage of other values in the data set falling below it. For example, a test score of 50 that falls into the 80th percentile means that 80% of the other scores are less than 50.
Persistent observation	Efforts by a researcher to define specific characteristics that are most closely related to the problem area under investigation. This allows for a better in-depth understanding of the issues surrounding the problem area.
Personal history stories	See *Biographical narrative*.
Phenomenological reduction	See *Epoché*.
Phenomenological research	The act of investigating and reporting on the lived experiences of a group toward a unique event or object.
Pie chart	A circular chart divided into segments with each representing the percentage of a given value in a data set.
Placebo	A treatment designed to have no effect on the dependent variable. These are often used to compare the efficacy of a real medication (experimental group) versus a placebo (control group).
Platykurtotis	A bell-shaped distribution that is too flat (i.e., fewer values around the mean of the distribution than is expected) to be perfectly normally distributed.
Pooled standard deviation	An estimate of the population standard deviation based on a weighted average from a set of sample standard deviations.
Population	All members of a group being investigated.
Population parameter	Any value known about a population.
Positive correlation	The relationship between two variables that move together in the same direction. A positive correlation shows that when one variable decreases, so does the other; when one variable increases, so does the other.
Positively skewed	Skewed to the right (i.e., there are more values above the mean of a quantitative data set than there are below the mean).

GLOSSARY

291

Possible range	The set of values a data set theoretically covers. For example, on most examinations, the possible range is 0–100.
Post hoc test	See *Multiple comparison test.*
Posttest-only control group design	A true experimental design where participants are randomly assigned to groups, exposed to an intervention, and posttested.
Power	The ability of a statistical test to identify when there is a true significant difference in the values being compared. It is computed by subtracting beta from 1.00; this means that as power increases, the probability of making a type II error decreases.
Practical (applied) research problem	See *Practical significance.*
Practical significance	The determination that the results of a research study are practically important or that they can be useful in real life.
Predictive validity	A form of criterion-related validity measuring how well a test can be used to predict a certain outcome or future event.
Predictor variable	The independent variable in a correlation procedure. It is used to predict values of the criterion variable.
Pre-experimental design	A research method with only one independent variable with one level.
Pretest–posttest control group design	A true experimental design wherein members are randomly assigned to levels of the independent variable, pretested, exposed to an intervention, and posttested.
Pretest–treatment interaction	A situation wherein taking a pretest sensitizes the subject to act differently during the course of a study, thereby affecting the dependent variable.
Primary sources	Literature attributed to the primary author in a field. For example, in reading about psychoanalysis, Sigmund Freud would be a primary author.
Probabilistic sampling	See *Random sampling.*
Problem statement	The specific issue, concern, or controversy to be investigated. The problem statement as part of a dissertation includes a discussion of the background of the problem, the specific problem, and the literature discussing the significance of investigating the problem.

Projective test	An instrument used to measure constructs.
Prolonged engagement	A situation where a researcher spends an extended period of time with a study's participants in their everyday world. By doing this, the researcher can best understand the participants' behaviors, values, and social and professional relationships.
Purpose statement	A statement made that tells the reader why a study is being undertaken.
Purposive sampling	A form of intentional sampling used in many qualitative studies to allow the researcher to identify small, specific groups to work with.
Qualitative	Non-numeric data such as interviews, recordings, etc.
Qualitative data	Non-numeric data, such as interviews, recordings, etc.
Qualitative methods	Researched based on the collection and analysis of non-numeric data such as interviews, texts, broadcast media, etc.
Qualitative priority	Mixed methods design where priority is given to qualitative data during collection and analysis.
Quantitative	A generic label for any data that are on an interval or ratio scale.
Quantitative data	A generic label for any data that are on an interval or ratio scale.
Quantitative methods	Research based on the collection and analysis of numeric data such as test scores, time taken for an action, etc.
Quantitative priority	Mixed methods design where priority is given to quantitative data during collection and analysis.
Quantitative research	Research based on the collection and analysis of numeric data such as test scores, time taken for an action, etc.
Quartile	The range of data representing 25% of the distribution.
Quasi-experimental design	Research design wherein random assignment to group membership is not possible.
Quasi-experimental research	Research designs wherein random assignment to group membership is not possible.

Quasi-experimental research	Research designs wherein random assignment to group membership is not possible.
Quota sampling	Similar to stratified sampling, except that, after stratification, members of the sample are selected based a prespecified proportion.
Random sampling	A sampling technique where all members of the population have a chance of being selected for a sample taken from it.
Range	The set of values that a data set actually covers. For example, if the lowest value in our data set is 30 and the highest value is 70, our range is 40 (highest minus lowest).
Rank data	See *Ordinal (rank) data.*
Ranking scale	Numeric scale used to rank items from least preferred to most preferred.
Ratio data	One of two types of data (see *Interval data*) that can be classified as quantitative. Ratio-level data can be divided into equal intervals and allow for direct comparison. For example, a person who weighs 150 pounds is twice as heavy as a person who weighs 75 pounds. There is an absolute zero point in ratio-level data.
Reactive arrangement	A threat to the external validity of a study caused by changes in a subject's personal demeanor. See *John Henry effect* and *Novelty effect.*
Referential adequacy	A process whereby a qualitative researcher, before beginning data analysis, retains and stores a sample of the data. After analysis, and the development of preliminary findings based on the remaining data, the archived data are then analyzed and examined, in order to test the validity of the overarching findings.
Regression to the mean	The tendency for an extreme value in a data set to be closer to the mean in a subsequent measurement.
Reject the null hypothesis	A decision made, based on the computed and critical value of a statistic, that indicates that differences between values being compared are true and not due to chance.
Relative frequency	The percentage of occurrences of various values in a data set.
Reliability	The characteristic of a data collection instrument that shows consistency in measuring a content area.

294

Reliability coefficient	A measure of the consistency and accuracy of a measuring instrument wherein the instrument is taken twice by a group and the two sets of measures are correlated. Coefficients approaching 1.0 indicate higher instrument reliability.
Research hypothesis	A synonym for the directional or nondirectional hypothesis being investigated. The research hypothesis is the antithesis of the null hypothesis.
Research question	A question derived from the problem and research purpose that drives a specific aspect of the investigation of a study.
Review of literature (ROL)	The reporting of the synthesis of literature read for a research study. The ROL is generally the topic of Chapter 2 in a dissertation proposal.
Sample	A subset of a population being studied.
Sample statistic	Any value known about a sample of data.
Sampling bias	See *Sampling error.*
Sampling distribution of the means	The resulting distribution when repeated samples are drawn from a population and their mean is calculated and plotted. Given enough samples, this will result in a perfect normal distribution.
Sampling error	The error inherent in measuring only a selected group (sample) from a population.
Sampling frame	See *Population.*
Sampling validity	An assurance that all content to be evaluated in an examination is covered.
Scatter plot	A graph that shows the relationship between sets of quantitative data.
Scheffé test	Multiple comparison test commonly used with an analysis of variance.
Secondary sources	Literature read that discusses and reports on the work of primary authors in a given field. See *Primary sources.*
Selection–treatment interaction	A threat to the external validity of a study due to the purposive sampling, and subsequent treatment and testing, of subjects.
Semistructured Interview	An interviewing protocol where the interviewer asks specific questions but is then allowed to ask follow-up or probing questions.

Sequential–explanatory design	A design wherein qualitative data are collected and analyzed in order to help explain the prior collection and analysis of quantitative data.
Sequential–exploratory design	A design where the collection and analysis of qualitative data is followed by the collection and analysis of quantitative data. This approach is especially effective while developing new instrumentation or investigating a phenomenon.
Significance of the problem	Evidence provided to show that investigating a problem is worthwhile.
Significantly different	A difference between two variables being measured that cannot be attributed to sampling error. The values are different due to reasons other than chance and would cause a null hypothesis to be rejected.
Simple frequency	The actual count of the number of occurrences of a given variable in a data set.
Simple-random sampling	See *Random sampling.*
Skewness	Degree to which a data distribution deviates from being a normal distribution (i.e., mound shaped) by having too many values in one end of the distribution or the other.
Skewed left	See *Negatively skewed.*
Skewed right	See *Positively skewed.*
Slope	The degree of inclination of a line of best fit.
Snowball sampling	A sampling process where an initial subject is identified with that participant subsequently identifying other potential participants. This process can continue until an adequate sample size is reached.
Solomon four-group design	A variant of the pretest–posttest control group design wherein only half of the subjects in each of the groups are pretested.
Spearman's rho	A correlational procedure used with ordinal level data. Rho can range from zero to +1.00. The closer rho is to +1.00, the stronger the correlation.
Specificity of variables	A threat to the external validity of a study due to using specific subjects, data collection instruments, or protocols during the study.

Split-half reliability	The degree to which selected sections of an instrument correlate with one another. For example, if a 50-item exam was developed and administered, the instrument developer might correlate scores between the first 25 questions and the latter 25 questions. Higher correlation coefficients reflect a higher degree of instrument reliability.
Standard deviation	Used to describe how spread out a data set is. It can be thought of as the average distance of any data point in a distribution from the mean of the data set. Obviously, the larger the standard deviation, the more spread out the data set is. The standard deviation is the square root of the variance.
Standard error of the mean	The standard deviation of a sampling distribution of the means.
Standard error of mean difference	The standard deviation of the sampling distribution of the mean differences used in a *t* test.
Stanine	A measure of relative standing involving the division of a distribution of quantitative scores into nine parts.
Static group comparison	A pre-experimental design involving two nonrandom groups. One group is exposed to an intervention and both groups are posttested.
Statistic	Any value we know about a sample of data.
Statistical regression to the mean	A phenomenon where subjects who score the highest and lowest on a pretest tend to score closer to the mean on a posttest.
Strands	In mixed methods research, the process of developing a data collection instrument, collecting and analyzing the data, and reporting the results. A strand represents only one type of data at a time.
Stratified sampling	Randomly selecting participants from unique subgroups in a population. This is most often done to ensure that smaller groups within the population are proportionately represented in the sample.
Structured interview	An interviewing technique where subjects are asked specific questions with no probing or follow-up questions.
Sum of squares	The sum of the within-groups and between-groups sum of squares; used in the analysis of variance.
Survey	An overarching term inclusive of content and construct data collection tools.

Survey research	The collection and analysis of data used to describe the current status of the event being measured.
Systematic sampling	The creation of a sample by identifying a starting point in the population and then selecting each nth subject to be included in the sample.
t distribution	The resulting distribution when repeated samples are drawn from a population and their t score is calculated and plotted. Given enough samples, this will result in a perfect normal distribution.
T score	A measure of relative standing based on a scale of 20–80. *Caution:* This is not the t value computed as part of a t test.
t table	A table showing the critical values of t for various alpha values and degrees of freedom.
Testing	A threat to the internal validity of a study due solely to the reaction, by study participants, to being tested.
Test–retest reliability	This process measures the consistency, over time, of the same test given at least twice to the same population of students. Results indicating a strong positive correlation of scores support the reliability of the test.
Theoretical (basic) research problem	See *Theoretical significance*.
Theoretical significance:	Research results that may be useful in testing a current theory or the development of a new theory.
Thick description	The addition of carefully researched detail to a report you are writing; this contributes to the validity of your work.
Threat to validity	Anything that happens during the course of an experimental study that affects the generalizability of its results.
Time-series design	A quasi-experimental design wherein one group is measured multiple times on the content area, construct, or activity of interest both before and after the treatment.
Transferability	See *Generalizability*.
Treatment diffusion	Anything occurring during the course of a study that negatively affects the effect of the independent variable.

Triangulation	The use of two types of research methodologies or data sources to increase the validity of a study by ensuring the results of each are similar.
True experimental design	See *Experimental design*.
Trustworthiness	See *Validity*.
Two-tailed hypothesis	See *Nondirectional hypothesis*.
Type I error	Rejecting the null hypothesis when we should not reject it.
Type II error	Failing to reject the null hypothesis when we should reject it.
Type I error rate	The probability of rejecting the null hypothesis when we should not reject it (i.e., rejecting the null hypothesis when it is true). The type I error rate is synonymous with our alpha value.
Type II error rate	The probability of failing to reject the null hypothesis when we should reject it. This is sometimes referred to as our beta value.
Unit of analysis	In qualitative research, the major construct about which data are collected and analyzed.
Univariate	Dealing with one independent and one dependent variable.
Unstructured interview	A data collection technique where respondents are asked only one overarching question with no follow-up or probing questions.
Upper-confidence limit	The highest value in a confidence interval.
Validation	In qualitative studies, the consistency of the data collection process.
Validity	The idea that a data collection instrument measures what it is supposed to measure. This comprises sampling validity (Is the entire content area covered?) and item validity (Does each item measure something specific to the content area covered?).
Variance	A measure of dispersion that is determined by squaring the standard deviation. Used in computations, such as the ANOVA, where negative numbers are not allowed.
Within-group degrees of freedom	An integral part of the calculation of F values; computed by subtracting 1 from the number of groups (i.e., levels of the independent variable) in the ANOVA.

Within-group variance	The amount of variance that occurs within one of the groups of data represented by a level of an independent variable.
Wilcoxon *t* test	Nonparametric alternative to the dependent-sample *t* test.
X axis	The horizontal axis of a plot.
Y axis	The vertical axis of a plot.
z score	A measure of relative standing computed by subtracting the mean of a bell-shaped data set from the observed score and dividing by the standard deviation.
z table	A table showing the critical value of *z* for all values in a normal distribution.

References

Abernathy, R. (1991). *And the walls came tumbling down: An autobiography*. New York: HarperCollins.

Adams, E. (2012, March 31). ADEM reports potential hazards in leakage near REEF. *The Daily Home*, p. 1.

Alabama Department of Environmental Management. (2006, October). Hazardous waste: The basics. Available at *www.adem.alabama.gov/programs/land/landforms/hwbasics.pdf*

Almeyda, J. (2020). *A COVID-19 induced shift from introducing high school females to computing careers to an assessment of technological readiness among STEM teachers* (Publication No. 28155983). [Doctoral dissertation, Nova Southeastern University]. ProQuest Dissertations and Theses Global.

Angrosino, M. (2007). *Doing ethnographic and observational research*. Thousand Oaks, CA: SAGE.

Babbie, E. (2012). *The practice of social research* (13th ed.). Belmont, CA: Wadsworth.

Barbour, R. (2007). *Doing focus groups*. Thousand Oaks, CA: SAGE.

Baxter, P., & Jack, S. (2008). Qualitative case study methodology: Study design and implementation for novice researchers. *The Qualitative Report, 13*(4), 544–559. Available at *www.nova.edu/ssss/QR/QR13-4/baxter.pdf*

Bazely, P. (2004). Issues in mixing qualitative and quantitative approaches to research. In R. Buber, J. Gadner, & L. Richards (Eds.), *Applying qualitative methods to marketing management research* (pp. 141–156). London: Palgrave Macmillan.

Beck, A. T., Steer, R. A., & Brown, G. K. (1996). *Manual for the Beck Depression Inventory-II*. San Antonio, TX: Psychological Corporation.

Beck, A. T., Ward, C. H., Mendelson, M., Mock, J., & Erbaugh, J. (1961). An inventory for measuring depression. *Archives of General Psychiatry, 4*, 561–571.

Belmont Report. (1979). The Belmont Report: Ethical principles and guidelines for the protection of human subjects of research. Retrieved December 21, 2014, from *hhs.gov/ohrp/humansubjects/guidance/belmont.html*

Berner, E., & Graber, S. (2008). Overconfidence as a cause of diagnostic error in medicine. *American Journal of Medicine, 121*, S2–S23.

Bhargava, A., Kirova-Petrova, A., & McNair, S. (1999). Computers, gender bias, and young children. *Information Technology in Childhood Education, 1*, 263–274.

Billups, F. D. (2021). *Qualitative data collection tools: Design, development, and applications*. Thousand Oaks, CA: SAGE.

Bogdan, R., & Biklen, S. (2007). *Qualitative research for education: An introduction to theory and methods* (5th ed.). Boston: Allyn & Bacon.

Booth, W. (1995). *The craft of research*. Chicago: University of Chicago Press.

Bracht, G. H., & Glass, G. V. (1968). The external validity of experiments. *American Education Research Journal, 5,* 437–474.

Bronstein, D. (2007). *The efficacy of a web-site evaluation checklist as a pedagogical approach for teaching students to critically evaluate Internet content*. Unpublished doctoral dissertation, Nova Southeastern University, Ft. Lauderdale, FL.

Buck, J. (1992). *The house–tree–person projective drawing technique: Manual and interpretive guide* (rev. ed.). Los Angeles: Western Psychological Services.

Butler, D. (2000). Gender, girls and computer technology: What's the status now? *The Clearing House, 73*(4), 225–229.

Campbell, D., & Stanley, J. (1963). *Experimental and quasi-experimental designs for research*. Chicago: Rand-McNally.

Carter, K. (2009a, March 24). Citizens file lawsuit against company because of odor. *The Daily Home*, p. 1.

Carter, K. (2009b, March 25). Hundreds complaining of bad smell. *The Daily Home*, p. 1.

Casciaro, A. (2006, May 23). Avondale closing Sylacauga, Pell City plants. *The Daily Home*. Available at *http://nl.newsbank.com/nl-search/we/Archives?p_action=list&p_top-doc=31*

Charmaz, K. (2014). *Constructing grounded theory: A practical guide through qualitative data analysis* (2nd ed.). Thousand Oaks, CA: SAGE.

Chen, P., & Krauss, A. (2004). Simple correlation/regression. In M. S. Lewis-Beck, A. Bryman, & T. F. Laio (Eds.), *The SAGE encyclopedia of social science research* (pp. 1036–1037). Thousand Oaks, CA: SAGE.

Cheong, Y. F., Pajares, F., & Oberman, P. S. (2004). Motivation and academic help-seeking in high school computer science. *Computer Science Education, 14*(1), 3–19.

Clandinin, J. (2013). *Engaging in narrative inquiry (developing qualitative inquiry)*. London: Routledge.

Cohen, D., & Crabtree, B. (2006). Qualitative research guidelines project. Available at *www.qualres.org/HomeLinc-3684.html*

Cole, J. S., & Denzine, G. M. (2004). "I'm not doing as well in this class as I'd like to": Exploring achievement motivation and personality. *Journal of College Reading and Learning, 34*(2), 29–44.

Comprehensive Environmental Response, Compensation, and Liability Act of 1980. (1980). 42 U.S.C. 9601 et seq.

Cooper, H. (1998). *Synthesizing research: A guide for literature reviews* (3rd ed.). Thousand Oaks, CA: SAGE.

Creswell J. (1994). *Research design, qualitative and quantitative approaches*. Thousand Oaks, CA: SAGE.

Creswell, J. (2014). *A concise introduction to mixed methods research*. Los Angeles: SAGE.

Creswell, J., & Guetterman, T. (2018). *Educational research: Planning, conducting, and evaluating quantitative and qualitative research* (6th ed.). Los Angeles: SAGE.

Creswell, J., & Plano Clark, V. (2017). *Designing and conducting mixed methods research* (3rd ed). Los Angeles: SAGE.

Creswell, J., & Poth, C. (2017). *Qualitative inquiry and research design: Choosing among five approaches* (4th ed.). Los Angeles: SAGE.

Creswell, J. W., & Creswell, J. D. (2020). *Research design: Qualitative, quantitative, and mixed methods approaches* (5th ed.). Thousand Oaks, CA: SAGE.

Deci, E. L., & Ryan, R. M. (1985). *Intrinsic motivation and self-determination in human behavior*. New York: Plenum Press.

DeVellis, R. (2011). *Scale development: Theory and applications* (3rd ed.). Thousand Oaks, CA: SAGE.

Eide, E., & Showalter, M. (1998). The effect of school quality on student performance: A quantile regression approach. *Economics Letters, 58*, 345–350.

Elias, S. M., & Loomis, R. J. (2002). Utilizing need for cognition and perceived self-efficacy to predict academic performance. *Journal of Applied Social Psychology, 32*, 1687–1702.

Emurian, H. (2004). A programmed instruction tutoring system for Java: Consideration of learning performance and software self-efficacy. *Computers in Human Behavior, 20*(3), 423–459.

Environmental Protection Agency. (2013). Hazardous waste recycling regulations. Available at *www.epa.gov/osw/hazard/recycling/regulations.htm*

Fetterman, D. (2010). *Ethnography: Step-by-step* (3rd ed.). Thousand Oaks, CA: SAGE.

Fidelman, U. (1985). Hemispheric basis for schools in mathematics. *Educational Studies in Mathematics, 16*(1), 59–74.

Fink, A. (Ed.). (2003). *The survey handbook* (2nd ed.). Thousand Oaks, CA: SAGE.

Fink, A. (2016). *How to conduct surveys: A step-by-step guide* (6th ed.). Thousand Oaks, CA: SAGE.

Fowler, F. (2013). *Survey research methods* (5th ed.). Thousand Oaks, CA: SAGE.

Franklin, B. (2019). *The autobiography of Benjamin Franklin*. CreateSpace Independent Publishing Platform.

Friday Institute for Educational Innovation. (2012). *Middle and High School Student Attitudes Toward STEM Survey*. Raleigh, NC: Author.

Galvin, J. (2012). *Writing literature reviews: A guide for students of the social and behavioral sciences* (5th ed.). Glendale, CA: Pyrczak.

Gay, L. R., Mills, G. E., & Airasian, P. W. (2012). *Educational research: Competencies for analysis and application* (10th ed.). Boston: Pearson.

Gibbs, G. (2007). *Analyzing qualitative data*. Thousand Oaks, CA: SAGE.

Glaser, B., & Strauss, A. (1967). *The discovery of grounded theory—strategies for qualitative research*. Chicago: Aldine.

Gottfried, A. E. (1983). Development of intrinsic motivation in young children. *Young Children, 39*, 64–73.

Harris, C., & Hester, E. (1958). *U.S. Patent No. 2854812 A*. Washington, DC: U.S. Patent and Trademark Office.

Henry, G. (1990). *Practical sampling*. Thousand Oaks, CA: SAGE.

Hesse-Biber, S., & Leavy, P. (2011). *The practice of qualitative research* (2nd ed.). Thousand Oaks, CA: SAGE.

Holsti, O. R. (1969). *Content analysis for the social sciences and humanities*. Reading, MA: Addison-Wesley.

Howles, T. (2007). *A study of attrition and the use of student learning communities in the computer science introductory programming sequence*. Unpublished doctoral dissertation, Nova Southeastern University, Ft. Lauderdale, FL.

Jesson, J., & Matheson, L. (2011). *Doing your literature review: Traditional and systematic techniques*. Thousand Oaks, CA: SAGE.

Johnson, B., & Turner, L. (2003). Data collection strategies in mixed methods research. In A. Tashakkori & C. Teddlie (Eds.), *Handbook of mixed methods in social and behavioral research* (pp. 297–318). Thousand Oaks, CA: SAGE.

Johnson, R., & Onwuegbuzie, A. (2004). Mixed methods research: A research paradigm whose time has come. *Educational Researcher, 33*(7), 14–26.

Jones, J. (1993). *Bad blood: The Tuskegee syphilis experiment*. New York: Free Press.

Kipling, R. (1940). *Rudyard Kipling's verse*. Garden City, NY: Doubleday.

Kohler-Riessman, C. (2008). *Narrative methods for the human sciences*. Thousand Oaks, CA: SAGE.

Kolb, D. (1984). *Experiential learning: Experience as the sources of learning and development.* Englewood Cliffs, NJ: Prentice-Hall.

Kvale, S. (2007). *Doing interviews.* Thousand Oaks, CA: SAGE.

LaPlante, E. (2016). *Seized: Temporal lobe epilepsy as a medical, historical, and artistic phenomenon.* Plano, TX: Open Road.

Lincoln, Y., & Guba, E. (1985). *Naturalistic inquiry.* Newbury Park, CA: SAGE.

Machi, L., & McEvoy, B. (2012). *The literature review: Six steps to success* (2nd ed.). Thousand Oaks, CA: Corwin.

Mahoney, J. (1999). *The effects of air traffic controllers' cognitive style, learning strategies and performance within a multimedia training environment.* Unpublished doctoral dissertation, Nova Southeastern University, Ft. Lauderdale, FL.

Margolis, J., & Fisher, A. (2002). *Unlocking the clubhouse: Women in computing.* Cambridge, MA: MIT Press.

Merriam, S. (2009). *Qualitative research: A guide to design and implementation* (2nd ed.). San Francisco: Jossey-Bass.

Milgram, S. (1974). *Obedience to authority: An experimental view.* London: Tavistock.

Moore, D. (2014). *An investigation of the attrition of African-American students in an online undergraduate program.* Unpublished doctoral dissertation, Nova Southeastern University, Ft. Lauderdale, FL.

Morse, J., & Niehaur, L. (2009). *Mixed methods design: Principles and procedures.* Walnut Creek, CA: Left Coast Press.

Moustakas, C. (1994). *Phenomenological research methods.* Thousand Oaks, CA: SAGE.

Munhall, P., & Chenail, R. (2008). *Qualitative research proposals and reports: A guide* (3rd ed.). Sudbury, MA: Jones & Bartlett.

Murchison, J. (2010). *Ethnography essentials—designing, conducting and presenting your research.* San Francisco: Jossey-Bass.

National Geographic. (2013). Toxic waste: Man's poisonous byproducts. Available at *http://environment.nationalgeographic.com/environment/global-warming/toxic*

Neuendorf, K. (2002). *The content analysis guidebook.* Thousand Oaks, CA: SAGE.

Neuman, W. L. (2011). *Social research methods: Qualitative and quantitative approaches* (7th ed.). Upper Saddle River, NJ: Pearson.

Newton, P., & Shaw, S. (2014). *Validity in educational and psychological assessment.* Thousand Oaks, CA: SAGE.

Nicholson, J., Gelpi, A., Young, E., & Sulzby, E. (1998). Influences of gender and open-ended software on first graders' collaborative composing activities on computers. *Journal of Computing in Childhood Education, 9*(1), 3–42.

Ollhoff, J. (2011). *How to write a literature review.* Farmington, MN: Sparrow Media Group.

Onwuegbuzie, A., & Leech, N. (2006). Linking research questions to mixed methods data analysis procedures. *Qualitative Report, 11*(3), 474–498.

Pan, M. (2014). *Preparing literature reviews: Qualitative and quantitative approaches* (3rd ed.). Los Angeles: Pyrczak.

Patton, M. Q. (2001). *Qualitative evaluation and research methods* (3rd ed.). Newbury Park, CA: SAGE.

Plus, A. (2013). *Literature reviews.* Fourply.

Poorandi, M. (2001). *The impact of graphing calculators in teaching mathematics.* Unpublished doctoral dissertation, Nova Southeastern University, Ft. Lauderdale, FL.

Ragsdale, S. (2013). *Pursuing and completing an undergraduate computing degree from a female perspective: A quantitative and qualitative analysis.* Unpublished doctoral dissertation, Nova Southeastern University, Ft. Lauderdale, FL.

Raines, B. (2012, October 5). State and federal officials initiate emergency measures to contain pollution at abandoned REEF environmental facility in Sylacauga. Available at *http://blog.al.com/live/2012/10/state_and_federal_officials_in.html*

Raloff, J. (2009, June 6). School-age lead exposures most harmful to IQ. *Science News*, p. 13.

Resource Conservation and Recovery Act. (1976). 42 U.S.C. §6901 et seq.

Rovai, A. (2002). Development of an instrument to measure classroom community. *Internet and Higher Education, 5*(3), 197–211.

Rugutt, J. K., Ellett, C. D., & Culross, R. (2003). Discriminating student learning and efficacy levels in higher education: Contributions of classroom environment and teaching and learning effectiveness. *Planning and Changing, 34*(3), 229–249.

Salkind, N. (2012). *Exploring research* (8th ed.). New York: Pearson.

Schrum, L., & Levin, B. (2013). Preparing future teacher leaders: Lessons from exemplary school systems. *Journal of Digital Learning in Teacher Education, 29*(3), 97–103.

Schunk, D. H., & Pajares, F. (2001). The development of academic self-efficacy. In A. Wigfield & J. Eccles (Eds.), *Development of achievement motivation* (pp. 15–31). San Diego, CA: American Press.

Sekaran, U., & Bougie, R. (2013). *Research methods for business* (3rd ed.). Chichester, UK: Wiley.

Shadish, W., Cook, T., & Campbell, D. (2001). *Experimental and quasi-experimental designs for generalized causal inference* (2nd ed.). New York: Houghton Mifflin.

Skaggs, G. (2022). *Test development and validation*. Thousand Oaks, CA: SAGE.

Skoe, E., Krizman, J., & Kraus, N. (2013). The impoverished brain: Disparities in maternal education affect the neural response to sound. *Journal of Neuroscience, 33*(4), 17221–17231.

Snyder, T. D., & Willow, S. A. (2010). *Digest of education statistics 2010*. Washington, DC: U.S. Government Printing Office.

Sokolowski, R. (1999). *Introduction to phenomenology*. New York: Cambridge University Press.

Spielberger, C. (1975). The measurement of state and trait anxiety: Conceptual and methodological issues. In L. Levi (Ed.), *Emotions—their parameters and measurement* (pp. 713–725). New York: Raven Press.

Spielberger, C. (1983). *State–Trait Anxiety Inventory for Adults*. Palo Alto, CA: Mind Garden.

Spradley, J. (1980). *Participant observation*. Orlando, FL: Holt, Rinehart & Winston.

Stake, R. E. (1995). *The art of case study research*. Thousand Oaks, CA: SAGE.

Stake, R. E. (2005). *Multiple case study research*. Thousand Oaks, CA: SAGE.

Stevenson, T. (2014). *Serving military families: Using solution-focused therapy in a virtual environment*. Unpublished doctoral dissertation, Nova Southeastern University, Ft. Lauderdale, FL.

Student, A. (1909). The distribution of means of samples which are not drawn at random. *Biometrika, 7*(1/2), 210–214.

Superfund Amendments and Reauthorization Act of 1986. (1986). 42 U.S.C. §§ 9601–9675.

Superfund National Accomplishments Summary Fiscal Year 2012. (2012). Available at *www.epa.gov/sites/default/files/201509/documents/annperreportfy2012.pdf*

Tashakkori, A., & Teddlie, C. (2003). *Handbook of mixed methods in social and behavioral research*. Thousand Oaks, CA: SAGE.

Teddlie, C., & Yu, F. (2007). Mixed methods sampling: A typology with examples. *Journal of Mixed Methods Research, 1*(1), 77–100.

Terrell, S. (1992). *An investigation of cognitive evaluative theory: The effect of graphic feedback on student motivation and achievement*. Unpublished doctoral dissertation, Florida International University, Miami, FL.

Terrell, S. (2011). Face-to-face in writing: My first attempt at conducting a text-based online focus group. *Weekly Qualitative Report, 2*(14), 83–88.

Terrell, S. (2012). Mixed methods research methodologies. *Qualitative Report, 17*(1), 254–280.

Terrell, S. (2014). The use of experiential learning styles to predict attrition from a limited residency information systems graduate program. *Online Journal of Applied Knowledge Management, 2*(1), 1–10.

Terrell, S. (2021). *Statistics translated: A step-by-step guide to analyzing and interpreting data* (2nd ed.). New York: Guilford Press.

Terrell, S., Dringus, L., & Snyder, M. (2009). The development, validation, and application of the Doctoral Student Connectedness Scale. *Internet in Higher Education, 12*, 112–116.

Terrell, S., Krause, D., & Campbell, B. (2019, January). *Developing an after-school program to increase STEM interest, awareness and knowledge of young Hispanic females in a Title I middle school.* Paper presented at the annual conference of the Florida Distance Learning Association.

Terrell, S., & Rendulic, P. (1995). The use of technology to increase achievement in elementary school children. *Journal of Instruction Delivery Systems, 9*(4), 13–16.

Tuskegee University. (2022). About the USPHS Syphilis Study. Retrieved May 29, 2022, from *www.tuskegee.edu/about-us/centers-of-excellence/bioethics-center/about-the-usphs-syphilis-study*

Vrijheid, M. (2000). Health effects of residence near hazardous waste landfill sites: A review of epidemiologic literature. *Environmental Health Perspectives, 108*(1), 101–112.

Walker, C., & Baxter, J. (2019). Method sequence and dominance in mixed methods research: A case study of the social acceptance of wind energy literature. *International Journal of Qualitative Methods, 18*, 1–14.

Wang, L., Ertmer, P., & Newby, T. (2004). Increasing preservice teachers' self-efficacy beliefs for technology integration. *Journal of Research on Technology in Education, 36*(3), 231–244.

Wayman, E. (2013). Toxic waste sites may cause health problems for millions. *Science News, 183*(10). Available at *www.sciencenews.org/article/Toxic-waste-sites-may-cause-health-problems-millions*

Willging, P. A., & Johnson, S. D. (2004). Factors that influence students' decision to drop out of online courses. *Journal of Asynchronous Learning Networks, 8*(4), 105–118.

Yale University. (2022). Primary and secondary sources. Available at *https://primarysources.yale.edu*

Yin, R. (2013). *Case study research: Design and methods* (5th ed.). Thousand Oaks, CA: SAGE.

Zarocostas, J. (2009). Health effects of toxic waste dumped in Côte d'Ivoire need urgent examination, UN expert says. *British Medical Journal, 339.*

Index

About the Author

Steven R. Terrell, PhD, is Professor Emeritus at Nova Southeastern University. He has taught quantitative and qualitative research methods since the 1980s and is the author of over 150 journal articles, book chapters, conference papers, and presentations, as well as the widely read textbook *Statistics Translated, Second Edition: A Step-by-Step Guide to Analyzing and Interpreting Data*. Dr. Terrell is a member of the American Counseling Association and the American Psychological Association, and served as the Chair of the American Educational Research Association's Online Teaching and Learning Special Interest Group. He serves on the editorial boards of several national and international journals and was recently named a Fellow and Distinguished Scholar of the International Institute for Applied Knowledge Management. He is currently serving as part-time faculty in the School of Computing at Middle Georgia State University.

Made in the USA
Coppell, TX
22 August 2024

36302916R00177